ANTONY
&
CLEOPATRA

For Charles, Karen, Graeme and Jacqui,
for enormous amounts of help and encouragement.

Not forgetting Cleo and Tiddy who always help by sitting on the exact section that
I'm trying to read, and prodding the keyboard.

ANTONY
&
CLEOPATRA

PATRICIA
SOUTHERN

TEMPUS

First published 2007

Tempus Publishing
Cirencester Road, Chalford
Stroud, Gloucestershire, GL6 8PE
www.tempus-publishing.com

Tempus Publishing is an imprint of NPI Media Group

British Library Cataloguing in Publication Data.
A catalogue record for this book is available from the British Library.

ISBN 978 0 7524 4383 6

Typesetting and origination by NPI Media Group
Printed and bound in Great Britain

Contents

Acknowledgments 7

Introduction: The Background 9

1 Caesar's Lieutenant: Mark Antony c.83–47BC 19
2 Caesar's Lover: Cleopatra 69–47BC 61
3 A Time in Rome: Antony and Cleopatra 47–44BC 95
4 Separate Ways: Antony and Cleopatra 44–41BC 121
5 Reunion: Antony and Cleopatra 41–35BC 165
6 Caesar's Heir: Antony, Cleopatra and Octavian 35–30BC 201

Notes 231
Bibliography 255
Abbreviations 263
List of Illustrations 265
Index 271

Acknowledgments

This book owes its origin to a suggestion made by Peter Kemmis Betty of Tempus that the two biographies of Antony and Cleopatra, produced by this author some time ago, could be combined to tell the stories of each of these larger than life personalities in a single volume. The several authors, past and present, who deal with either Antony or Cleopatra individually are obliged to include much information concerning the other partner, but a swift trawl through both current and previous publications revealed that there does not seem to have been a joint biography – correct me if I'm wrong – since Shakespeare wrote his famous play. Having such an illustrious predecessor is somewhat daunting, but there is a perennial fascination with the story, and this book makes no pretence of measuring up to the aforementioned genius. It serves a different purpose and caters for a different audience, made up of people who have heard of Mark Antony and Cleopatra and would like to know a bit more, and students of the period who would like to know where the information comes from. On this last point it should be noted that the information that has survived is limited and also biased, because history is recorded by the winners, and the losers suffer as a consequence. There is a greater preponderance of sources regarding Antony, while for Cleopatra there are a few literary references, her papyrus records, her coins, and her alleged portraits, not all of which are securely identified.

There are several people to thank for their help in producing this book. Jonathan Reeve of Tempus answered all my questions promptly, and artists Jacqui Taylor and Graeme Stobbs produced the drawings of various coins and the maps. I would also like to thank those who wrote to me after the production of the previous two books, especially the scholar who pointed out that I had managed to prolong the life of the unfortunate Calpurnius Bibulus beyond the battle of Pharsalus and then forgotten to put him into the index. Being a loyal Caesarian ought not to have interfered with accuracy, and any mistakes in this book are solely due to the author.

Introduction:
The Background

The legendary 2,000 year-old tale of Antony and Cleopatra has
never faded through the centuries. It is an epic, a love story, and
a tragedy, three elements guaranteeing perennial fascination, as
evidenced in a steady accumulation of novels, plays and films. Each
new portrayal displays a slightly different interpretation of the character and motives of the main *dramatis personae*; villains and heroes
change places, depending on the prevailing opinion of the times or the
individual author. For the Romans, steeped in Augustan mythology,
the villains were Cleopatra above all, and to a lesser extent, poor
beguiled Antony, who perhaps would never have gone so much astray
if it had not been for the malign influence of the wicked Egyptian
Queen and her unbridled ambitions. The hero was of course
Octavian, the new Gaius Julius Caesar, transformed into Augustus by
a grateful Senate a mere three years after Antony and Cleopatra were
buried together in their Alexandrian tomb. Other interpretations are
possible, based on a more world-weary cynicism that casts suspicion
on the surviving evidence, most of it one-sided and loaded with
autocratic self-justification.

The link between Antony and Cleopatra was Julius Caesar, and the catalyst that ultimately threw them together was the civil war between Caesar and Pompey the Great. When Pompey fled to Egypt after the battle of Pharsalus, looking for money and a new army, Caesar followed and became embroiled in the civil war between Cleopatra and her brother Ptolemy XIII. From then onwards Cleopatra was closely associated with Caesar, and after his death with Mark Antony.

Antony and Cleopatra grew up in different parts of a world dominated by Rome, at a period when Rome herself was dominated by a succession of determined, enterprising politicians who bent or broke the rules to accrue enough personal power and influence to reshape the Republic and its functions, in accordance with their own ideas. It was all done for Rome first and personal credit second, or at least that is how it was represented. Opposition was often aimed at the person rather than the programme, and on occasion even blatantly necessary, perfectly justifiable measures were quelled because of personal animosities. The response to such opposition was often heavy handed, involving escalating factional strife to which the Republic was subject for much of its existence. This state of affairs frequently lent itself to the emergence of a single dominant figure who swept aside opposition. Julius Caesar was an exception in that he did not allow the massacre of his opponents in authorised proscriptions such as those of his predecessors Gaius Marius and Lucius Cornelius Sulla, and his successors Antony and Octavian.

The political organisation that allowed for such proceedings had a long history. According to hallowed tradition, at the end of the sixth century BC the Romans expelled the tyrannical kings who oppressed them and formed themselves into a Republic, with a new system of government designed to ensure that no single individual acquired supreme power, except for short periods by means of the office of Dictator, held for no more than six months. The chief organ of government was the Senate, dealing with all aspects of administration, including finance, legislation and important trials for conspiracy and assassination, and foreign embassies. The leading senators tended to be landowners, but this did not mean that it was an exclusively aristocratic organisation, even though membership was based on wealth. The men who fell below the property qualification of the senators ranked as equestrians (*equites*), who played no formal part in politics but often dealt with the business interests of senators with whom they were associated. Access to the senate was not denied to equestrians but many of them preferred to pursue their monetary careers. From the early Empire, when the standing army was created, officers were increasingly drawn from this class.

The power of the Senate was balanced by the more limited power of the People. The initials SPQR on monuments and documents stand for *Senatus Populusque Romanus*, the Senate and People of Rome. During the Empire, the power of the people was curtailed, and even in the Republic, it was limited to voting for candidates for office, or accepting or rejecting proposals put to them by the magistrates. There were two main popular assemblies; the *comitia curiata*, which was the oldest, based on the thirty *curiae*, or divisions of the people, and the *comitia centuriata*, based on the electoral and military centuries. The *comitia curiata* confirmed the appointment of the magistrates, and conferred *imperium* on them, or the power to command armies, while the *comitia centuriata* could make laws, and could reject or accept proposals for war.

The chief magistrates were the two consuls, elected annually, answerable to the Senate and People of Rome. Their responsibilities covered civil and military functions, embracing all political activities during the year of their office, and they also commanded the armies. Troops were levied each year if there was war, and Rome rarely passed a year without a war. Subordinate to the two consuls there were several less important annually elected magistrates with varied responsibilities, such as praetors whose duties were primarily legal, but who could also command armies, quaestors who administered the treasury and finances, and aediles who looked after the buildings and streets of the city, kept public order, regulated the markets, and took care of the water supply. An important innovation with long lasting consequences was the institution of the office of tribune of the plebs, probably in 494BC when the plebeians of Rome went on strike and refused to serve in the army. The *tribuni plebis* were elected by the plebs and were sacrosanct while in office. Their primary duty was to protect the plebs and their property from oppression by the patricians, facilitated in the political sphere by the tribunician right of veto, which enabled them not only to overturn any proposals, but also to reverse any laws already passed by the magistrates in office.

By the first century BC Rome had become much more than a fairly well-organised, adaptable city state with pre-eminence over her neighbours. She had acquired territories beyond her boundaries, and even beyond Italy, sometimes almost by accident under the heading of the search for secure borders, sometimes as a result of war dressed up as justified aggression, sometimes by default when kingdoms were bequeathed to Rome. Empirically and exponentially, the Romans learned how to adapt their political and military organisation, designed for a single city and its satellites, to suit the needs of an Empire. When the amount of daily business increased, they increased the number of personnel, and empowered them to deal with it. The institution of the pro-magistracy was a major innovation that simultaneously allowed for almost seamless continuation of government of the city and the growing number of provinces, and provided wider experience for aspiring Roman politicians and generals. The first extension of powers in this way occurred towards the end of the fourth century BC. In 326BC the consul Quintus Publilius Philo was still engaged in the siege of Naples when his consulship was technically due to expire. Normal procedure would have been to elect new consuls and send one of them to replace the commander, thereby risking loss of continuity, and perhaps detrimentally interrupting the siege. An innovation with long lasting consequences was established to circumvent the problem. Two new consuls were elected, and Philo was given the rank and title of proconsul, indicating that he was not actually consul, but retained consular power so that he could command the army. The proconsulship separated the powers from the annual office, allowing the proconsul to step down from office, but to be invested with authority to complete existing tasks or to undertake new ones for which there were not enough suitably qualified officials.

The promagistracy was also extended to the praetors, and also the total number of praetors rose steadily, whereas the number of consuls never exceeded two at any one time. In the early Republic there was only one praetor, who was invested with *imperium*, or the power to command an army, and he also dealt with all aspects of the legal system. When the consuls were away from Rome, as they frequently were in times of war, the praetor acted as chief magistrate. By the middle of the third century BC there were two praetors, one for internal affairs and one to look after the interests of foreigners. The total was increased to four when Rome annexed Sardinia and Sicily, thus requiring two extra men with military and legal powers to govern and defend the new territories.

After their term of office as consul or praetor, the proconsuls and propraetors took on a specific task usually allotted to them by the Senate as need arose, such as supervision of the corn supply, management of woodlands, caring for the roads, or the government of one of the provinces. The term *provincia* was at first applied to any of these tasks, and only after the passage of time and the growth of the Empire did the word acquire its territorial connotations. Governing a province was the most lucrative task for the promagistrates. Despite the laws that were passed to prevent extortion, and several notorious trials to punish those guilty of it, provincial governors could enrich themselves and pay off the debts that they had incurred in getting themselves elected in the first place. It became a way of life, and Caesar was no exception, relying on his appointment as propraetorian governor of Further Spain to gather funds, though he perhaps avoided outright extortion of the provincials and instead perhaps accepted gifts from people who were grateful that he had suppressed the Lusitanian bandits, or found in their favour in the courts.

Other governors were less scrupulous, like the infamous Verres, the plunderer of Sicily who was prosecuted by Cicero. Provincials could appeal to Rome, and in this instance the Sicilians won their case after only the first of Cicero's prepared speeches. Verres was condemned and Cicero published his subsequent speeches, slightly piqued that he had not had a chance to proclaim them out loud in public.

When Pompey and Caesar entered on their careers, the Republican system still operated as it had always done since its foundation, but the flaws had begun to appear. In theory a career path had evolved for senators, combining a sequence of military and civil posts. Candidates for the high offices who followed this course ought to have reached their early forties and gained considerable experience before they took up the reins of state as consuls. Laws were passed setting age limits on the various magistracies and military commands, but in practice this legislation and even the electoral process meant very little. In desperate times, very young men could be awarded military commands and political offices without going through the process of election. During the wars against the Carthaginians, when Hannibal was wreaking havoc in Italy, Scipio Africanus was appointed to command Roman armies in Spain at the age of twenty-six, and he was granted consular powers without having held the office of consul. He went on to command in Africa, drawing Hannibal out of Italy and finally defeating him at the battle of Zama. In the turmoil and lawlessness of the feud between Gaius Marius and Lucius Cornelius Sulla, a young plebeian noble called Gnaeus Pompeius, more familiarly known as Pompey, commanded armies from the age of twenty-three. Political procedure was adapted to legalise his position.

When the danger was past, adulation of the hero was usually replaced by fear of his power, so the Romans frequently turned against the men they had elevated to high office and removed them before they could turn into replicas of the tyrannical kings. After defeating Hannibal, Scipio Africanus was prosecuted and exiled. Pompey lost favour when he was not needed to save the Roman

world, and gained it again when the ruling classes chose him to fend
off Caesar.

Even in more peaceful times, burning political issues polar-
ised senators and people alike. Bribery and main force ensured the
election of the most determined men as consuls, who manoeuvred
their friends into other key posts, so that their political programmes
could be implemented within their year of office. Rivals could be
silenced by perfectly legal means by using the power of veto of
the tribunes of the plebs. Whilst this power was still exercised for
its original purpose of protecting the common people, towards the
end of the Republic unscrupulous politicians regularly employed or
bought the services of well-disposed tribunes to disrupt proceedings
and prevent their rivals from putting their proposals into effect.

An accepted method of gaining notoriety was to carry out a successful prosecution of one or more of the leading politicians, past or present,
and then to go on to hold office in Rome and a military command in
the provinces. Successful command in a foreign war was the supreme
shortcut to fame and power, so there was a scramble for such appointments when opportunity arose. In 89BC war was declared against
Mithradates VI Eupator of Pontus, who was aggressively extending his
influence over many of the eastern kingdoms. He ordered a massacre
of all Romans and Italians in the province of Asia, so war was declared
and a Roman general was required to mount a punitive expedition.
The ensuing struggle for the supreme command between the foremost
generals of the day, Marius and Sulla, led to riots. The Senate awarded
the post to Sulla, but one of the tribunes vetoed the award, and instead
it went to Marius. The response was revolutionary, as Sulla gathered his
army, marched on Rome, killed the tribune and his associates, drove
Marius out of the country, and enacted several laws while his troops
looked on to make sure that they were passed. Everyone was deeply
shocked, including his adherents. All except one of his military officers
refused to march on the city. But the precedent had been set.

When Sulla departed with his army for the eastern campaigns,
chaos reigned once again in Rome. One of the consuls, Gnaeus

Octavius, was well disposed to Sulla, but the other consul, Lucius Cornelius Cinna made no secret of his opposition. He had made a promise, which he had no intention of keeping, that he would not overturn the measures that Sulla had put into place. Octavius drove him out of Rome, but the rebound was horrendous. Cinna had friends, among them Gaius Marius, and between them they attacked and took Rome. Marius exacted a bloody and indiscriminate revenge on his enemies, turning a blind eye if other people seized the opportunity to rid themselves of a few rivals, unnoticed in the general carnage. Fortunately it was short lived, and ended with the death of Marius only a few days after he had entered the city.

It was against this background that the sixteen year-old Caesar and twenty year-old Pompey embarked on their careers, Caesar as an adherent of Marius who was married to his aunt Julia, and Pompey firmly in Sulla's camp. Given that this is how they started out, on opposite sides in an era of prolonged bitter strife, it is hardly surprising that they ended by warring against each other, but political life in Rome was never so straightforward. Alliances were sealed or shattered according to the needs of the moment.

Pompey started out as a teenage soldier in the camp of his father Pompeius Strabo, and largely because of the tumultuous times in which he lived he never pursued a normal career. In his early twenties, he raised three legions from his estates in Picenum on behalf of Sulla when he returned from the Mithradatic war. He defeated successive anti-Sullan armies sent against him in the north of Italy and was given a command with praetorian rank against Sulla's enemies in Sicily and Africa. After the death of Sulla in 79BC, the Senate appointed Pompey to the command of armies in Spain from 77BC to 71BC, with Metellus Pius as colleague, campaigning against the Roman armies and Spanish allies of Quintus Sertorius, an intransigent supporter of Marius. Consequently Pompey's early experience was exclusively military. He came late to politics and did not enjoy the same success in the Senate as he had on his campaigns.

Unlike Pompey, Caesar started out as a politician and came late to soldiering, but typically he made a thorough job of both careers. When Pompey was most in need of someone to help him in the Senate, Caesar had just returned to Rome after a term as propraetorian governor of Further Spain. He was elected consul for the year 59, a lively year during which Caesar revealed his talents for persuasion and his sometimes reckless determination and impatience to get things done. His opponents repeated the process that had delayed Pompey, by debating every single sentence in an attempt to talk the bills into oblivion, a particular talent of Marcus Porcius Cato. Caesar tried for a short time to go through the traditional procedures to put his proposals into effect, then lost patience with the unnecessarily prolonged debate, and resorted to other methods. He did not line the streets with troops, but he bypassed the Senate and had his acts passed by the popular assembly. It was not illegal, but it was definitely not approved.

By the end of his consulship Caesar had converted his land reforms and other proposals into law, and Pompey had obtained ratification for his administrative organisation of the eastern provinces, had started to settle his veterans on the land, and had married Caesar's daughter Julia. For himself, Caesar had obtained the provinces of Cisalpine and Transalpine Gaul as his proconsular command, which he took up without a break, directly after his consulship came to an end. He retained this command for the next ten years. As a result of his military and political success, enhanced by his capacity for self-advertisement, Caesar gradually began to eclipse Pompey and to irritate many other senators, because even while he was in Gaul, Caesar influenced the political life of Rome. Without leaving his province he could arrange unofficial meetings with his supporters and canvass to bring about the election of his adherents to significant posts where they could be of use to him in several ways, including the prolongation of his command. Among other things it was this that contributed to the outbreak of the civil war.

Mark Antony entered recorded history with a few brief notices in Caesar's commentaries on the war in Gaul, and continued as a firm adherent of Caesar until the Ides of March, 44BC. He fought with Caesar in the first phase of the civil war against Pompey, and administered Italy while Caesar fought against the Pompeians in Africa and Spain. Cleopatra entered Roman history shortly after the battle of Pharsalus, with one or two laconic statements in Caesar's account of the Alexandrian War. The celebrated association of Antony and Cleopatra began after the murder of Caesar in 44BC. When Caesar's will was read out in the Senate, it was revealed that he had adopted his nineteen year-old great nephew, Gaius Octavius. The boy was an insignificant youth who was perpetually ill, but he grasped his inheritance with tenacity and determination, representing himself as the new Gaius Julius Caesar. The story of Antony and Cleopatra reveals how Caesar's lieutenant and Caesar's lover entered upon their legendary relationship, and eventually found themselves at war with Caesar's heir.

I
Caesar's Lieutenant:
Mark Antony *c.*83–47BC

When the defeated Roman commander Marcus Antonius committed suicide in 30, he could not know as he lay dying in the arms of
Cleopatra, as the legend tells us, that his name would be remembered
through the centuries, sometimes with affection, sometimes with
admiration, sometimes with disapproval. Many people who neither
know nor care about the Romans are nonetheless aware of his heroic,
ultimately tragic, bond with Cleopatra. It may have amused Antony
to know that an Elizabethan Englishman called William Shakespeare
would read the ancient accounts of his life and then write a play
about him and Cleopatra, and that this play would still be performed
several centuries after it was written.

Any assessment of Antony's character attracts hyperbole. He was
larger than life, ostentatious, appreciative of the finer things in life,
cheerful, a hard drinker, and a consummate womaniser. He was a
loyal subordinate, an implacable enemy, boisterously affectionate,
quick to anger. He had a sense of humour, liked to play practical
jokes and did not mind being on the receiving end when jokes were
played on him. Generous like his father, he would give his friends his

last denarius, but he was always down to his last denarius, and never out of debt. His dissolute youth in the wrong company[1] divorced him for ever in the eyes of his contemporaries from the solid Roman virtues of *dignitas* and *gravitas*, and yet he was well educated, spending two years in Athens, the university city of the Roman world, and he was noted for his eloquence and talents in public speaking. He was nobody's fool, consistently at his best in a crisis, a good soldier, resourceful and responsible when necessary. Unfortunately his flaws were all too obvious and he did nothing to conceal them, so his enemies were legitimately able to emphasise them to depict him in the worst possible light, as a perennial drunkard, hot tempered, irresponsible, and easily led. This is how the Romans explained his slavish attachment to Cleopatra. To contemporaries, his relationship with the Queen was reprehensible if not downright vile, and the fact that he preferred to remain with her and to spurn Rome was beyond comprehension. By contrast, to some modern audiences, his loyalty to Cleopatra is his redeeming feature. Somewhere between the villain of Augustan propaganda and the heroic, ultimately tragic failure, there was a living, breathing, vivid personality.

The year when Antony was born is not established. Most modern scholars opt for 83, but two other dates are possible, 86 and 81. The discrepancy arises because the ancient authors disagree about his age when he committed suicide in 30. According to Plutarch[2] he was fifty-six years old when he died, but according to an alternative tradition[3] he was fifty-three. Appian[4] says that when Antony met Cleopatra at Tarsus in 41, he was aged forty, perhaps better interpreted as 'in his forties'. Fortunately, it is known that Antony's birthday was 14 January, because after his death this day was declared *nefastus*, or unholy, a day on which no public business could be carried out.[5] Antony's memory was supposedly obliterated by a decree of *damnatio memoriae* passed by the Senate, as part of Octavian's self-justification for the war against a fellow Roman.

The Antonii were plebeian nobles, neither fabulously wealthy nor politically prominent. Antony's father was Marcus Antonius Creticus, and his mother was Julia, the daughter of Lucius Julius Caesar, and third cousin to Gaius Julius Caesar. Antony's grandfather, also called Marcus Antonius, was the first of his line to reach the consulship in 99. He was an orator and lawyer, but like most Romans he also served in a military capacity. He was sent to round up the pirates based in Cilicia, where he commanded from 113 to 112. After his consulship in 99 he was appointed censor in 97. There was a census every five years and the two censors were responsible for conducting it and registering the people in their voting tribes. The censorship was a prestigious office, but since the censors also had the task of ejecting men from the Senate if they were deemed unsuitable, they made enemies. Ten years after his censorship, Marcus Antonius was killed in the bloodbath of 87, when Gaius Marius was brought back to Rome by the consul Cornelius Cinna. In the notorious proscriptions that followed many leading senators were killed. Antonius left Rome to hide on a farm, but when the farmer, trying to please his unbidden guest, sent to his local inn for a better wine than he normally bought, suspicions were aroused, and the slave sent to fetch it revealed who was hiding with his master. Marius was informed. When the soldiers came, Antonius tried to talk his way out of execution, until the commanding officer inquired why it was taking so long, and killed him. Antonius's head was sent to Marius.[6]

Antony's maternal grandfather, Lucius Julius Caesar, was also a victim of the proscriptions, so before Antony was born, both his grandfathers were dead, a harsh lesson in the pitfalls of Roman party politics. Rugged individualism or neutrality was of no help to men who wanted to rise via a senatorial career. It was necessary to attach oneself to the right party, and the consequences of belonging to the wrong one were sometimes fatal.

The elder Marcus Antonius, Antony's father, was impulsive, generous, disorganised and, ultimately, a failure, and the anecdotes that were told of him were readily accepted because they demonstrated so aptly the old adage 'like father, like son'. Plutarch[7] relates how a friend called on Antonius one day to ask for a loan. With no cash to spare, Antonius sent a slave to fetch a silver dish, which he presented to his friend, telling him to sell it and keep the money. Some time later, when Julia missed the dish and accused the slaves of theft, Antonius had to confess.

Marcus Antonius reached the praetorship in 74, and in the following year he was given a command against the pirates in Crete, but in contrast to his father the consul, he enjoyed little success. The Cretans defeated him, and he made an ignominious treaty. He earned the victory title Creticus,[8] but to all contemporaries it would serve as a reminder that mere pirates had defeated a Roman general. Creticus died while still in office in 71. Antony, now aged about eleven, and his younger brothers Gaius and Lucius, were burdened by their father's defeat in battle, and his poverty. Antony did not inherit any of his father's property, and chose to be labelled a bankrupt.

As a widow with three young sons, Julia did not remain unmarried for long. Her next husband was Publius Cornelius Lentulus Sura,[9] a senator of some standing who had committed some indiscretions as quaestor in 81. He was praetor in 74, and consul in 71, the year in which Creticus was killed. Antony and his brothers were brought up in Lentulus' house, and they seem to have been fond of their stepfather. It could have been the beginning of a significant career for Antonius, if only Lentulus had been in the right faction. Mistakes and misdemeanours could be glossed over if one belonged to the faction that came out on top.

The consuls for the year 70 were Pompey, now self-styled Magnus the Great, and Marcus Licinius Crassus, whose recent exploits gave them the dubious distinction of saving the state from the slave army led by Spartacus. Pompey's reputation as a general was secure, but Crassus continually sought a more dignified command that would bestow upon him the military distinction that he desired. Pompey, as always, was in an anomalous position. Up to now his career had been quite abnormal. He had never been elected quaestor or praetor, the requisite preliminary offices to the consulship. Consequently he had no administrative experience, and he had to persuade his literary friend Varro to write a handbook for him on senatorial procedure.

Many of the senators distrusted both Crassus and Pompey, especially since they were blatantly intent on destroying Sulla's work in strengthening the Senate. As part of this policy they needed to disempower Sulla's supporters. It was at Pompey's insistence that censors were appointed to revise the list of senators. Among others, Lentulus Sura and Antony's uncle Gaius Antonius Hybrida[10] were weeded out of the Senate, and had to begin their careers all over again. It was a serious setback to Lentulus, and also to Antony, whose circumstances conveyed no hope of a brilliant future. By 63 Lentulus had worked his way upwards again and had become urban praetor, which was a lowly enough post for a man who had been consul eight years earlier.

While he was growing up, Antony would have become increasingly aware of factional strife in Rome, and by education and observation he would note how it was possible to rise to power via command of armed forces, and how such distinction abroad brought prominence at home. A successful general would always be popular whenever there were enemies to fight, so Pompey went from strength to strength. He never asked for commands, but waited until situations became desperate and then used third parties to argue for his appointment. Through his adherents in the Senate, he was given the command against the pirates in the Mediterranean, for which he needed special dispensation to grant him the power and authorisation to give orders to the provincial governors of territories all round the Mediterranean coast. This amounted to a command over most of the Roman world. The piecemeal attempts to eradicate the pirates had proved ineffective in the long term, so there was a definite need for an extensive unified command with a single powerful leader at the head, directing the operations of a number of subordinates in order to cover the vast expanse of sea and land. Pompey was authorised to appoint twenty-four legates[11] of his own choosing to command the various sectors of the fleet and the army. An important factor was that these men were answerable to himself and not the Senate. Pompey's Mediterranean command was quite unprecedented in the extent of the wide ranging powers that it gave him, and the number of very distinguished men who served under him as his legates. It provided a framework for government that was adapted by Augustus.

Once he had all the relevant powers, personnel and equipment, Pompey was as good as his word. He divided the Mediterranean into thirteen sectors, placed squadrons in each of them under his legates, and made rapid sweeps of the entire Mediterranean and the surrounding coastal areas. In less than two months he had rounded up all the pirates and made the Roman world safe, and the food supply secure.[12] His next project was even more ambitious. He angled to deprive Lucius Licinius Lucullus of the eastern command against Mithradates VI, now recovered from his defeat by Sulla, and aggressively expanding his territory. Pompey had acquired a long standing reputation as a victorious commander, and he had also shown that he had a talent for organisation and administration, so the troops had more faith in him than in Lucullus, which caused great animosity between the two generals. By 62, Pompey brought forcible peace to the eastern provinces and made arrangements for the future administration of the whole area.[13]

In Pompey's absence, other politicians were striving for position and mapping out their careers. Marcus Licinius Crassus was jealous of the seemingly endless successes of Pompey the Great, and formulated schemes to gain military glory, as well as using his vast fortune to bind aspiring Romans to him by financing their careers. Another ambitious soul was Marcus Tullius Cicero, regarded with disdain as a *novus homo*, or a new man, with no illustrious consular ancestors. He had no ambition to command armies or govern provinces. He was an orator, steadily gaining fame via his work in the law courts, and determined to reach the consulship via this path. The most potentially dangerous of all, though it was not immediately apparent just yet, was a rising politician, the nephew of Gaius Marius, who was seeking power in whatever way he could get it, and was drawn to Crassus as his financial backer. Gaius Julius Caesar would very shortly become a name to reckon with in Roman politics.

Besides these ambitious men there were many discontented citizens in Rome, Marians who had suffered at the hands of Sulla, penniless veterans from Sulla's armies, dispossessed farmers, impoverished aristocrats, and those like Antony's stepfather and uncle who had fallen victim to Pompey's purge of the Senate.[14] The situation was ripe for agitation, creating uncomfortable suspicion of anyone who looked as though he might make a bid for domination. A following was guaranteed to any suitably qualified and disgruntled leader who championed the cause of the poor, the debtors, the dispossessed, or the veterans. Cicero saw such a man in the form of Lucius Sergius Catilina,[15] who had been prosecuted for extortion after governing the province of Africa for two years. He was not condemned, but while the trial was going on and until he was acquitted he was not allowed to stand for the consular elections in 66 and 65.

Cleared of all charges, Catilina presented himself as a candidate for the elections in 64 for the consulship of 63. The other candidates were Antony's uncle Gaius Antonius Hybrida and Cicero. Hybrida had already been ejected from the Senate, and Cicero was an outsider whose ancestry was undistinguished. The dilemma of the senators was that they wanted Catilina even less than they wanted the other two, so Hybrida was duly elected along with Cicero.[16]

In 63, Catilina failed to be elected consul for 62. He was already under suspicion, probably without foundation, of involvement in some sort of plot three years earlier, though precisely who was conspiring to do what, and how, and when, remains unexplained.[17] After failing at the elections, Catilina began to stir up the poorer classes, with a proposal to cancel all debts, which was a fairly common rallying cry in Rome, but particularly pertinent at this time, since even Cicero acknowledged that the burden of debt was extreme. Cancellation of debts was even more pertinent to Catilina himself, an impoverished aristocrat who had borrowed more than he could pay back, gambling on achieving the consulship and then a proconsulship as governor of a province, where he could reimburse himself. Desperate now, and harassed by Cicero who had caught a whiff of conspiracy, Catilina left Rome towards the end of 63. He gathered a motley collection of senators, plebeians, foreigners and slaves, and started to recruit veteran soldiers in Etruria.[18] Whether he intended to use armed support and overthrow the state is not certain, and the question has to be asked, would there have been a so-called Catilinarian conspiracy without Cicero's suspicions and consequent actions?

At this point Antony's stepfather Lentulus Sura enters the scene. He was praetor in 63, and allegedly the chief of the conspirators in Rome. It was said that when Lentulus and his colleague Cethegus received news of Catilina's arrival at Faesulae, they were to call on Cicero with knives concealed in their clothing and murder him. At the same time, fires were to be lit in several different places in Rome, and in the confusion Catilina was to take over the state. There was no real evidence of a conspiracy, until Lentulus tried to subvert a party of Allobroges from Gaul, who had come to Rome to petition the Senate for redress for wrongs done to the tribe. They were unsuccessful, and Lentulus judged that they might be sufficiently disgruntled to be converted to the cause of rebellion,[19] perhaps providing some of their famed mounted warriors to add to Catilina's army. It was a miscalculation. After some soul-searching the Allobroges informed Quintus Fabius Sanga, their patron in Rome, who passed on the information to Cicero. Meanwhile the Allobroges played the parts of double agents, leading the conspirators on until Cicero had some solid evidence which justified his arrest of the suspects.

Catilina escaped and survived until January 62, when the consul Antonius Hybrida marched against him. He was suspected of complicity in the plot, and of having sworn an oath to Catilina, because when the battle started, he claimed an attack of gout, so the command devolved upon his subordinate Marcus Petreius, who won the victory. Catilina was killed.

Before Hybrida set off with his army, Catilina's associates, among them Antony's stepfather, were immediately arrested and imprisoned in the houses of the praetors. A riot broke out when the slaves, freedmen and adherents of Lentulus and Cethegus stormed the houses where they being held and tried to rescue them.[20] When order was restored, Lentulus was brought before the Senate, deprived of his office and rank, and questioned. Cicero wanted the death penalty, immediately. The first senator to speak was Silanus, the consul elect for the next year, and he too advocated the death sentence. Another senator advised that the conspirators should be tried in court, according to proper procedure. Julius Caesar, who was now Pontifex Maximus or High Priest, spoke in favour of a milder penalty, namely imprisonment under close supervision in the Italian towns until Catilina should be apprehended or killed, and then all the conspirators should be subject to due process of law. No one heeded him. Hysteria had taken too strong a hold. The moment was Cicero's finest hour. He had discovered a conspiracy, patiently watched it grow, arrested the culprits in the nick of time, and he was not to be cheated of their deaths. He carried the day, and the conspirators were executed, without a proper trial. Cicero ought to have gone through laborious but requisite legal procedure and arranged for prosecution and defence, but he was in too much of a hurry. As a lawyer he knew that there was many a slip twixt prosecution and conviction. Condemnation was never a foregone conclusion even for the blatantly guilty, and if people had time to think and ask questions, loopholes might appear in the evidence, and the end result might be very far from the punishment Cicero so desired. Acquittal would tarnish his exploits in saving the state.

Lentulus was the first to be killed. He was taken to the Tullianum prison and despatched by strangulation. Antony always declared that Lentulus's body was not released to the family for proper funeral rites, except after pleading with Cicero's wife. Ancient authors did not believe the story, but significantly this was not a point that Cicero chose to refute when he referred to the incident much later in the *Philippics*. The most important point is that Antony firmly believed that Cicero would go so far as to deny his stepfather a Roman funeral.[21] All that Antony would be able to see was his stepfather suddenly executed without the opportunity to plead his case and then refused burial. Logic would not enter into his calculations; the man who had caused the death of his stepfather without a fair trial was Marcus Tullius Cicero, a new man from outside Rome, and no better than the Antonii or the Lentuli. It was unlikely that Antony would ever forgive him.

Two important characters had now entered Antony's life, Cicero as an enemy and Gaius Julius Caesar as a potential ally. Caesar had risked his reputation and perhaps even his life by speaking in favour of a lighter penalty for the conspirators, because it left him vulnerable to the accusation that he had somehow been party to the plot. Nonetheless he spoke out in public, in effect pleading for the lives of condemned men, and perhaps trying to divert Cicero from a potentially disastrous action that might rebound on him later.

Possibly at this time Antony married his first wife, though some authors date the marriage to 53 or 52. He was alleged to have first married a lady called Fadia, and had children by her, but nothing else is known of her. His new bride was his cousin Antonia, daughter of the consul Gaius Antonius Hybrida. Antonia gave birth to a daughter, also called Antonia, of whom little is known, except that in 44 Antony betrothed her to the son of his future colleague in the Triumvirate, Marcus Aemilius Lepidus. The marriage never took place, and eventually she became the wife of a wealthy aristocrat from a city in the eastern Roman Empire, possibly as part of an agreement made by Antony when he was reorganising the eastern provinces and allied states after the civil wars.

Marriage and fatherhood did not deter Antony from his normal pursuits. In the company of his great friend Gaius Scribonius Curio, Antony joyously frittered away his early adult life in drinking, gambling and womanising. Curio was just as badly behaved as Antony, but wealthier and better connected and therefore much more likely to emerge unscathed. Some ancient authors, notably Plutarch, portray Antony as weak willed and easily led, and put the blame on Curio for leading Antony astray, but it is highly unlikely that

Antony needed any encouragement in this sphere, nor is it likely that he lacked the courage to resist friends who were leading him where he did not want to go. Later on when he was a little older, he extricated himself from association with his notorious friend Clodius. No source illuminates precisely why he did so, except that Cicero[22] implies that the falling out occurred because Antony had an affair with Clodius's wife, Fulvia.

In the company of Curio Antony tried to match expense for expense and escapade for escapade. Proudly he refused to sit in the seats at the theatre reserved for bankrupts, the status that he had inherited from his father, while at the same time borrowing more and more. Curio offered to stand surety for Antony's debts, a gesture not to be underestimated, and testimony to Antony's capacity to inspire friendship. Curio's father found out, and banished Antony from the house and his son's presence. Antony never renounced Curio's friendship altogether, remaining on good terms with him until the latter's death. Cicero in the *Philippics* suggests that Antony actually sold himself to Curio and had homosexual relationships with many other young men, but this was a standard derogatory charge that lost much of its impact through indiscriminate overuse. Caesar was accused of the same thing, and so was Octavian – by Antony himself, when the two were battling for supremacy after Caesar's death.[23]

Apart from his association with Curio, virtually nothing is known of Antony's life at this period. He had witnessed the highly charged suppression of the supposed conspiracy of Catiline, which affected his family very closely, and he may have decided to maintain a low profile and stay out of politics, rather than struggle against his already clouded reputation to attempt to gain one of the junior posts that would lead to the quaestorship and entry to the Senate. One way of beginning a career was to take up a post as military tribune of a legion, a post geared to administrative duties rather than command in the field. Roman generals often appointed to this post young men who were known to them or recommended to them, and after serving for about a year the tribunes often stood for election as quaestor in Rome. Antony did not pursue this career path in his early youth and had no political significance until he came to prominence under Caesar.

Antony was about twenty years old when Pompey returned to Rome in 62, and everyone held their breath in case the victorious general should choose to march on Rome at the head of his troops, then force through legislation to suit his needs, just like another Sulla. Unexpectedly, Pompey quietly disbanded his soldiers, laid down his command, and then entered Rome perfectly legally, as a private individual, confident that the sheer magnitude of his achievements and his undoubted supremacy would protect him from prosecution and facilitate all his eastern administrative arrangements and the provision of land allotments for his veterans. He was to be sadly disillusioned. He had enriched himself and the state, but got no credit for it, and the Senate would not ratify his acts without first debating endlessly each minor point. Since he was no friend of Pompey, Antony may have inwardly rejoiced that the great man was being thwarted, but the episode had much to teach, not least about how senatorial narrow-mindedness and pique could override good practice, common sense, and even the welfare of the state. When he engaged in his Parthian campaign some years later, Antony took the precaution of having all his arrangements for the eastern territories ratified in advance.

Pompey was losing prestige and needed an ally in the Senate. Gaius Julius Caesar had meanwhile launched himself on his political career. He had been praetor in Rome in 62 and propraetorian governor of Further Spain from 61 to 60, and in that short time he had managed to raise the cash to pay off most of his considerable debts. On his return he demanded a triumph for his military exploits in suppressing the bandits who infested Lusitania, and also the right to stand for the consulship of 59. As a returning general at the head of an army he was not allowed to enter the city, so he kicked his heels while the Senate considered, then refused, his request to hold a triumph and also stand for the consulship. Quite unruffled,

Caesar readily abandoned the triumph, and threw himself instead into the more pertinent matter of the consular elections, backed by Pompey and Crassus. The association of these three men in 60 was described by contemporaries as *Tricaranus*, the Three Headed Monster.[24] The modern, artificial, terminology for this alliance is the first Triumvirate. There was no legal basis for the mutual agreements made by Pompey, Caesar and Crassus, unlike the so-called second Triumvirate of Antony, Octavian and Aemilius Lepidus, whose alliance was ratified by a law, sanctioned by the Senate, and described by the official formula *tresviri rei publicae constituendae*, or three men charged with restoring the Republic.

Caesar was duly elected consul for 59 with Calpurnius Bibulus as colleague, but he was soon acting almost independently, ignoring Bibulus and most of the Senate. Roman wits referred to the consulship of Julius and Caesar, instead of Caesar and Bibulus. Not all Caesar's actions were selfish, even though he acted in a blatantly dictatorial manner. He recognised the need for administrative reforms and then pushed them through with determination. Pompey's eastern arrangements were ratified en bloc, at last. A dynastic marriage was arranged to bind Pompey and Caesar closer together. Pompey had divorced his wife Mucia as soon as he returned to Rome, and was now the most eligible bachelor in the world, so Caesar offered him the hand of his only child, Julia. Though it was a dynastic marriage and not a love-match, both partners were genuinely fond of each other.

Caesar engineered his own appointment as proconsular governor of the provinces of Cisalpine Gaul and Illyricum, which would give him command of troops. The command was extended when the governor of Transalpine Gaul died in office, and at Pompey's suggestion the extra province was granted to Caesar with one more legion. It remained for Caesar and Pompey to reduce the power of their individual and mutual rivals. To this end, they promoted Publius Claudius Pulcher, a patrician who had changed his name to the plebeian form of Clodius.[25] Both Caesar and Pompey supported

Clodius in his aim to be elected tribune for 58, but there was a problem, in that as a patrician he was ineligible for the office. Undeterred,
Caesar as Pontifex Maximus presided over the necessary adoption of
Clodius into a plebeian family in March 59. It was an unscrupulous
manipulation of the regulations, but it was not illegal, and not an isolated case. Cicero's son-in-law, Cornelius Dolabella, was adopted into
the family of the Lentuli, so that he could stand for the tribunate in
49. With Clodius as tribune Caesar had an ally in Rome who would
be sure to keep his enemies under control while he was in Gaul.

Clodius was one of Antony's most infamous friends, with whom
he associated more often after he was deprived of Curio's company.
He presumably made the acquaintance of Fulvia, Clodius's wife,
but whether or not he had an affair with her at this time, leading
to a rift with Clodius, must remain conjectural. At any rate, Antony
knew Fulvia well enough to become, eventually, her third husband.
Clodius's behaviour was never anything less than scandalous. In
December 62 he had been discovered dressed in female attire during
the religious festival of the Bona Dea, observed exclusively by women.
Caesar was Pontifex Maximus, and the festival was celebrated in his
house, where his mother Aurelia presided over the ceremonies. She
discovered Clodius and ejected him for his sacrilegious act. It was
said that Clodius was having an affair with Caesar's wife Pompeia (no
relation to Pompey), so Caesar divorced her, famously declaring that
'Caesar's wife should be above suspicion'. A great deal of suspicion
attaches to the incident. Although Clodius was plainly guilty, Caesar
would not assist Cicero in prosecuting him, for reasons which he
kept to himself.[26] The trial took place in 61, and Cicero gave almost
conclusive evidence of Clodius's guilt, but doubtless after extensive
bribery, the jury acquitted him. The only result was that Clodius
became a bitter enemy of Cicero.

There is every likelihood that Caesar was the author of at least some
of Clodius's political agenda as tribune in 58, since some of the laws
that he promulgated were designed to prevent the kind of unscrupulous, but legal, obstructive behaviour in which anti-Caesarians

had indulged themselves in the previous year. Some of Clodius's legislation was less general, framed with deliberate targets in mind. Almost as soon as he was in office, Clodius removed Cato, who had employed his particular talent for endless uninterrupted talking to block Caesar's legislation. He was sent to take over the new province of Cyprus.[27] Cicero's fate was worse. Clodius passed a law (*lex de capite civis*) aimed directly at Cicero, proclaiming that anyone who had put to death Roman citizens without due process of law was to be outlawed.[28] In the current political climate in Rome Cicero suddenly found that he had no friends. Even those with whom he had been most closely associated refused to speak for him. Caesar merely said that he did not approve of laws applied retrospectively, presumably speaking with his tongue firmly in his cheek, since he had no intention of obstructing Clodius. When Cicero tried to visit Pompey to ask for his assistance, Pompey saw him approaching, and fled by the back door as Cicero was shown in at the front. In order to avoid prosecution, Cicero went into exile at Thessalonika. His banishment was formally ratified after his departure, and his houses were destroyed. He was convinced that Antony had been one of the prime movers behind his exile. This may have been true, since Antony was one of Clodius's friends, and if the subject of Cicero was discussed, he may have expressed his opinion in rather vivid terms, but Antony had no political influence, and besides, Cicero had irritated too many people to require Antony's assistance in his loss of favour.

Caesar waited in Rome until Cicero had left Italy, and then departed for Gaul. In that same year, 58, Antony went to Greece, to study at Athens.[29] He may have had enough presence of mind to see disaster looming. It was rumoured that Antony had tired of Clodius' irresponsible violence, but another factor was that Pompey was in charge in Rome, and the last time that Pompey enjoyed unrivalled power he had not been well disposed to Lentulus Sura or Antony's uncle Hybrida.

Antony's grandfather had been a distinguished orator, and although they never knew each other Antony would have absorbed the tradition, which may have influenced him in making his decision to embark on a course of higher education. It was common for Roman youths to learn Greek and other subjects at home with a tutor and then go on to the equivalent of a university education at Athens or Rhodes. In Athens, Antony's course of study, according to Plutarch[30] consisted of gymnastic and military exercises and the practice of the florid Asiatic style of oratory which was so suited to Antony's character, full of swagger and melodrama. This is perhaps a case of matching known facts about Antony to a style which suited him, rather than a true depiction of his oratory. Suetonius[31] says that Augustus considered that Antony was a madman, because in his writing he preferred being admired to being understood, implying that he was verbose and florid, but this merely highlights the contrast with the straightforward unembroidered style cultivated by Augustus himself. From a few ancient sources it is known when and why Antony made speeches, but none of the content survives, except in fabricated versions in the ancient sources. Dio's version of what Antony said to his troops before the battle of Actium is a device for discussing Antony's situation.[32]

Up to this point, Antony had not revealed any desire for a military career, but his ambitions were aroused when Aulus Gabinius, consul in 58, arrived in Greece in 57, on his way to take up his post as governor of Syria. Gabinius was in Pompey's faction. He had been instrumental in obtaining Pompey's command against the pirates in 66, and had accompanied him to the east for the campaign against Mithradates. Julius Caesar had supported him when he stood for the consulship in the elections of 59. Gabinius's father had served under Antony's grandfather in the campaign against the pirates in 113–112, and Gabinius himself knew Clodius, who was tribune of the plebs in the year of Gabinius's consulship; they may have discussed Antony, and when he reached Athens Gabinius may have sent for him.

At first, Antony was not tempted by the offer of an administrative post in Gabinius's army, though his education best qualified him for

such an appointment. Then Gabinius offered him the command of
the cavalry, and the young man came into his own as *praefectus equitum*. Whatever he had been aiming for, his future life was determined
now, when he left Greece as a cavalry commander with Gabinius's
army. He had no military training in the modern sense. Roman boys
performed their military-style exercises, on horseback and on foot,
and Antony's studies at Athens continued these exercises, but there
was no military academy. Except for a few military manuals, there
were no theoretical courses on how to be a general, and no passing
out parade of the annual quota of newly qualified officers. Military
appointments were made on personal recommendations and letters
of introduction, and the appointees were simply expected to know
how to command troops.

Antony and Gabinius travelled together to Antioch, where they
were greeted with the news that there was a civil war in Judaea. The
situation there was volatile, and called for Roman intervention to
protect the interests of Rome as much as the citizens of Judaea. It was
within the brief of the governor of Syria to monitor Judaean affairs
and to keep order. The problem dated back to Pompey's conquest.
The Roman favourite was Hyrcanus, who was both High Priest
and ruler, but he was opposed by Alexander, the son of Aristobalus,
who was languishing at Pompey' pleasure in prison in Rome. Once
in Judaea, Antony was sent ahead with the cavalry and some light
armed infantry to find Alexander's rebel army, and then to wait for
the arrival of the rest of the Roman troops. There were two battles,
one near Jerusalem and one on the road to Jericho, in which Antony
distinguished himself.

Peace was restored for a short time, only to be disturbed all over
again when Aristobalus escaped from Rome and tried to re-establish
himself in Judaea. This time Gabinius stayed at Antioch and sent three
commanders, one of whom was Antony, to deal with the situation.[33]
When Aristobalus was forced to fall back on the ruins of Machaerus,
Antony led the assault on the town. He had thus revealed qualities of
bravery and leadership, had gained the respect of the soldiers. He had

also gained some experience of eastern affairs, soon to be enhanced in an expedition to Egypt.

As yet Rome had no direct control over Egypt, but indirectly she already controlled much of what went on in the kingdom. Several wealthy Romans lent money to the Ptolemaic kings and some of them entertained hopes of eventually gaining complete control of the whole land. The Senate refused to acknowledge Ptolemy Auletes on his accession in 80, but in 59 Caesar as consul shored up his rule over Egypt by formally recognising him as a 'friend and ally' of the Roman People, at a price. Suetonius[34] says that he extracted 6,000 talents for himself and Pompey. The money was raised on Ptolemy's behalf by the banker Gaius Rabirius Postumus, and in order to pay Rabirius, Ptolemy increased existing taxes and raised new ones, which made him so unpopular that he was forced to flee to Rome to seek help. Pompey was sympathetic, and so was the Senate, but then senatorial sympathy waned, and at this stage Pompey was not willing to compromise himself in the eyes of the senators. The matter dragged on for more than a year. Ptolemy left Rome and turned up at Gabinius's headquarters in Antioch, seeking military assistance, for which he promised to pay. Tacitly, Pompey condoned the idea because the restoration of Ptolemy could still be achieved and therefore his loan repayments would not be interrupted, but there would be no direct evidence that Pompey was behind it all. The ready cash to effect the restoration of Auletes was advanced by Rabirius Postumus, who had already raised the six thousand talents to pay Caesar and Pompey in 59 for recognition of Ptolemy as an ally of Rome. Rabirius recouped his outlay by going to Egypt to gather taxes as Ptolemy's treasurer, after the restoration.

Gabinius had no authority to intervene in Egypt. The Senate had already forbidden any attempts to reinstate Ptolemy, and besides it was illegal for a provincial governor to leave his province and enter another without the sanction of the Senate, so technically Gabinius could not legally enter Egypt even if he went with a small entourage, but what was proposed was an invasion with an army. Tempted by the fabulous wealth of the country, and allegedly in receipt of ten thousand talents[35] as a gift from Ptolemy, Gabinius set about putting the Egyptian ruler back on his throne, taking Antony with him. It was said later that Antony had been the catalyst in helping Gabinius to make up his mind, because he was an irresponsible hothead eager for adventure. This early contact with Egypt, retrospectively applied, indicated that there had always been a penchant for Empire building in Antony's character, especially when it concerned Egypt and its ruler.

It is not an easy task to invade Egypt by land, since it is protected on both sides by deserts, and the Nile Delta is an obstacle in itself, especially when patrolled by watchful ships. Antony crossed the difficult terrain, combining desert and marsh using Jewish guides. He sustained only a few casualties, and went on to capture Pelusium, the gateway to Alexandria. From Pelusium the Roman army fought and skirmished its way to Alexandria. Antony was instrumental in preventing a vengeful massacre of the inhabitants by Ptolemy Auletes after the ringleaders of the attempted coup were executed, earning for himself a reputation for courage and fair play. Remaining for a while in Alexandria, Antony impressed the inhabitants and the Roman soldiers with his exploits. He was in his late twenties, with a body like an athlete, which Plutarch[36] says that he liked to show off by wearing very short tunics. It may all be part of the stock image, describing a character who was larger than life, but Antony's popularity with his men, his generosity, roistering and womanising, is quite credible because it was all genuine and sincere, and not done for effect.

It is assumed that Antony met the princess Cleopatra while he was in Alexandria. She was about fourteen years old. Appian[37] insists that he fell head over heels in love with her as soon as he saw her, but this is retrospective fabrication. If they did meet, it is unlikely that they would have made much impression on each other, apart from the important fact that Antony had managed to prevent Ptolemy Auletes from exacting a bloody revenge on the rest of his family and the

Alexandrian citizens. By origin, upbringing, education, ambitions and above all, rank, Antony the cavalry commander and Cleopatra the princess in waiting were poles apart. It was much later, when mutual needs drew them together, that the eternal combination began.

Antony's stay in Egypt was confined to restoring Ptolemy Auletes on his throne. A second revolt against Hyrcanus broke out in Judaea in spring 55, so Gabinius left a contingent of soldiers in Egypt for the protection of Ptolemy and his family, and marched his remaining troops back to Judaea, Antony and the cavalry included. When the revolt was put down, Gabinius returned to Syria. Antony remained under his command for another year, without recorded incident.

In Rome, there had been significant developments. Cicero had been recalled from exile as a result of the belated efforts of Pompey. In 56, Caesar had taken time off from the conquest of Gaul, and travelled to Cisalpine Gaul to meet Pompey at Lucca. He talked with Crassus as well, but it is not certain whether all three men had a conference together. In a famous letter written in 54, two years after the meetings, Cicero[38] informed Lentulus Spinther, governor of Cilicia, that Caesar met with Crassus first at Ravenna, and then at Lucca he talked with Pompey, who had diverted from his journey to Sicily and Africa to meet Caesar. However it was accomplished, Pompey, Crassus and Caesar arranged the fate of the world for the next few years, mainly for their mutual benefit. They possessed enough corporate influence and wealth to guarantee that whatever they desired would happen, even to the extent of engineering the elections of magistrates. It was agreed that Crassus and Pompey should become consuls for 55, and that Caesar should be confirmed as governor of Gaul for another five years. He had no intention of leaving the conquest half finished, because that would give someone else the chance to mop up what he had begun, and then take all the credit for it.

Crassus was already making plans for his proconsulship. Originally he was to govern Spain and Pompey was to govern Syria, but these arrangements were reversed. Crassus saw his chance to make his mark. As governor of Syria, he intended to conquer Parthia, the one power that could rival or even outshine Rome in the extent of her Empire and in her sophisticated organisation. He began to recruit an army while he was still consul, and took over Gabinius's troops when he arrived in Syria, not without a struggle, because at first Gabinius refused to hand over his command. No source indicates whether Antony was offered and declined a post under Crassus, or whether he asked for one and was rejected, but he left Syria in the same year that Crassus arrived. Evidently he had decided that his future lay in independent action. Perhaps through good fortune, or perhaps through an intelligent grasp of Roman politics, he decided not to return to Rome in the entourage of Gabinius. It was said that he dared not face his creditors, which is quite likely, but he also knew that the Egyptian venture would draw criticism if not prosecution, which would perhaps extend to him as well as Gabinius. Consequently Antony did not want to be too closely involved with his former commander, who was put on trial for leading his army out of Syria without authorisation from the Senate. On that particular charge Gabinius was acquitted, but was promptly put on trial again for accepting bribes from Ptolemy. Cicero undertook the defence, at Pompey's insistence, but uncharacteristically he did not perform very well, and Gabinius was condemned and exiled on a charge of extortion.

Antony now required employment, preferably distant from Rome and the men to whom he owed money. He went from Syria to Gaul, via the overland route through Asia Minor and Greece. Presumably he did not simply set off on this journey vaguely hoping that Caesar would welcome him. Before he left Syria, or while he was travelling, he probably contacted Caesar himself, or one of Caesar's adherents, though it is not known who might have recommended him. The details of Antony's journey to Gaul, the date of his arrival there, and Caesar's opinion of him, have not been recorded, nor is it known what he did for the next two years.

By the end of those two years he had attained a position of importance as one of Caesar's generals, sometimes entrusted with semi-independent commands which called for initiative and courage. How he arrived at this position of trusted officer is not documented. While older and more experienced officers like Titus Labienus planned and executed brilliant strategic actions in virtually independent commands, Antony served an unrecorded two-year apprenticeship under the eye of Caesar, and impressed him sufficiently to gain promotion. The first mention of Antony by name in Caesar's commentaries is in the account of the siege of Alesia, when Antony and Trebonius, called *legati* or legates, shrewdly anticipated trouble and kept troops at the ready, with which they were able to fight off a night attack on the siege works. It was only a minor action, but Caesar had noted it.[39]

The years which Antony spent in Gaul with Caesar were eventful ones for Rome. The marriage alliance between Caesar and Pompey was ended when Julia died in childbirth in 54. The child died too, so there was no family connection that may have bound the two men together. Though Julia's death did not create an immediate rift between Pompey and Caesar, it removed a possible soothing influence which she may have exerted upon her father and husband when it came to open war. The situation did not deteriorate overnight, but an inexorable series of developments eventually forced Rome's greatest general into the arms of the Senate and divorced him from the brilliant, determined, ruthless, self-advertising, conqueror of Gaul. Pompey was not tempted by further offers of marriage with relatives of Caesar, and instead married Cornelia, the daughter of Metellus Scipio. Although it has been interpreted as a deliberate snub, this new alliance with a member of the senatorial aristocracy did not necessarily indicate an immediate breach with Caesar.

Nor did the death of Marcus Licinius Crassus necessarily sever relations between Pompey and Caesar. In 53, Crassus was disastrously defeated in Parthia. His dream of conquering the Parthian Empire was shattered; Crassus lost his army and died swallowing molten gold, forced down his throat by the Parthians in reference to his love of wealth. The defeat and death of Crassus begged for revenge, and when the civil wars were over, Caesar made preparations for a Parthian campaign which he intended to start in 44. By this time he had raised the troops and the cash, and he had sent his great-nephew Gaius Octavius to Macedonia where five legions were stationed in readiness, but his plans were terminated by his assassination. Caesar may have discussed the country, the terrain and the enemy army with Antony in Gaul and in Rome after the civil war. When he embarked on his own Parthian campaign, Antony claimed that he was carrying out Caesar's plans.

Even when Crassus was removed from the scene, there were as yet no indications of a serious rift between Pompey and Caesar, much less one that would ultimately lead to war. As long as Caesar devoted himself single-mindedly to the conquest of Gaul, and Pompey devoted himself to keeping order in Rome, the possibility of conflict between them was postponed. Everything depended on what happened when Caesar's term as governor expired. The potential problems did not solely concern the termination of Caesar's command, but centred on his plans to step without a break from his proconsulship to a second consulship. He could not legally enter Rome until he relinquished his command, so he sought permission from the Senate to stand for the consular elections *in absentia*, remaining in his province while the elections were held. Caesar's wish to remain in command of troops until he could take up office as consul derived from his reluctance to enter Rome as a private citizen for the elections. As provincial governor in command of troops, and as consul, he would be immune from prosecution under any heading, but as a mere *privatus* he could be legally prosecuted by anyone who wished to do so. This was a tacit admission that he had left behind him a trail of several dubious actions that merited prosecution, and he was in no doubt that some of his enemies would bring one or more cases against him. His assumptions have been challenged and translated into mere excuses for not laying down his command. The likelihood of prosecution has been played down and the possibility of condemnation in the courts has been dismissed.[40] This perhaps

misses the point. It is possible that Caesar entertained no worries at
all about condemnation, but if he had to undergo a trial or multiple
trials he would not be able to stand as a candidate for the consular elections. Catilina lost two years through such procedures, and
Caesar never felt inclined to waste two years.

While this potential source of trouble was still fomenting, Caesar
fostered Antony's career, not entirely altruistically, since Caesar
required magistrates in Rome who were sympathetic to his cause.
Antony was despatched home in the last months of 53, to stand as
a candidate for the quaestorship for the following year. He went
immediately to see Cicero, who refers to the visit in the *Philippics*,[41]
revealing that Caesar had written to him to ask him to receive Antony
and support his candidature for the quaestorship. It was probably a
short time after he arrived in Rome when Antony met Clodius in
the street and a fight broke out. Antony chased him, sword in hand,
into a bookshop where Clodius took refuge on the upper floor, but
Antony backed off, and Clodius survived.[42]

Antony was elected quaestor for 52, a year of escalating violence.
For the last two years there had been so much corruption, bribery
and violence in the city that the consular elections had been postponed each year, and in 52 it seemed that they would have to be
postponed indefinitely. Pompey had lost much of his popularity
and had suffered from a series of political attacks on himself and
his associates, following the example set by Clodius as tribune in
58. In retaliation, Pompey had fostered Titus Annius Milo who was
tribune in 57. With Pompey's undeclared approval, Milo formed an
armed gang to counteract the disruptive activities of Clodius. By
54 Clodius and Pompey had reached an unofficial truce. Pompey's
elder son Gnaeus married Clodius's niece, the daughter of Appius
Claudius Pulcher, Clodius's brother.

Although Clodius had ceased to focus on Pompey, he had never
become reconciled with Milo, and at the beginning of 52, the two
of them, each with their entourage, met at Bovillae on the Via Appia,
about ten miles outside Rome. There was a brawl that turned into

a small battle, in which Clodius was killed. His body was carried into Rome, where the populace, always loyal to him because of the benefits he brought them, gave him a splendid unofficial funeral in which they managed to burn down the Senate House. Fulvia, widow of Clodius, married Antony's good friend Curio.

During the disturbances of the previous few years, rumours had circulated that Pompey wished to be made Dictator.[43] He denied it, but it was his recognised technique to declare that he was not seeking posts and then to accept them when they were offered. While the Clodian gangs attacked Milo's house and his supporters, Calpurnius Bibulus proposed that Pompey should be made sole consul in order to empower him to bring order to the city. The consulship was more acceptable than the Dictatorship, because the powers were limited. Pompey as Dictator would have been subject to no other authority, but as consul he could be called to account, and the tribunes could still veto his actions. He accepted and at once set in motion the necessary measures, one of which was to bring his erstwhile agent Milo to trial. He surrounded the court with soldiers and intimidated Cicero, who had been asked to defend Milo. The noted orator could not speak with his usual authority and he lost the case. Antony made a speech against Milo. He may have fallen out with Clodius for personal reasons but he had once been his friend, and neither Pompey nor Cicero ever fell into that category.

As consul, Pompey passed several laws, three of which directly or indirectly concerned Caesar. The so-called law of ten tribunes started out as a proposal to recall Caesar from Gaul to Rome so that he could be appointed Pompey's colleague in the consulship. While this would have facilitated the direct passage from proconsulship to consulship, Caesar was not yet ready to leave Gaul. The conquest was not complete, so if he left too soon and uprisings broke out, all his work would be undone and someone else would have to be sent out to deal with it. In place of the first law, Caesar and Pompey proposed another, that Caesar could stand for the consulship without presenting himself personally in Rome. This law was passed and all seemed to be going smoothly, then Pompey passed two more laws designed to bring order out of chaos and reduce the opportunities to bribe the electorate to gain magistracies and provincial commands, but these laws seemed to be designed to embarrass Caesar. The *lex de iure magistratuum* stipulated that candidates for any office must come to Rome for the elections. Pompey added a codicil to this law specifically exempting Caesar, which meant that the law of ten tribunes could stand, but he wished to make it clear that this was an exception, and would be the last time that anyone could stand for election *in absentia*. Interpretation of Pompey's actions vary. He has been dismissed as careless, with a bad memory for laws that he had only very recently passed. Worse still, he has been accused of devious double dealing, attempting to deceive Caesar by surreptitiously overturning the law allowing him to stand for election *in absentia*, then when the little subterfuge was discovered, of backing down and writing a codicil. This is patently not tenable; Pompey deserves more credit for common sense.[44]

The next law that appeared to thwart Caesar's plans was the *lex de provinciis*, establishing a five year gap between holding office in Rome and becoming a governor of a province. It was designed to put an end to the rampant bribery, and the borrowing that supported it, by removing the possibility of rapid reimbursement by exploitation of the unfortunate provincials. The law obviated the need to allocate consular provinces before the elections, putting an end to the pre-election squabbling and scrambling for commands, and it also overturned the law passed by Gaius Sempronius Gracchus forbidding tribunician veto on the allocation of consular commands. One of the immediate results of this law was that for the next few years there were not enough suitably qualified personnel to govern the provinces, so men who had no ambition to be provincial governors had to be rounded up and persuaded to go abroad. Cicero, whose epicentre of the universe was Rome and who could not endure life beyond a short radius outside the city, had to go and govern Cilicia for a year, returning to Rome in summer 50.

Some modern scholars have interpreted Pompey's law as a contradiction of his agreement with Caesar, because in theory the Senate could now appoint a new governor to the Gallic provinces at any time, forcing Caesar to give up his command. It was not a serious threat, since any of the tribunes would have been able to block the proposal. Pompey had not turned against his ally, and was still doing everything in his power to help Caesar, though later historians such as Dio traced the beginning of the civil war to the period of Pompey's sole consulship when he appeared to be making laws designed to thwart Caesar's ambitions. In reality, there were no misgivings among contemporaries that it would all end in civil war a few years later.[45]

As quaestor, Antony's responsibilities were mainly financial and judicial. Senior magistrates in Rome or commanders of armies outside Rome could ask for particular quaestors to serve under them, for a theoretical period of two years. In Caesar's commentaries Antony is described as quaestor, usually translated as quartermaster general, and although his functions were largely administrative, primarily to keep the financial accounts, Antony was obviously much more than a chief clerk, since he was placed in charge of troops and despatched on special missions.

Caesar's promotion of Antony was most probably due to his education, and to long term observation of his abilities coupled with an assessment of his loyalty. There were other officers in Caesar's army who were entrusted with semi-independent commands, but not all of them were selected for political advancement. Antony was now properly launched upon his political career, and indelibly dyed as one of Caesar's protégés. During the winter of 51 he was put in charge of the winter quarters near Bibracte (modern Autun),[46] while Caesar fought a rapid campaign in December against the Bituriges, whose lands were fertile, and provided a lucrative source of supplies. Antony was placed in command of the Twelfth legion in a campaign against the Eburones, who dwelt between the river Meuse and the Rhine.[47] After this campaign, he remained in northern Gaul, in command of fifteen cohorts, the equivalent of one and a half legions.[48] In this part of Gaul, just south of the Rhine, the last spark of Gallic resistance to Roman domination was finally obliterated. For some time Commius, the leader of the Atrebates, had resisted the Roman advance, liaising with the Germanic peoples across the Rhine, whose aid he sought more than once in his struggle. When threatened he simply fled across the Rhine to his allies. He was a constant thorn in Caesar's side, clever, resourceful and justifiably bitter. He had made the mistake in the previous year of agreeing to talk to the Roman envoy Gaius Volusenus Quadratus, unaware that Caesar's trusted lieutenant, Titus Labienus, had arranged an ambush.[49] Unfortunately for Caesar, but fortunately for Commius, the centurion appointed to despatch him bungled the job, so Commius got away with a head wound and a lifelong grudge.

As commander of the northern region, Antony soon came into conflict with Commius, who waged a perpetual guerrilla war, damaging communications and supply lines by raids with his swift horsemen. Gaius Volusenus was now Antony's cavalry commander, and was given the task of frustrating Commius's raids. The two met in a skirmish, in which Commius personally led the charge against the Roman horsemen, wounding Volusenus in the thigh.[50] Eventually Commius agreed to terms with Antony, sending hostages as guarantee for his good behaviour. Unfortunately it is not known what part Antony played in bringing about this capitulation. Commius migrated to Britain, and the peoples of Gaul finally accepted Roman rule. Antony's contribution in ending the war was hardly one of resounding military or historical importance, but he had shown that he could act on his own initiative and it was clear that Caesar trusted him.

Antony returned to Italy in 50 to stand for election as augur. This was a religious office which he retained all his life. He may have sought the appointment in 53 when he came to Rome to stand for the quaestorship, because a vacancy had occurred after the death of Crassus' son in Parthia. If he stood for the office at that time clearly he did not obtain it. In 50 there was another vacancy when Cicero's friend, the orator Quintus Hortensius died, and on this occasion Antony was successfully elected.[51] Caesar canvassed for his election vigorously, and as usual by now, Caesar's support won the day. Antony's main rival was Domitius Ahenobarbus, whose candidacy was favoured by Cato and the senatorial party, all of them anti-Caesarians to the last man, so Antony's success was all the more remarkable. In the last book of the *Gallic Wars*, Aulus Hirtius comments that Caesar was happy to use his influence to benefit a close friend, and was also pleased to secure the election of Antony in opposition to those people who desired to reduce his influence when he returned from his province.[52]

The duties of the augurs were to observe and interpret the heavenly signs from the gods, which could be revealed to them in the skies or in the flights of birds. Taking the auspices, or divination of the will of the gods, was an important feature of Roman life, rooted in the distant past; the word auspices derives from *auspicium* or *avispicium*, denoting the observation of birds (*avis*, bird; *specio*, I look). No magistrate would embark on serious business without taking the auspices first, so the augurs who were entrusted with interpretation of the signs could exert significant power over public life. If the omens were unfavourable they could suspend all public business, or even retrospectively invalidate actions or decisions that had already been taken. With Antony as augur, there would have been several advantages for Caesar if ever need arose, even if only to extricate himself from temporary difficulties. For both Caesar and Antony, the appointment was not just an empty honour, it was a useful political tool. It is certain that without the slightest hesitation, Antony would interpret the signs in accordance with Caesar's wishes.

Antony's appointment as augur was aided and abetted by his old friend Curio, who was tribune in 50, the year of the elections. He too was Caesar's man, either by inclination, or as some men said, Caesar had bought him. The two friends worked towards the same end, protecting Caesar's interests. This was a crucial time for Caesar.

The problems over his tenure of Gaul had already begun in 51 when the consul Marcellus suggested that Caesar should be recalled in that year. Pompey tried to put an end to vacillation, and opted for a definite terminal date of 1 March 50, on the reasonable grounds that in 55 the command of Gaul had been granted to Caesar for a second term of five years. This postponed the thorny decision for a while, and clung firmly to the letter of the law.

The terminal date of 1 March 50 came and went without the outbreak of serious hostilities. For the rest of the year, whenever the matter of Caesar's recall was raised in the Senate, Curio as tribune vetoed the proceedings if there was the slightest hint of a threat to Caesar. Through the agency of Curio, Caesar offered a compromise solution on 1 December 50. He proposed that he would disband his army before he entered Rome to stand for the consulship, if Pompey would also disband his troops as a reciprocal gesture.[53] Many senators approved of this plan but the consuls sabotaged it. This simply gave Caesar the excuse to claim that if he came to Rome to stand for the consulship, disbanding his army as he was legally obliged to do, then he was potentially at risk from Pompey who had access to troops. Pompey's standing in Rome was made clear by his appointment as sole consul in 52, while at the same time he was governor of Spain where he commanded troops, two departures from the norm which had not been condoned in the past, since there should have been two consuls, and a commander of troops should not even enter the city, much less act as one of the current magistrates. The senate had willingly legalised Pompey's anomalous position, but refused to entertain Caesar as proconsul and candidate for the consulship at the same time. The discrepancy did not go unnoticed and could be utilised when Caesar needed to justify himself.

Curio was nearing the end of his office as tribune. Since it was unlikely that the agitation to recall Caesar would cease, it was important to replace Curio with another compliant Caesarian. Antony in his turn became tribune for 49, taking up office on the traditional date of 10 December of the previous year.[54] Antony could be relied upon to veto any suggestions that threatened to damage Caesar, but such a state of affairs could not continue indefinitely without escalating protests from Caesar's enemies, who manoeuvred to find a new loophole as fast as his friends manoeuvred to close the last one. On 21 December Antony made a speech attacking Pompey, denouncing all his activities since his youth. The content of the speech has not survived but Cicero reported the incident in a letter to his friend Atticus, together with Pompey's reaction.[55] The incident seemed to strengthen Pompey's resolve for war. He asked Cicero, rhetorically, what would Caesar be capable of, if 'this ineffective quaestor' could behave in such a manner.

There followed a proposal in January 49 that Caesar should be forced to disband his army by a certain date or be declared *hostis*, an enemy of the state. The tribunes Mark Antony and Quintus Cassius Longinus vetoed the proposal, but feelings were running very high, and the Senate was not willing to compromise. Antony and Cassius were thrown out of the Senate House, with the threat that their safety could not be guaranteed if they tried to re-enter.[56] They left Rome in a hurry, disguised as slaves, and accompanied by Curio they made their way to Caesar, who was at Ravenna. When he heard the news that the tribunes had been threatened and that the Pompeians were indulging in ominous spear rattling, Caesar made a speech to the troops and marched to Ariminum in Italy. Though Caesar does not say as much in his self-justificatory account of the civil wars, this entailed crossing the river Rubicon, in geographical terms a rather insignificant stream, so insignificant that no one today can say with certainty where it is, but in political terms it was supremely important because it marked the boundary between his province and northern Italy.[57] To march across it at the head of troops was an unequivocal declaration of war.

When Antony, Cassius and Curio arrived at Caesar's camp at Ariminum, dishevelled and tired, Caesar quickly grasped the opportunity to show them to the troops in their sorry state, and made Curio explain to the soldiers just how shabbily the tribunes had been treated.[58] He had all the evidence that he needed to work up the troops with the news that Antony and Cassius, trying to protect the interests of Caesar and therefore of the army, had been forcibly ejected from the Senate and hounded out of Rome in fear for their lives. Not only that, but Caesar was now declared a public enemy and by extension of that idea the soldiers too were enemies. This was their reward for fighting hard for the greater glory of Rome for the past eight or nine years – to be declared enemies and therefore outlaws. Having dealt with the soldiers, Caesar attended to his political image. When he wrote his commentary on the civil wars, he explained that he wished to protect the sacrosanctity of the tribunes, a theme which he reiterated more than once.

While Caesar concentrated on raising more troops, Antony was sent on an independent mission, to secure Arretium (modern Arezzo) with five cohorts under his command.[59] When the town was won, and Caesar had his troops, the two of them reunited 150km from Rome at Corfinium. The citizens of the town of Sulmo declared themselves ready to submit to Caesar, but they were held back by the senator Quintus Lucretius. Antony was despatched with five cohorts of the Thirteenth legion, but there was no fighting. The citizens opened the gates, welcomed and congratulated Antony, and he set off to rejoin Caesar. Cicero gloomily reported the incident to his friend Atticus.[60]

Already one of Caesar's trusted lieutenants, Antony may have been drawn closer to Caesar after the departure of Titus Labienus. Until now Labienus had always been associated with Caesar, but he came from Picenum, Pompey's homeland, and his allegiance wavered. Caesar heard the rumours but did not believe them, until Labienus joined the Pompeians. From then onwards he was the most implacable of Caesar's enemies. He may have been jealous that Antony's promotion came without long and hard service in the army, but no one knows why Labienus left Caesar when the civil war began; perhaps not even Caesar knew the reason.[61]

Pompey meanwhile had been caught off guard by Caesar's rapid advance from the north. He had done nothing to raise an effective army, having proclaimed proudly but misguidedly that he only had to stamp his foot and troops would spring up in Italy. Stamp as he would, few troops sprang up. Having no army of sufficient calibre to match Caesar's battle-hardened soldiers, Pompey abandoned Rome and withdrew to the south. He needed to delay the start of the war, and take time to train his army. Eventually he set sail from Brundisium and transferred the whole of his army to Greece. Many senators, forced to make a choice, followed him. Caesar was now supreme in Italy, but he was flanked on east and west by armed enemies. Pompey was governor of Spain *in absentia*, so the troops there were loyal, and held the province for him. Caesar acted decisively. He decided to deal with Spain first, summing up the situation with one of his usual succinct phrases, 'I am going to fight an army with no commander, then I will deal with the commander with no army'.

Caesar made his dispositions, sending various officers to secure certain territories. Curio was sent to Sicily, and Antony's brother Gaius Antonius to Illyria. Caesar gave Antony propraetorian powers, placing him in charge of all the troops stationed in Italy,[62] which effectively gave Antony control of the government, with the exception of the city of Rome, where Marcus Aemilius Lepidus as urban praetor was responsible for day to day administration. Antony was quite capable of keeping order, both among the civilian communities and in the army. Energetic and committed, he fulfilled his duties with determination and vigour, but without the oppressive and stern attitude that would have ruined his attempts to reconcile opposing factions. He travelled the length and breadth of the country visiting the troops.

There were still several important people who had not yet joined the Pompeians, so it was important for Caesar to cultivate people and dissuade them from taking money and materials to Pompey. Antony's education had equipped him for persuasive letter writing, and he tried quite eloquently to convert Cicero to the Caesarian cause, by alternately cajoling and then by making veiled threats about what might happen if he decided to join the Pompeians.[63] In another letter to Cicero, Antony revealed that Caesar had ordered him to keep a close watch on the ports to prevent anyone from leaving Italy. He suggested that perhaps Cicero should write to Caesar himself.[64] In the end, Cicero did leave Italy, but his initial vacillation probably did not impress Pompey very much, and after he had lived with the army for a while, he was disgusted at everyone's behaviour.

Much later, after Caesar's assassination, Cicero tried to blacken Antony's name in connection with his command of Italy. He emphasised the fact that Antony ignored the needs of the civilians in the Italian towns while he attended to the troops, and had scandalised the aristocracy of the municipalities by appearing at official receptions in the company of his mistress, an actress no less.[65] His treatment of town officials and the leading representatives of local councils was shameless, for instance he summoned some of them to meet him one morning but stayed in bed and told them to come back the next day.[66] It is significant that even at his most vitriolic Cicero could find nothing more serious with which to charge Antony. If there had been death and destruction, pillage and looting, or the slightest misdemeanour to report, Cicero would not have wasted his time thinking up fulsome phrases to describe loose morals and actresses. Antony's conduct in Italy may not have been exemplary in the social sphere, but he would understand the importance of winning over the population of the Italian municipalities, not least because they provided the main recruiting grounds for soldiers and political supporters. The town of Bologna provided many of Antony's own political clients. As he toured Italy, Antony would be constantly aware that he represented not just Rome, but Caesar himself, and without Caesar, and Caesar's money and Caesar's support, he would be alone; he would have no hope whatsoever of furthering his political progress by changing his allegiance, since he was by now too much involved with Caesar to make a credible convert to any other party, and in this case there were definitely only two sides to choose from. Cicero's accusation that Antony shirked his duties at this time cannot be substantiated; it would have been foolish in the extreme to have neglected any groups of people in Italy who could cause trouble, or conversely provide Caesarian supporters.

There were some reverses for the Caesarians abroad which affected Antony on a personal level. His friend Curio had been sent to Sicily, and from there he had crossed to Africa with two legions to fight the Pompeians who had allied with Juba, king of Numidia. The expedition was a complete disaster, and Curio was killed.[67] Fulvia was therefore a widow for the second time. Antony's brother Gaius[68] was captured by the Pompeians, and remained a prisoner until after the final battle at Pharsalus. His troops were recruited into Pompey's army. Nearer home, Caesar had to deal with a mutiny among his own army. The soldiers had fought in Spain and on the way home they had taken Massilia, which had stood against Caesar. They had made some profit from this exercise, but now they were tired, had nothing to show for their efforts and did not want to fight anywhere else. Caesar singled out the Ninth legion and threatened to decimate it, lining up the soldiers and killing every tenth man. Before he did so he made a speech to the soldiers, addressing them as citizens, as though discharge were an accomplished fact. In calling their bluff Caesar rapidly brought them to their senses; very soon they were clamouring to fight wherever he sent them. Caesar tidied up by executing a few ringleaders and turned his attention to Rome.

Politically Caesar was now supreme. Lepidus as urban praetor proposed that Caesar should be made Dictator. In this instance Caesar's tenure of the post was even shorter than the normal six month period, since he laid down the office and left Rome after only eleven days in the city, having first secured his election as consul for 48, with Servilius Isauricus as colleague. By the time he entered upon his consulship, he was on his way to Greece. There was little time to lose, since Pompey had been recruiting and training his army for a year. Caesar's greatest problem was his lack of ships. He set sail with seven legions and the cavalry, leaving five legions under Antony, to be ferried across the Adriatic.[69] Caesar planned to send his transports back for the rest of his army, but Bibulus, his embittered

consular colleague and commander of the Pompeian fleet, managed
to destroy most of them, cutting Caesar off from the rest of his army.
But Caesar proved himself as resourceful as ever. He evaded capture
and landed near Palaeste, and soon won over Oricum and Apollonia,
where he made camp. He sent messages to Antony to embark the
five legions as soon as possible and sail to Oricum. Caesar was in a
perilous position, with only half his army holding onto a narrow strip
of territory. He sent envoys to Pompey with proposals of peace, and
was rebuffed. It served to delay an outbreak of fighting for which he
was not prepared. He could not seriously have intended or expected
to bring the war to a conclusion in this way.

When Antony did not appear, Caesar may have begun to wonder
if his lieutenant was perhaps hanging back on purpose, waiting to
see who would emerge as the victor.[70] Famously, Caesar tried to set
sail in an open boat to cross the Adriatic and hurry the troops along,
but the weather and tides conspired against him, forcing him back to
land. This story as told by Caesar himself puts a rather more heroic
interpretation on the event. He encouraged the captain of the ship
with the famous phrase, 'Have no fear, you carry Caesar and his fortune'. This time, however, Fortune failed him, and he had to rely on
Antony's ingenuity instead.

Antony was experiencing frustrating delays, blockaded in
Brundisium by squadrons of the Pompeian fleet under the command
of Libo, who occupied the island of Santa Andraea as a base. This was
a very strong position for the fleet, but the one commodity that the
Pompeians lacked was fresh water. Antony knew this. He guarded all
the landing places where the Pompeians might come in for water,
and waited. Libo was eventually forced to withdraw to find water
elsewhere, and Antony seized his chance.[71] He set sail for Apollonia,
but the wind was in the wrong direction, and forced him towards
Nymphaeum, north of Dyrrachium.[72] He made a good landing,
skilfully avoiding the Pompeian fleet, and while he was hurriedly
disembarking his troops, the wind changed, blowing the enemy ships
onto the shore, where they lost several vessels. He put ashore three

veteran legions, one legion of recruits, and eight hundred cavalry. Then he sent most of the ships back to Italy to bring over the rest of the infantry and cavalry, leaving the pontoons at Lissus, so that if Caesar had to return to Italy in an emergency he would at least have some form of transport.[73] Unfortunately, a short time later, Pompey's elder son Gnaeus discovered the pontoons at Lissus and burnt them.

After disembarking Antony sent a message to Caesar to explain the arrangements he had made, and then lost no time in setting off southwards to join Caesar's army, while at the same time Pompey marched north to intercept him. The potential trap did not work; either Caesarian troops reached Antony to warn him, or he sent out reliable scouts who discovered the Pompeian army. Forethought and knowledge of the enemy plans saved Antony from ambush. It was now Pompey himself who had to give up the pursuit and make his escape, since he was between two armies, having lost the opportunity of eliminating them one at a time. A heroic stand was out of the question. Pompey withdrew to fight elsewhere.

If Caesar had harboured any doubts about Antony, they ought to have been dispelled after these episodes, which demonstrated that in Antony, Caesar had a capable and reliable lieutenant, who would do as he was asked to the best of his ability, and who displayed courage and considerable intelligence in carrying out his orders. Antony had used guile, patience, and his knowledge of geography to outwit Libo, instead of tackling him head on, inviting a battle, and probably losing ships and men in the process. He had embarked as soon as Libo moved off, and after landing at Nymphaeum he had managed to avoid walking straight into Pompey's ambush. Mark Antony, for all his love of wine, women and song, and his dissolute behaviour, had a level head and knew when to remain patiently inactive and when to burst into action.

Reunited with Antony, Caesar marched off. As soon as Pompey realised where he was heading, he followed in hot pursuit, so the two armies raced for Dyrrachium.[74] Caesar reached the destination first, but Pompey seized the high ground of Petra, while retaining access to the sea. Caesar dug in around the enemy camp, blockading it on three sides with siege works running right round them from the sea shore in the north to the sea shore in the south. The result was stalemate, and the campaign now hinged on supplies. Pompey was surrounded, but his troops could be supplied by sea; Caesar on the other hand was free to come and go, but his troops steadily ate their way through the available food and had to go further and further away to find supplies. The situation was compounded by the fact that the Pompeian army had already stripped the immediate territory of most of its available food while Caesar fought the war in Spain.

There were two possible solutions. One was to risk everything on a pitched battle, but Pompey wisely avoided committing himself, so Caesar could not bring him to anything more than a minor skirmish. The second solution was simply to wait. Time would tip the balance, for two reasons. Firstly, in the fertile plains at Caesar's back, the crops would eventually grow again, enabling him to feed both men and horses. Secondly, though Pompey could feed his troops on seaborne supplies, he had no fodder for his horses, so it would eventually be Pompey, not Caesar, who found himself in serious difficulties. It was in Caesar's interests to wait and try somehow to survive the starvation of the first months. Before the waiting game bore fruit, Pompey tried to break out. A plan to lure Caesar into a trap was foiled by hard fighting. Next, Pompey attacked the weakest point in Caesar's lines, at the south end near the sea.[75] At this point, Caesar had constructed two lines of defences, one facing inwards to complete the siege works, and one facing outwards to guard against the possibility of a Pompeian attack from behind. The theory was sound, but the lines simply extended down to the sea, and had not yet been closed off with a trench and palisade joining the two parallel defences together. It was possible, therefore, to penetrate between the two lines from the coast. Two Gallic chieftains, deserting from Caesar for reasons unknown, gave Pompey all the information he needed to exploit this weak spot. There was an added advantage in that Caesar's main camp was at the extreme northern end of the siege works, while the southern tip was guarded by the quaestor Lentulus Marcellinus, who was ill.

Pompey's attack began in the middle of the night. He ferried sixty cohorts to the point of attack, complete with ladders and light artillery. He had ordered the men to put wicker shields on their helmets to protect them from missiles thrown by the Caesarian troops. He co-ordinated the attack from the sea with another attack from within the Pompeian camp, so the Caesarians found themselves in a desperate position, with the enemy to their front and rear, and also between the two lines. The Caesarians broke and ran. Marcellinus' cohorts were unable to reverse the position, but Antony came up from the outposts with twelve cohorts and managed to stabilise the lines.[76] This was no mean feat. If Caesar did not exaggerate wildly, then Antony was outnumbered four to one, and had to instil confidence in men who were badly frightened and had given up. But he did it, somehow. By now he would be a well known figure, with a reputation for courage and ingenuity. Men would trust him to be able to do something in adverse situations like this. If they had no faith in him, they would have carried on running away. Eventually Caesar himself arrived, hurrying down from the northern sector, and the Pompeians were beaten off.

Pompey had so nearly won this last battle. His next move was to camp near the siege works, a short distance from the sea, where he could supply his troops and provide fodder for his horses. Caesar tried to storm the camp in a surprise attack, but his troops were routed. If Pompey had followed up this victory immediately it is doubtful if Caesar would have survived; even in the absence of a vigorous pursuit, Caesar decided to raise the siege. He did so in progressive stages. First the baggage, then most of the army left, except for two legions. Caesar intended to keep Pompey guessing until he could get most of the army away; at the last moment, Caesar departed for Apollonia, where he lodged the wounded men. Pompey followed, usually not quite as rapidly as Caesar moved. After it became clear that this was a definite withdrawal and not a short promenade, Pompey was further delayed because his troops had not brought all their baggage with them, and went back to the camp at Dyrrachium for their belongings.

The two armies came to a halt near Pharsalus, where they both made camp. Each day Caesar drew up his army in battle order, but could not tempt Pompey to risk a fight. He decided to march away. On the very day appointed for the Caesarians to break camp, Pompey came out in style. Caesar rapidly changed his plans. Thus the battle of Pharsalus began. Antony commanded the left wing, with two legions, the Eighth and the Ninth, but they were depleted by their losses at Dyrrachium and their combined strength amounted to only one legion.[77] This is the sum total of knowledge about Antony's part in the battle. The decisive action was on Caesar's right, where he had shrewdly placed eight cohorts of his normal reserve. He brought them into the battle just at the right moment, as the Pompeian cavalry drove the Caesarian horsemen back, exposing the whole of the right wing to attack. The reserve stood their ground with their spears stuck into the earth to form a bristling defensive line. Gradually the tables were turned, and it was the Pompeian left flank which was exposed to attack, but Pompey's troops did not hold their positions. Long before it was over Pompey left the field, because he knew that all was lost. He rode back to camp, then almost immediately left it in haste, disguised as a trader or a slave, just as the Caesarians broke in. Antony was given the task of pursuing the fleeing Pompeian army, which he did with relentless efficiency. It was an important task, and contributed to the completeness of the victory; too many stragglers left to their own devices could reunite, and become a dangerous element, fighting on in the name of Pompey, or Rome, or the Republic. Caesar needed to kill or capture as many as he could.

Pompey himself evaded capture. He took ship and headed to Egypt, and Caesar followed, because in Egypt Pompey could rely upon his connections with Ptolemy Auletes, borrow money and recruit another army, and continue the war. Caesar could not let this happen. He may have hoped to meet Pompey and reach an agreement that would end hostilities. He could not know at this point that Pompey would meet death at the hands of the Egyptian courtiers, putting a grisly end to the first phase of the civil wars, and leaving unfinished business with Pompey's sons and adherents. When news of the battle of Pharsalus reached Rome, the Senate appointed Caesar Dictator for one year, twice the normal tenure. He accepted the post but could not return to Rome to exercise it. While he chased after Pompey one of Caesar's most pressing requirements was for someone with authority to look after affairs in Italy, and for this task he chose Antony, sending him back to Italy as soon as possible, and appointing him *magister equitum*, or master of horse, the traditional deputy of the Dictator. There was a debate in the Senate about Antony's appointment, which technically ought to have expired after six months, but Dio[78] points out that since Caesar's dictatorship had been confirmed for a year, and the office of *magister equitum* expired along with the Dictatorship, it was hardly necessary to quibble about the duration of Antony's command as his deputy.

As master of horse, Antony once again commanded troops in Italy, which emphasised the fact that he was Caesar's lieutenant in the military and political spheres. Unfortunately, largely through circumstances beyond his control, everything started to go wrong and there were riots in Rome that he had to suppress, somewhat bloodily, and Antony found himself out of favour and unemployed when Caesar returned to Rome.

2
Caesar's Lover:
Cleopatra 69–47BC

Cleopatra belonged to one of the highest ranking dysfunctional families of the ancient world, descended from a dynasty of Macedonian Greeks who had been murdering each other with alarming regularity for nearly three hundred years before she was born. She was one of several children of Ptolemy XII Auletes (the Flute Player) who came to power in 80 and tenaciously held onto his throne through a series of near disasters and attempted coups for the next three decades. The reputation of her father for incompetence and cruelty did very little to raise the profile of Cleopatra, who is portrayed in the meagre ancient sources as untrustworthy, scheming, power crazed, with the avowed intent of obliterating Rome. This one-sided portrait derives from the biased and hostile Roman sources. The works of later Roman and Greek historians subscribe largely to the official version promoted by Octavian, who geared the Romans for war, not against his fellow Roman Antony, who was dismissed as a poor bewitched hanger-on, but against Cleopatra, who was female, foreign, and the ruler of a wealthy country that several Romans had been trying to bring within their grasp for many years.

The Ptolemaic dynasty, of which Cleopatra was the last representative, was founded at the end of the fourth century BC. The Ptolemies were not of Egyptian extraction, but stemmed from Ptolemy Soter, a Macedonian Greek in the entourage of Alexander the Great. Alexander's Empire was quickly won, but consisted of various disparate territories that were not firmly welded together at his death in 323. His closest friends and generals were left without leadership, but they soon rallied, and split up to take over parts of the territories he had conquered. These new kingdoms, known as the Successor kingdoms, enjoyed different fates. Some of the Successors like Ptolemy Soter founded long-lasting dynasties that survived for centuries. They all adopted the customs and institutions of their new domains, and superimposed on them Greek forms of administration.

Ptolemy Soter kidnapped Alexander's corpse and transported it to Egypt, first to Memphis and then to Alexandria, where he deposited the body in a famous tomb in the centre of the city. He had to use force to eject Cleomenes, the official Macedonian administrator, and thereafter founded a dynasty that survived for not quite three centuries until Rome put an end to it. Ptolemy chose Egypt for many reasons. It had tremendous advantages. Thanks to the Nile, it was extremely fertile, and consequently very wealthy.

The first Ptolemy ruled Egypt via an amalgamation of Macedonian administrative systems and Egyptian practices. Greek was the official legal and administrative language, but he ensured the survival of the native Egyptian language, culture, and religion. He preserved both Royal Greek and Pharaonic Egyptian ceremonials and respected Egyptian traditions, but he moved the capital from Memphis to Alexandria on the coast, bringing Egypt into closer contact with the Mediterranean world. For the first two decades of his reign Ptolemy I Soter concentrated on the defence of his kingdom against the aggressive and acquisitive urges of his rivals. By the beginning of the third century BC he was secure enough to extend his power over Cyprus and the Aegean islands, important for trade and control over weaker neighbouring powers.

The fertility and wealth of Egypt did not go unnoticed by the Romans. When Ptolemy I Soter appointed himself as ruler, Rome was still groping towards domination of Italy, but by the time that Cleopatra's father Ptolemy XII Auletes inherited the Egyptian domains, Rome had become a world power, and the Romans, particularly one or two leading senators such as Pompey and Caesar, were not slow to recognise the advantages of bringing Egypt within their growing Empire. Plans for annexation were formed on more than one occasion but not put into effect. In 65 it was suggested that Julius Caesar should take over the country and its satellite territories. That suggestion came to nothing, then in the following year a tribune of the plebs proposed a law for agrarian reform, for which purpose a Board of Ten should be created to decide which lands belonged to Rome, and among the recommendations was another suggestion that Egypt should be annexed. Cicero talked this law to death, and for the next few years, leading Romans extended credit to Ptolemy Auletes to enable him to keep his throne.

Cleopatra was born in 69, in a world increasingly dominated by Rome. She was the seventh royal descendant of the Ptolemies to bear her name. No one knows who was the mother of Cleopatra VII, so speculation that she was half Syrian or half Ethiopian must remain unproven. The story that Cleopatra was the daughter of a mistress of Ptolemy Auletes can be dismissed. Except for an intriguing statement of Strabo's[1] that Auletes had three daughters and the only legitimate one was the eldest (Cleopatra was the middle daughter), the charge of illegitimacy was apparently never made against Cleopatra, and it is surprising, if it were true, that her Roman enemies failed to use it. Octavian-Augustus would probably have made some mileage out of such information in his virulent propaganda against her. The lack of scurrilous tales about Cleopatra's illegitimacy, and her high status within the family makes it clear that her mother was legally married to Auletes. The question is, who was the mother?

Ptolemaic marriages tended to be complicated and after two thousand years they are not well documented. Marriage was kept largely within the family. Brother-sister marriage was practised, uncles married nieces, stepmothers married stepsons. Each Ptolemaic ruler might marry two or three wives in succession, so that matching the children to their mothers can be difficult if not impossible. Cleopatra's brothers and sisters were not the offspring of the same mother, and it is possible that there were more children of Auletes and different wives than those that are known by name. The two boys were both called Ptolemy, and of the girls Berenice was the eldest child, followed by Cleopatra and Arsinoe. These were common girls' names among the Ptolemies.

The sources are more confusing than helpful about Cleopatra's maternal origins. According to one version, in 78 Ptolemy XII married his sister Cleopatra Tryphaena, who disappeared from the official records after 69, but no one knows how or why. The year is significantly that of the birth of Cleopatra VII, so it is not impossible that Tryphaena died in childbirth, but there are a few complications to upset this simplistic explanation. An inscription from Edfu records the completion of the great temple in the twenty-fifth year of the reign of Ptolemy Auletes, who was in exile in Rome at the time. The text of the inscription mentions Ptolemy and his sister Queen Cleopatra Tryphaena by name, indicating that she was still alive after 69. Another tradition maintains that during the exile of Auletes from 58 to 55, Cleopatra Tryphaena and her younger sister Berenice were co-rulers, implying that this Tryphaena was the eldest daughter of Ptolemy Auletes. The multiplicity of Cleopatras within one family gives rise to suspicion.[2] There may indeed have been three of them, one being Cleopatra Tryphaena the wife of Ptolemy Auletes, the other two being their eldest daughter also called Cleopatra Tryphaena, and Cleopatra VII. This would make Berenice the second daughter. It is more likely that the co-rulers in the absence of Auletes were in fact mother and daughter, not sisters. The omission of any details in the papyrus records of Cleopatra Tryphaena from 69 onwards may be accounted for by divorce, and her reappearance on a later inscription may mean that during the exile of Auletes she had assumed or been granted the power of regent with her daughter Berenice as co-ruler. None of this speculation can be proven, nor does it answer the question whether Tryphaena was also the mother of Cleopatra VII, whose origins remain obscure.

According to the ancient sources, Cleopatra was not stunningly beautiful. Plutarch[3] admitted that she was not the sort of beautiful woman who instantly attracts attention, but in person she was irresistible because of her charm, her movements, and especially her voice. It is not certain that all or even any of the alleged portraits of her are securely identified, but those which have gained general acceptance as depictions of her do not portray a woman of marked physical beauty. They show an ordinary face, most often, but not always, with a prominent and somewhat hooked nose, which she inherited from her father. This feature is most visible on her coin portraits, some of which are decidedly unflattering. Sculptures portray her with a not-quite-straight mouth that almost smiles, and unremarkable eyes. She was nonetheless fascinating and extremely clever. It was said by the ancient authors that Cleopatra's charming manner and her animated conversation, combined with her intelligence and education, elevated her beyond the realm of physical perfection.

Cleopatra's early life and upbringing were inauspicious. Since she was among the younger members of the family, she could not realistically expect to inherit the kingdom while her brothers and her elder sister still lived. As a child, she witnessed and survived treachery and bloodshed, most of which originated with members of her own family. This was not a new phenomenon among the Ptolemies. Her great-grandfather Ptolemy VIII was continually at odds with the Alexandrians and caused tremendous destruction to the city and surrounding countryside during and after a civil war in 132–130. Her grandfather Ptolemy IX succeeded in 116, initially sharing the kingdom with his mother Cleopatra III, but she expelled him from Egypt and replaced him with his brother Ptolemy X Alexander. Cleopatra III died in 101, and it was believed that Alexander had murdered her. In 88 Ptolemy IX returned, expelled Ptolemy X, and regained his kingdom, fighting off repeated attacks from the sea and from Syria by his brother. He died in 80, during the supremacy of the Roman general Lucius Cornelius Sulla, who placed the younger son of Ptolemy IX on the throne as Ptolemy XI, with Roman support, for which the newly elevated Ptolemy showed his gratitude by allegedly making a will leaving the whole country to the Roman People. He lasted only a few months. He killed his wife, who was also his stepmother, and then in turn the Alexandrians killed him.

The kingdom of Egypt was inherited in 80 by Ptolemy XII Auletes, who also inherited a struggle to keep it. The Romans were already deeply enmeshed in Egyptian politics and government, and refused recognise him as the official ruler, but nor did they seize the kingdom that Ptolemy XI had bequeathed to them. The question of taking control of Egypt continued to surface now and then in Roman politics, so Ptolemy XII spent a lot of time, effort and money cultivating influential Romans to maintain friendly relations and to stave off annexation. Cleopatra was born eleven years after her father's accession. As soon as she was old enough to understand the situation she would know that Rome was the most important power in the Mediterranean world, and had to be appeased and watched closely for signs of acquisitive desires. The moods of the native population required monitoring and, much more urgently, the mixed and highly vocal and volatile population of Alexandria could be fatal. The Alexandrians had expelled more than one ruler of Egypt in the past.

Auletes was the root cause of the unrest. He was neither effective nor decisive, and never developed a ruthless talent for business and profit such as Cleopatra revealed when she was established as ruler and set about reconstituting her country's wealth. Her father had started badly by frittering away his income in search of Roman support. In the beginning he was backed by the wealth of Egypt, so debts scarcely worried him, but the drain of his country's resources in this fashion could not continue unchallenged for ever. During Cleopatra's early childhood he was almost totally dependent on

Rome and the support of influential Romans such as Pompey the Great. The Egyptians and Alexandrians saw the fruits of their labours being regularly siphoned off to pay Ptolemy's Roman creditors, apparently for no other purpose than the continued comfort and enjoyment of their ruler. Though apologists for Auletes recognise in his policies sensible aims and plans for the development of Egypt, to a large extent self-interest seems to have ruled him.

When Gaius Julius Caesar was consul in 59, he arranged for the formal recognition of Ptolemy Auletes as a friend and ally of the Roman People.[4] It was a formal phrase applied to the various so-called client kings allied to Rome. The favour had a price tag attached to it, six thousand talents for Caesar and Pompey, according to Suetonius. Whilst this status as an ally of Rome put an end to the uncertainty of Roman recognition, it did not preclude eventual annexation. The Romans were quite adept at absorbing the territories of their 'friends' (*amici*) on one pretext or another. Nor did recognition by Rome solve the problem of acceptance at home in Egypt, nor the mounting debts. In 58, Auletes owed so much to important Romans that the citizens of Alexandria, losing patience at being taxed to pay these Romans, rebelled and drove their ruler out of the country. Naturally he went to Rome, as the guest of Pompey and others to whom he owed virtually everything, including money, his throne and even his life. While there he spent his time trying to persuade influential politicians to put him back on his throne.

Initially the Senate received the proposals with sympathy, and most senators were ready to restore Auletes, with Pompey the Great urging them on. The choice of who was to carry out the restoration fell on Publius Lentulus Spinther, who was about to set out to govern the province of Cilicia.[5] Once there, he would be close enough to Egypt and would have access to troops, but he never started on his task. Terrible omens gave the opposition a chance to put a stop to proceedings in January 56. On the Alban Mount outside Rome, the statue of Jupiter, Rome's chief deity, was struck by a thunderbolt. The famous Sibylline Books were consulted. These sacred texts had been bequeathed to Rome in the distant past, full of prophecies that guided the Romans in times of stress. Cato was the chief architect of this manoeuvre, triumphantly claiming that the prophecy instructed the Romans to extend friendship if the King of Egypt should ask for assistance, but not to help him by means of an armed force, because danger would threaten. The Senate now forbade anyone to restore Ptolemy, and though the tribunes exercised their veto on this resolution, no moves were made to help him. Ptolemy left Rome under a cloud. An embassy had been despatched from Egypt to Rome to try to dispose of him, and he had arranged for the murder of several of its members.[6] He went to Ephesus, and sometime later Pompey went to visit him there.

It is not known whether Cleopatra VII travelled to Rome with her father. Whether she accompanied him or whether she remained at home, she would learn just how fragile was her father's grasp on the country, and just how intense was Rome's acquisitive interest in Egypt and its wealth, and though she was only about eleven or twelve years old, she would make notes for the future. If she remained in Egypt, no one can say how she survived the three years of her father's absence, or whether she was involved in the palace revolution in 56 when her elder sister Berenice tried to seize power. Cleopatra Tryphaena, who may have ruled with Berenice, is not mentioned; perhaps she had died by this time. To regularise her position Berenice required a consort and an ally, so she investigated princes from other lands. She looked first to the Seleucid kingdom founded by Seleucus, one of the successors of Alexander the Great. Unfortunately her chosen consort died before arrangements had been completed, and the second choice met opposition from Rome and backed down. Her next prince, probably an illegitimate son of one of the Seleucid kings, actually arrived in Egypt, but he proved to be quite unsuitable because of his coarse appearance and uncouth manners, and was quietly strangled on the orders of Berenice. Finally she married Archelaus, of Greek descent, and by the grace of Pompey elevated to the rank of priest king of the temple of the Great Mother at Komana in Pontus.

This marriage was viewed in Rome with some alarm as a threat to Roman stability, but still there was no official sanction by the Senate to mount an expedition to depose Berenice or restore Auletes. Pompey had been forbidden to act in person, but he had connections, one of whom was Aulus Gabinius, the tribune who had proposed the law that gave him the command against the pirates in 66. Conveniently, Gabinius was governor of Syria. Things began to move. It was rumoured that Ptolemy offered Gabinius ten thousand talents if he would march with his troops and replace him on the throne of Egypt. Pompey probably did well out of the transaction but ten thousand talents is a grossly inflated figure.[7]

When Gabinius arrived in Egypt, there was some skirmishing, but it was soon over. A relatively unimportant cavalry officer called Mark Antony spearheaded the invasion from Syria, capturing Pelusium on the east of the Nile Delta before the rest of Gabinius's army had arrived, and opening up the route to Alexandria for the main body of the army. More importantly, he kept the peace after Auletes had executed Berenice and her immediate supporters, and was about to embark on a vengeful massacre of the population of Alexandria. Antony organised a proper funeral for Berenice's husband Archelaus, who had been killed in the fighting, and he also protected the soldiers of the garrison of Pelusium. The rest of the family may or may not have been implicated in the rebellion, but since it is unlikely that all the siblings could act in concert for any length of time without squabbles, it is also unlikely that they all presented a united front against their father. Their young ages probably saved them. The two boys were just young children, and the younger girls were adolescents, Arsinoe aged about eleven, and Cleopatra was about fourteen.

The death of her sister Berenice may have affected Cleopatra very deeply, or it could have left her totally unmoved. Later, when she was established as Queen, she allegedly pronounced her sister disloyal, but that may have been an opinion derived from political necessity rather than personal emotion. Perhaps she learned very early the value of tacit neutrality until the proper time for revealing her hand, when she was certain of success. At fourteen, she was old enough and shrewd enough to realise that after the removal of her elder sister Berenice, and the restoration of her father, her position had improved. Her siblings were all younger than she was herself and she had not lost favour with her father. Cleopatra was now an important and potentially powerful individual.

Conscious of her elevated but precarious position, and wary of upsetting the Alexandrians by too deep or obvious a relationship with the visiting Romans who had replaced her father on the throne, Cleopatra may not have deigned to notice Aulus Gabinius or his dashing young cavalry officer who was currently impressing all of Alexandria with his reckless generosity, his Herculean drinking prowess and athletic form. Mark Antony threw himself passionately into whatever fate decreed for him, and he lived life to the full. He appreciated a feminine form as much as, probably more than, the next man, but in spite of Appian's assertion that he fell in love with Cleopatra at first sight, he was a realist whose aspirations at this time probably did not stretch as far as a lifelong involvement with a princess of the Nile. Similarly the ambitions of the aforementioned princess probably did not include bestowing her favours on a well-built, hard-drinking cavalry officer with no political influence or economic stability. Antony and Cleopatra had nothing to offer each other at this stage. If they met at all in those days, it would be on a formal and very restricted basis, and they would each have noted a name and a face, little more.

Once the object of the expedition was achieved and Ptolemy Auletes was back in control of his kingdom, Gabinius and his officers returned to his province, leaving behind some of the troops in Egypt.[8] The presence of Roman soldiers lent support to Auletes during the last years of his reign, especially as they contracted marriages with local women and raised families. To the Romans this was a shocking dereliction of duty, since soldiers were forbidden to marry, and marriage between Roman citizens and foreigners was illegal. From Auletes' point of view the liaison between Roman soldiers and native women was an advantage because it lent cohesion and stability to the Roman units, which he incorporated into his own army, and employed with success. In his account of the Alexandrian war after the defeat of Pompey, Caesar hints at some sort of civil strife, when he says that the soldiers of Gabinius fought the Egyptians on behalf of Auletes. It is unlikely that this refers to a serious civil war. There may have been discontent and rioting occasioned by Auletes' financial demands, involving the Roman soldiers in police work and crowd-control. For a short time after his restoration, Ptolemy was forced to appoint the Roman financier Gaius Rabirius Postumus as his treasurer, in order to allow him to recoup the money he had lent to pay Caesar and Pompey on behalf of Auletes in 59, and whatever sum that Ptolemy had promised to Gabinius. Rabirius extracted the money so efficiently that the Egyptians finally erupted in protest and he had to leave with indecent haste. The management of the debt for the remaining sums owing to Rabirius were taken over by Caesar, which gave him a perfect excuse to intervene in Egyptian affairs. Magnanimously he reduced the amount by half when he arrived in Egypt after Pharsalus.

The extent to which Auletes may have been preparing Cleopatra for eventual succession to his throne is uncertain. Retrospective evidence, taken out of context, suggests that Cleopatra was always in line for the succession, and no doubt knew of it. The author of the Alexandrian War, probably Aulus Hirtius using Caesar's notes, says that Auletes declared in his will that he wished the country to be ruled by his elder son Ptolemy and his daughter Cleopatra, and moreover Auletes appealed to the Roman people to honour and uphold this wish.[9] This may be Caesarean propaganda, to advertise to both Egyptians and Romans that when he appointed Cleopatra as Queen of Egypt he had the backing of the legitimate testimony of the last ruler. The Egyptians would more likely acquiesce if they believed that the decision to promote Cleopatra derived from the declared intentions of Ptolemy XII rather than an uninvited Roman general, and the Roman people would also acquiesce in the decisions taken by Caesar if they imagined that they had a part to play in these measures.

At the beginning of the year 51 Auletes died, probably in the early spring of that year, perhaps in May, but the precise month is unknown. Evidence from papyrus records indicates that the thirtieth and final regnal year of Auletes was also counted jointly as the first year of Cleopatra's reign, implying that for a brief period there was in fact a joint reign.[10] Normal Ptolemaic procedure was to begin new regnal years from the day when one ruler died and another succeeded, without an overlap, so the papyrus evidence does not simply mean that Auletes died and Cleopatra succeeded him in the same year. Something more significant is implied, perhaps that Auletes recognised that his time was short and by making her co-ruler while he still lived, he declared quite unequivocally that his heir was to be Cleopatra.

More sinister interpretations have been advanced. The joint rule of Auletes and Cleopatra is still attested on papyrus records up to mid-July 51. Marcus Caelius Rufus wrote to Cicero from Rome on 1 August 51, adding in the last paragraph that it had been reported and accepted as fact that the king of Alexandria, meaning Auletes, was dead. He asked Cicero, who was governor of Cilicia and therefore closer to Egypt, to find out what was happening and who was in charge of the country. Seemingly he had not been informed that Queen Cleopatra was the ruler, with or without her father. On the basis of this evidence it has been suggested that Cleopatra may have kept the death of her father secret, until she was properly established and accepted as Queen.[11] The Ptolemies and other rulers had brought off such subterfuges in the past, but to sustain the lie for perhaps three months is a commendable feat.

Once the death of Auletes had been made public, Cleopatra honoured her father's memory. After the rebellion of Berenice had been suppressed, all the surviving children of Auletes had been given the name Philadelphus, indicating brotherly love and accord between them, and now Cleopatra and the elder Ptolemy adopted the title of

Philopator, denoting affection for their father. It may not have been an empty gesture, at least on Cleopatra's part. A granite sphinx with the head of Auletes was found in the harbour of Alexandria in 1998, during the ongoing underwater excavations there. If Auletes had been entirely incompetent or uncaring, it would not have been a shrewd policy for his daughter, newly established as ruler, to remind people of her ancestry. Perhaps circumstances were against Auletes. If he could have displayed any pronounced military or diplomatic skills he may have been able to obliterate his other deficiencies, but Egypt was not under dire threat requiring his military intervention, despite the depiction of him in standard Pharaonic pose on the temple of Horus at Edfu, smiting his enemies. He may have followed sound policies with regard to the well being of Egypt and the few foreign possessions he had been able to hold, but his historical reputation has subsumed whatever he may have achieved.

The kingdom that Cleopatra inherited was already old beyond reckoning, its administration very conservative, intensely regulated and centralised. The self-contained nature of Egypt made it easier to control, and the dependence of all the inhabitants upon the seasonal flooding of the Nile created mutual needs that positively demanded co-ordination by a central authority. The blend of many different races and cultures worked better in Egypt than elsewhere because of this mutual dependence, not that it was a peaceful co-existence, but priorities were food and trade. There was already a substantial Greek population in Egypt even before the arrival of Alexander. The city of Naucratis was a Greek trading settlement tracing its origins back to a colonising venture of the seventh century BC. The other mainly Greek cities were Paraetonium, founded by Alexander on the western edge of the Nile Delta, and Ptolemais founded by Ptolemy I Soter.

The greatest city of all was Alexandria[12] founded by Alexander in 332, and laid out on a grid plan by the Greek architect Dinocrates. Alexandria was a new city, built on the site of a village called Rhakotis, on the north-west side of the Nile Delta. The planners took advantage of all the modern ideas that were current in the fourth century BC. The city was well defended, situated on a strip of land between the sea and Lake Mareotis, but the coast could be dangerous for shipping until Ptolemy I Soter built the great lighthouse, on Pharos island protecting the northern approaches to the eastern harbour. [13] The famous monument took its name from the island. The Pharos was one of the Seven Wonders of the ancient world, and there are several surviving representations of it in paintings and mosaics, and on Roman coins. In 1997, underwater excavations conducted by French archaeologists revealed the foundations of the lighthouse, sunk beneath the sea after an earthquake in ancient times. The Pharos island and the mainland were connected by the Heptastadion, a man-made causeway which divided the coastal waters between the Pharos island and the city, and provided a double harbour. The eastern one, the Great Harbour, was a natural feature with breakwaters erected on either side of the entrance with the Pharos on the seaward side of the northern breakwater. The western harbour, called Eunostos, was an artificial creation. In addition to the sea going ships using the two harbours, traffic from the Nile was conveyed to Alexandria via a canal connecting the river to Lake Mareotis, the large sweet-water lake stretching along the southern, landward side of the city. Branches of the canal cut through the city on the east and west sides led to each of the two harbours, so the core of Alexandria was surrounded by water.

Alexandria was always, and still is, in a class of its own and a law unto itself. Most modern capital cities of the world share this characteristic of a certain degree of difference and separateness from the rest of the country, largely because of their composite, international make-up, but in ancient Alexandria this separateness was taken somewhat further. The population was very mixed, predominantly settled by enterprising and industrious Greeks with a large body of equally industrious Jews, but with many other races represented. People spoke of going from Alexandria to Egypt, a strange viewpoint to modern minds, akin to going from London to England or from Paris to France, which absurdity underlines the different ideology of the ancient Alexandrians. Their city was probably administered separately by the Ptolemies, and then by the Romans, whose governors were described as prefects of Alexandria and Egypt.

Trade was Alexandria's raison d'être, and was conducted with the Mediterranean countries and with Africa and Ethiopia. The volume of trade was enhanced after Alexander destroyed the important city of Tyre, bringing Phoenician trading activities to a standstill. In 146 the Romans destroyed Carthage and also Corinth, and while the Alexandrians may have sympathised with the inhabitants of these cities, they were not averse to taking over any extra trade that came their way as a result. One of Egypt's chief exports was papyrus, followed by grain, salt, olive oil, vegetable oil, linen, wool, and glass products. This is not an exhaustive list of products. The Ptolemies controlled all economic activity very closely, monopolising all trade and agriculture. They owned all the land, and leased some of it to peasants, even lending seed in return for a tax on the produce.

Alexandria was probably the largest city in the ancient world, with a teeming ethnically mixed population. Trouble occasionally flared up between these different groups, and the population as a whole was always very near the flash point. Several of the Ptolemaic rulers had used force to keep the peace in Alexandria. It was a city of extremes; transient pleasures, decadence, and vice were ever present, but there was also art and culture. The Museum, attached to the great and famous library, drew scientists, poets and artists from all around the Mediterranean, creating the largest body of researchers and *literati* in the civilised world. There was a freedom of thought and expression in Alexandria which Rome never enjoyed.

The Greeks in Egypt did not follow the example of their ancestors, in that they did not form separate city states. The mountainous landscape in Greece itself, and the scattered islands of the wider Greek world, fostered this fragmented political development, because communications between cities were not easy and transport was better by sea than overland, so that the cities looked outwards to the Aegean

and the Mediterranean rather than inward to any cohesive ideology of a single, united country. In Egypt, the opposite was true. The
country looked in upon itself, and the landscape favoured cohesion.
The Greek and Jewish population co-operated reasonably well with
each other and with the native Egyptians, not without occasional
serious disputes, but in general these problems were more domestic
than national. The Alexandrians were collectively more volatile and
dangerous than the native population of the rest of Egypt, because
of their numbers and co-ordination, and Cleopatra respected their
power. Whenever possible she accommodated the Alexandrians, but
mostly by manipulation rather than capitulation, by pre-empting
trouble rather than waiting for it to happen and then meeting it
head-on.

Cleopatra made a genuine effort to understand and empathise
with all the people in and around Egypt. She learned the native
Egyptian language, the first of the Ptolemies to attempt to speak to
her subjects in their own tongue. According to Plutarch she spoke
several other languages as well as Greek and Egyptian, including
Ethiopian, Hebrew, Aramaic, Syriac, Median and Parthian.[14] These
were the most important languages of the peoples around Egypt,
with whom she would need to conduct diplomatic business or to
arrange trading privileges. It may have been her father who encouraged her to learn these languages as part of a wider plan for Egypt.
He encouraged trading contacts with the east via the Red Sea and
the Indian Ocean, but his unfortunate reputation does not allow him
any credit for far-seeing or co-ordinated policies. The inevitability
of associating with Rome meant that all external policies and even
purely national policies came under scrutiny whether or not Rome's
'friends and allies' (amici) acquiesced in such scrutiny, so if Cleopatra
inherited any ideas from her father, she would have to subordinate
them to the wishes of Rome. Acquiring languages could have been
her idea from the start. It freed her from reliance upon interpret-
ers whenever she dealt with delegations or groups of people from
other countries. These would not necessarily always be politically

motivated encounters. She had a discerning financial sense, alert for any profitable venture, so more than ever she would need to know precisely what was being said. The closest modern analogy would be to imagine what it would be like to buy a used car in a foreign country without being able to speak or understand a word of the language.

Plutarch does not mention that Cleopatra spoke Latin, which seems a strange omission, since she spent most of her life dealing with Romans in one capacity or another.[15] Perhaps it is to be taken as read that she spoke both Latin and Greek, and in any case, even if she spoke no Latin in her early youth, by the time she needed to speak to the leading Roman general of the day in 48, it is fairly certain that she would have acquired enough of the language to meet him on advantageous terms. If she spoke no Latin at all, then the conclusion is that all her conversations with Caesar, Antony and their friends were conducted in Greek. Most wealthy and educated Romans spoke Greek as a matter of course, and Cleopatra would deal only with the wealthy and educated classes.

From the outset of her reign she established herself as an energetic ruler, with a mind of her own and decided opinions as to what she wanted and how she would achieve it. She fostered Egyptian ways of life and paid great attention to religious practices. There is some evidence, not without dispute, that in March 51 she travelled to Upper Egypt to attend the ceremony of the inauguration of the sacred bull Buchis at Hermonthis (modern Amant), near Thebes.[16] Bulls were held in high esteem in many parts of Egypt, and worshipped as a living symbol of the gods. The citizens of Memphis honoured their own bull, called Apis. When each animal died, a new one was installed in its place, the holy name was bestowed on him, and he was worshipped until he died. An inscription from Hermonthis indicates that Cleopatra, with the titles of Queen and Lady of the Two Lands (of Upper and Lower Egypt), rowed the sacred bull in the barge of Amon-Ra on the Nile. It has been suggested that this is all figurative, honouring Cleopatra in her absence, but there seems no reason to doubt that she went to the ceremony, without her father, who may have been too ill to attend, or as some would insist, already dead. Cleopatra's activities were appreciated by the people of Upper Egypt, who gave her sanctuary when she had been ejected from Alexandria by her brother, and in her last hour when she and Mark Antony were facing war with Octavian, the people declared themselves ready to rise up in arms to defend her. Her presence at this religious ceremony at Hermonthis, and perhaps at others elsewhere that have gone unrecorded by archaeological finds, need not be doubted.

Having achieved sole rule, Cleopatra was extremely reluctant to relinquish it. For the first three years of her reign there is no mention of her young brother who eventually became Ptolemy XIII, until the papyrus sources indicate that the third year of Cleopatra's rule was also the first year of Ptolemy's.[17] While exercising sole power, Cleopatra issued coins which displayed her head alone, an unprecedented move in a kingdom where Queens wielded considerable influence but definitely did not reign without a consort. It may be significant that Ptolemy XIII first appears as joint ruler only in troubled times. First of all there was a tense moment when Cleopatra faced potential trouble with Rome. In the aftermath of the disastrous defeat of Marcus Crassus by the Parthians in 53, Calpurnius Bibulus, the Roman governor of Syria, was threatened with a Parthian invasion of his province in 51. In the end the invasion turned out to be less serious than he had imagined but as part of his preparations Bibulus decided to recall the Gabinian troops who had originally been part of the provincial troops in Syria. Accordingly he sent his two sons to Egypt to oversee the evacuation of the soldiers of Gabinius' army, but these men had settled down in Egypt in the pay of Ptolemy Auletes and did not want to leave. They underlined their reluctance by murdering the two young men. At once, Cleopatra arrested the main culprits and despatched them to Bibulus, and fortunately the matter ended there. Bibulus acted with supreme correctness and sent the guilty men to be tried by the Senate in Rome.[18] Apparently he did not hold Cleopatra responsible, or at least that was the public face he assumed. Privately he may have harboured a tremendous grudge against her.

The new Queen was no doubt relieved that she was not held accountable for the murders of the two young Romans, especially as it indicated that she was unable to control her own army. At this moment she needed all the support she could muster, for internal problems beset her as well as external ones. At the beginning of her third year, Cleopatra was in control and her status as Queen was assured, but by the end of the year she was struggling not only for supremacy but also existence, as Ptolemy and his entourage gained more power and became more hostile. Bad harvests in the autumn of 50 threatened famine and potential food riots. Cleopatra took immediate control of grain production, and decreed that all the produce of Middle Egypt must be transported to Alexandria and not, as was more usual, to Upper and Lower Egypt. Channelling food into Alexandria was a safeguard. Most populations of ancient cities were extremely volatile during food shortages and the Alexandrians were an especially troublesome lot. Cleopatra was not prepared to take any chances with them. As well as ensuring that their food supplies did not fail, perhaps it was only now, if she had not already done so, that she brought her younger brother to political prominence both to satisfy hallowed custom and put an end to suspicion that she intended to rule alone for ever. Perhaps more importantly, she no doubt knew that it was not only the Alexandrian population who might have been harbouring suspicions about her intentions. Rome was watching fairly closely, and it was known in Rome that Ptolemy XIII had not yet been acknowledged as her colleague. Excuses about his extreme youth would be valid for only a limited duration.

There is an alternative interpretation of the events of 50, in that the Royal decree forbidding transport of grain to Upper and Lower Egypt may indicate that it was Ptolemy XIII, with his tutors and advisers, were in control of Alexandria, and the great quarrel between Cleopatra and her brother, noted by Caesar when he arrived in Egypt after Pharsalus, had already begun.[19] At some unknown date,

Cleopatra was banished from the city, perhaps taking refuge in Upper Egypt.[20] If it was Ptolemy who issued the edict on the control of the food supply he may have been trying to starve her out by removing food supplies from any part of the country where she might try to gather an army. Another advantage was that by bringing all the produce to Alexandria he could prepare for a siege of the city, if Cleopatra attacked.

Caesar makes a laconic statement in his account of the Civil War[21] that when he arrived in Alexandria Ptolemy and his friends had driven Cleopatra from her kingdom (*regnum*) 'a few months before'. Since the interval between the poor harvests of the autumn of 50 and Caesar's arrival in 48 cannot legitimately be described as a few months, it must be assumed either that Cleopatra was still in charge in 50, or that she had been driven first out of Alexandria into Upper Egypt, and then perhaps out of Egypt altogether, deposed as Queen and therefore without state or status. Her whereabouts are not known for certain until 48, when she made camp with her troops opposite Ptolemy's army at Pelusium. It is probable that she travelled abroad at some point at the end of 49 or the beginning of 48. She may have found refuge in Ascalon, a Philistine city which had ties with Egypt ever since the Ptolemaic rulers lent support against the aggressive intentions of the kings of Judaea. Presumably Cleopatra had some kind of military force with her, or she raised an army to fight her way back into Egypt. Appian says that she recruited soldiers in Syria.[22] But before she had made much progress her prospects began to change; in August and September 48, events in Greece began to unfold which swept her along with them and finally secured her throne as Queen of Egypt.

From 49 to 48 the whole of the Roman world was involved in the power struggle between the two greatest generals, Caesar and Pompey. If Cleopatra had been in Rome with her father from 58 to 56 she would have met Pompey, since it was mainly in his house in Rome that her father resided, and it was on Pompey that all her father's hopes were laid for restoration to his kingdom. She would also have heard of the proconsul Gaius Julius Caesar whose command in Gaul was proving so successful for Roman arms – at least by Caesar's own self-promoting accounts. Even if she had remained behind in Egypt while her father was absent, the association with Rome was so vital that she would no doubt have heard a great deal of these two political and military magnates.

For a few years, civil war between the factions was avoided. Caesar renewed his proconsulship and remained in Gaul to complete his conquests, while Pompey stayed in Rome, governing his province of Spain through legates, a hitherto unheard of arrangement. Gradually he was drawn into the anti-Caesarean camp, and the road to civil war began with efforts to recall Caesar from his province. When the war began, Pompey was not prepared, so he left Rome and then Italy, aiming for Greece, where he hoped to train and unite his army. By the summer of 48 Caesar too was in Greece facing Pompey, and in August he defeated him at Pharsalus. Pompey escaped by the skin of his teeth, took ship and headed for Egypt, where his connections ought to have been secure enough to borrow money and raise another army. He had recently been made guardian of the young Ptolemy XIII, so he expected a friendly reception.

Ptolemy's advisers saw the matter differently. Close behind the defeated Pompey there would be the victorious Caesar. The war would continue on Egyptian soil with Egyptian supplies and Egyptian cash requisitioned for the purpose. The Romans seemed not to mind where they fought their battles or whose kingdoms they destroyed or annexed in the process. Pothinus, Ptolemy's councillor, and Achillas, his general, advised that Pompey should be eliminated, because as Achillas reputedly explained, dead men don't bite. When Caesar arrived in Alexandria he was presented with Pompey's head and his signet ring. The first phase of the civil war was technically over, and the Alexandrians made it abundantly clear that they did not welcome the Roman consul or his display of Roman power. At that point, Caesar could have withdrawn from Egypt, but he chose to stay, sorting out internal Egyptian affairs on the pretext that he was collecting the debts owed to him by Auletes.

Cleopatra arrived at Caesar's headquarters, as the story goes, in a rolled up carpet carried by her faithful follower, the Sicilian Apollodorus.[23] The tale has all the stuff of legend, but it may be true. When the news of Pharsalus reached her, followed by the news of Pompey's death and Caesar's arrival in Alexandria, Cleopatra would need to assess her situation very carefully. She was twenty-one years old, but experienced beyond her years. She had no strong armies to use on her own account, and she would need help to regain and retain her throne. Her strongest hope of finding help in any part of the world at that moment lay with Caesar and his troops, and he was conveniently in Alexandria. This also meant that her brother Ptolemy XIII and his advisers now had immediate access to the Roman victor of Pharsalus, who might at any moment decide in Ptolemy's favour, swayed by the fact that it was in his name that Pompey had been so fortuitously removed from the scene, leaving Caesar blameless, exonerated and supreme in the Roman world. Next, there was the younger Ptolemy, aged about eleven, and their sister Arsinoe, now about eighteen years old. These individuals may have possessed no personal aspiration to rule, but Arsinoe in particular had already revealed signs of great ambition, and even if she relinquished all claims to the throne, that was not the end of the matter. In the Royal Palace there would be many influential Macedonian Greeks and Egyptian officials whose interests could be advanced by using any of the Royal children as figureheads. Factional strife was not to be ruled out, and Caesar was the obvious source of arbitration and support. According to Dio[24] Cleopatra sent word to him stating her claims to the throne, but this was probably only a stopgap, in case she could not reach him herself. She may have used messengers for this purpose, since letters were never reliable, for many reasons. It was essential therefore to get to Caesar before the others did, in person and alone, not to his generals or to any of his assistants, and definitely not to any Egyptian or Greek official in Alexandria. Cleopatra probably did not trust anyone except her own immediate retinue. It was to Caesar that she must go to state her case, and she needed to do it directly and quickly. The rolled-up carpet story is perfectly credible, and if it is a romantic fabrication it does not matter very much. Somehow, armed with nothing but confidence in herself and considerable personal charm, Cleopatra glided back into Alexandria, evading all potential opposition, and found Gaius Julius Caesar. She still had some problems to overcome, but from that moment onwards her throne was as secure as it could possibly be, and by the following year she was undoubted Queen of Egypt.

The Alexandrians objected to Caesar's presence even more strongly when they began to suspect that he intended to make Cleopatra Queen, perhaps without a consort. Caesar had to review the four surviving children and make a decision about their future. He had already summoned Ptolemy XIII, before Cleopatra arrived, and Arsinoe and the younger Ptolemy were also resident in the Palace. Each would have their own staff and courtiers, so the potential for intrigue was vastly increased. Some effort at reconciliation between Cleopatra and Ptolemy XIII had to be made, with Caesar's backing. Once this was achieved, Caesar had no reasonable excuse to remain in Egypt, and at this point he could have withdrawn, but past experience had proved that Rome and Egypt had mutual needs which would be compromised if Caesar simply turned his back and left the various factions to fight it out. So he stayed in Alexandria, and we can only conjecture what was the content of the interviews, conversations and finally pillow talk between Caesar and Cleopatra. They both had extremely strong interests in control of Egypt. From Cleopatra's point of view there could be no compromise. Either she ruled, and ruled unopposed, or she was as good as dead, so in seeking for support from Caesar she risked everything. If he refused her, favouring Ptolemy XIII and his motley crew, she had nowhere else to turn. It was clear that Ptolemy, accompanied by Pothinus and Achillas, would soon marginalise her or even eliminate her, therefore she required support, preferably armed support, until she was properly established, and Caesar was on the spot and tolerably well armed. From the Roman point of view, peace in Egypt was a priority, not from any humanitarian considerations, but purely from the selfish Roman outlook. A weakened Egypt preoccupied with fighting civil wars did not constitute a direct threat, but such a series of events would also weaken and perhaps destroy the source of wealth and food supplies that could benefit Rome, and much worse, allies from other eastern countries might be called in to fight on behalf of one of the factions, and thereby gain a foothold in the country. The Romans knew all about how that was done because they were adept at it themselves. If any of the eastern kings or petty princes followed the example of the first Ptolemy and made Egypt into a private kingdom, then Rome would have to tread very carefully, so it was better to avert that possibility before it happened.

Naturally, Caesar was not as altruistic as all that; personal interests entered into the picture as well as wider political concerns.[25] There would be tremendous advantages for him personally if he could keep the ruler or rulers of Egypt grateful to him for their thrones, and therefore under his thumb. Caesar would not be blind to all these considerations about Egypt when he first heard Cleopatra's story. They must have become lovers very soon after their first meeting. It may have been a part of Cleopatra's strategy to captivate the Roman general in order to win him to her cause, or it may have been part of Caesar's plans to charm Cleopatra and make her more compliant. On the other hand, political motives may have been swept aside by simple biological urges. Caesar was in his fifties, married more than once, experienced, charismatic, and a known womaniser.[26] Cleopatra was in her early twenties, not classically beautiful but extremely attractive, and perhaps almost as experienced as Caesar in the ways of the world. She had grown up in a hard and violent milieu, but whatever cynicism she might have developed did not overwhelm her. She was engaging and clever, and Caesar liked women who were clever. But it is unlikely that both participants lost their heads. They were both of them too shrewd, too self-controlled and too aware not only of their immediate needs but also the long-term consequences of what they did. They probably discussed the ground rules under a series of main headings and sub-clauses before they went to bed.

When he realised that his sister had already found more than just political favour with Caesar, Ptolemy staged a public tantrum, stirring up the population of Alexandria on the basis that he was being displaced by Cleopatra.[27] Caesar issued benign statements, followed by a cosmetic celebration of the joint rule of Ptolemy XIII and Cleopatra, with feasting and festivities that probably sounded very hollow. There remained the two siblings, Arsinoe and the younger Ptolemy. In settling their fortunes, Caesar hoped to reconcile both the Alexandrians and the Egyptians by setting up the two remaining Ptolemies as independent rulers of Cyprus.[28] This was a bold move. The island had only recently been wrenched from Ptolemaic control and arbitrarily annexed by Rome, and the stern Marcus Porcius Cato had been sent out as its first governor. Caesar ought to have involved the Senate in debate about returning Cyprus to the Ptolemies, but he had already revealed his lack of respect for this long-winded approach, and did not feel the need for seeking senatorial permission. Besides he had to act rapidly to assuage the volatile population of Alexandria and to try to avert Palace rebellions in the name of any of the four Ptolemaic heirs. In Alexandria he had to be seen to be trying hard to pour oil on troubled waters. If the Senate objected, he could always deal with the situation later when he returned to Rome.

The settlements were precarious at best and the balance could be easily upset. The political jostling was exacerbated by Pothinus, one of the most prominent members of Ptolemy XIII's entourage and his most influential and ambitious adviser.[29] To Pothinus it was an ideal situation. All the main protagonists were contained in one place, while Ptolemy's army was intact outside Alexandria under the command of Achillas. Pothinus sent a message to Achillas to bring the troops to Alexandria and besiege the Royal Palace. Pothinus was determined to place Ptolemy XIII firmly on the throne, with himself as chief adviser, courtier and councillor, and it would not matter to him who was the Royal consort, provided that it was not Cleopatra. If the siege succeeded he could remove at one stroke the Romans and all the opponents of his schemes. Accidents could happen to anyone during sieges; Cleopatra, Arsinoe and the younger Ptolemy could all conveniently disappear. It is even possible that Pothinus had thought ahead about what to do with Caesar, perhaps counting on the enormous wealth that would be at his disposal with which to bribe his way into power if Caesar survived. Hardened ascetic though he was, Caesar was still very interested in money for the power that it brought in its wake, so Pothinus perhaps construed the situation as cut and dried, imagining that Caesar could be easily bought off, if it proved impossible to kill him. More realistically, he probably determined at the outset to have Caesar killed, counting on the fact that the Roman Senate might actually be grateful if he removed Caesar.

Achillas duly placed the Royal Palace under siege.[30] Caesar was now at a grave disadvantage, outnumbered and enclosed. He could not simply walk out of the Palace and then the city, and access to the sea was denied, so escape was impossible, unless he could neutralise the Egyptian fleet. This was his first priority, and in a surprise attack he captured the fleet and burned the ships before Pothinus or Achillas could use them against him.[31] While the ships burned the fire spread to the city, and it is widely believed that the great library of Alexandria went up in flames. It is an enduring legend, and made good copy both at the time and down the ages. Something of the sort may actually have happened, but in the *Alexandrian War* it is reported that the buildings of Alexandria were almost fireproof, because they were all built using an arched construction and contained no wooden joinery.[32] Timber was not abundant, imports were costly, and building techniques accommodated the needs of the population and suited the climate. This statement may have been a veiled apology for the calamity, but it is unlikely that the entire library was burned. Perhaps some important books and documents were lost on board ship, awaiting delivery to or transport from the library.

If Achillas had acted quickly he could have recouped some of his losses by seizing the famous lighthouse, the Pharos, at the harbour mouth. If he had been able to do this, the advantage that Caesar had just gained in destroying the fleet would have been invalidated, since even without enemy ships to oppose him, he would not have been able to pass the Pharos unscathed, and therefore would still have been unable to escape via the sea, nor would he have been able to bring in reinforcements, or supplies. Consequently, without pausing after the capture of the fleet, Caesar acted with characteristic dash and seized the Pharos himself.[33] The first round had thus been won by Caesar. Now everything depended on the siege of the Royal Palace. Cleopatra will have observed everything with keen interest. Now that events had taken such a desperate turn, there could be little chance of a negotiated peace. If Caesar failed, she failed. Their futures were already interlocked.

All that Caesar could do for the time being was to create defences around the Palace, and fight off attacks. He was still outnumbered, and from the autumn to the winter of 48, that was how it remained. Then the antagonism between the Ptolemies and their rival factions played into his hands. Arsinoe fled to Achillas, perhaps hoping to persuade him to make her Queen, as consort to either of her brothers. She took with her one of her courtiers, Ganymedes. He and Achillas instantly fell out.[34] Their quarrel spread to their retinues and then to the army, with the result that each faction vied for command. Caesar no doubt quietly rejoiced at the disintegration of unity in the Ptolemaic army. He chose this moment to execute Pothinus for stirring up trouble and communicating with Achillas. It was not a sudden whim; Pothinus had always been a dangerous liability. Caesar later proclaimed that Pothinus would have killed him if he had not executed him first. All the time acting correctly, Caesar was probably merely awaiting the perfect opportunity, and there would never be a better one. Very gradually, the opposition to Cleopatra and Caesar was being eliminated. Arsinoe had shown her hand but not yet won the victory, and now Pothinus was dead.[35]

Beset by internal squabbles and without Pothinus to provide him with information, Achillas found everything unravelling all around him, and was soon murdered on the orders of Ganymedes, who took

command of the army.[36] For a while the new commander fought
intelligently and aggressively against Caesar, first trying to cut off
his supplies of fresh water by letting the sea into the sweet water of
Lake Mareotis. The Roman soldiers dug wells as fast as Ganymedes
spoiled the water supply but Caesar knew that this could not go on
indefinitely. Fortunately Roman reinforcements were sailing towards
Alexandria. They arrived in December. This meant that Ganymedes
had to face two contingents of Caesar's troops, and he was without
a fleet, but his situation was not as disadvantageous as it sounds and
there was still some hard fighting. Though he had captured the lighthouse at the harbour mouth, Caesar did not yet have full control of
the island on which the lighthouse was built. Consequently he was
not in complete command of the entire bay, and in trying to fortify
the causeway between the Pharos island and the Alexandrian mainland, he nearly lost his life. He ferried troops to the island on board
ship, captured it and destroyed the buildings, and next day began to
erect a rampart on the causeway connecting the island to the mainland. While the ramparts were being built up, the Egyptians attacked
from the landward side and from the sea. The Roman ships drew
off, everyone panicked because they thought they were about to be
abandoned, and too many men tried to board too few ships, which
started to sink. Caesar quickly realised that his own ship would cap-
size, so he dived into the water and swam for safety. This is the laconic
version of the *Alexandrian War* but other authors add more heroic
details, that Caesar swam with one hand while holding a bundle of
documents above his head to keep them dry. He also abandoned his
purple cloak, which the enemy displayed as a trophy.[37]

After more skirmishing of this sort, with little hope of a quick
victory for either side, the Alexandrians petitioned Caesar to let
Ptolemy XIII return to them.[38] The envoys told him that Ganymedes
was too tyrannical, and that being tired of war they would make a pact
with Caesar if Ptolemy ordered it. There was some play-acting and
crocodile tears as Ptolemy left, but once with his army he revealed
that he also had crocodile teeth, and renewed hostilities with great

determination. The final battle was approaching. At the beginning of the siege Caesar had sent a request to his ally Mithradates of Pergamum to Syria and Cilicia to round up reinforcements. Mithradates was an important and wealthy individual who had been adopted by king Mithradates the Great, from whom he took his name, one which carried a great deal of influence. He had collected a considerable army with which he now besieged Pelusium, east of Alexandria, guarding the approach overland from Syria. It was occupied by a garrison placed there by Achillas, but Mithradates soon overcame resistance and appeared at the Delta, where Ptolemy tried to stop him. Seizing his chance, Caesar left Alexandria and came up behind Ptolemy's army. During the battle of the Nile, fought in March 47, Ptolemy XIII was drowned.[39] Resistance was at an end, but not before Caesar ordered a search for the body of the king to prove that Ptolemy was dead and therefore mortal. The Egyptians believed that drowning in the Nile, so inextricably connected with the Osiris legend, conferred instant deification. Ptolemy as a living person had been problematic enough, but Ptolemy as a dead king converted into a living god would have been a very great obstacle for Cleopatra to overcome. Caesar would be aware of the legends, but it was probably Cleopatra who best understood the deep significance that her countrymen would attach to it, and probably she who persuaded Caesar to put an end to all doubts about Ptolemy's fate.

In the *Alexandrian War* there is no mention of Cleopatra throughout the siege, except for an almost casual note describing how Caesar made himself master of Egypt and Alexandria, and then appointed rulers as outlined in Auletes' will. Since the elder Ptolemy was dead, the kingdom was assigned to the younger Ptolemy, now Ptolemy XIV, and his sister Cleopatra, 'who had remained loyal' to Caesar.[40] This small statement speaks volumes for their political and personal relationship throughout the Alexandrian war. It is most likely Caesar's own comment, either in note form or possibly an oral statement. Whoever was the author of the *Alexandrian War*, no matter if it was, or was not, Caesar's friend Aulus Hirtius, he could have found a way of avoiding any comment at all on Cleopatra's loyalties. It is implied that she had remained in the theatre of war, with Caesar and the troops, and whilst it might be argued that in the siege of the Palace she had no choice, it is also a tribute to her personal courage and her steadfast adherence to her own and Caesar's cause.

Cleopatra had reached the pinnacle of success. She was Queen of Egypt, with the support of the most powerful general in the Roman world, thereby connected to everything that the nascent Roman Empire had to offer, and virtually unencumbered with rivals at home. Her consort, symbolically her husband in accordance with Egyptian regal practice, was her twelve year-old half-brother Ptolemy XIV. He did not feature very prominently in the administration of the kingdom, which implies that he was useful for ceremonials but was only retained for cosmetic purposes to mollify the population.[41] Having witnessed what happened to ambitious members of the Ptolemaic Royal family, perhaps he did not entertain high-flying aspirations, content to remain in the background. More importantly it seems that there were no politically ambitious personnel around him who wished to agitate on his behalf. Cleopatra's only surviving rival was her sister Arsinoe, who was declared a traitor and sent as a prisoner to Rome, where some time later she would appear in Caesar's triumph, led to the Capitol as a captive princess. The island of Cyprus, briefly granted to Arsinoe and Ptolemy XIII as independent rulers, was instead restored to the kingdom of Egypt under Cleopatra and Ptolemy XIV.

Both Caesar and Cleopatra now had what they wanted. Egypt had escaped formal annexation. That would come later when Octavian appropriated the country and its wealth. It suited Caesar's purpose not to annexe the country, and it is certain that Caesar was the driving force behind the treatment of Egypt, no matter how captivated he may have been with Cleopatra, nor how persuasive she was in angling for what she wanted. Cleopatra retained her position by a fortuitous combination of circumstances, for however much she charmed Caesar and however much he may have loved her, Caesar's political ideology always ruled whatever he did. Emotions played no part in his list of political priorities. If he had personally detested Cleopatra but considered her a useful ally, he would still have installed her as Queen; if he loved her but considered her incompetent and unsatisfactory, he would have made alternative arrangements, retaining as far as possible his influence over the chosen ruler. He avoided formal annexation because it would have removed Egypt from his control and placed it under the Senate. He chose to leave Egypt independent under its rightful Queen, over whom it is to be supposed that he had some personal influence, so he had the best of both worlds.

His only alternative apart from these semi-private arrangements would have been to convert Egypt into a province and try to ensure that he governed it himself via legates, as Octavian did after the fall of Alexandria in 30. Caesar adopted a diluted form of this sort of government, leaving troops behind when he left Egypt under an officer called Rufio, who had risen from the ranks, and who had every reason to be loyal to Caesar for his advancement. The motive for lending armed support to Cleopatra was double-edged. She needed to keep the population of Alexandria under control, and to weed out undesirable elements in her court so that she could establish complete authority over her entourage. Rufio was no doubt a good officer and respectful to Cleopatra, and he and his troops would help her to maintain control, but he would also keep Caesar informed of what developments took place in Egypt. If Cleopatra began to show dissident tendencies – that is, dissident from Caesar's world-view – then there would be a means of curbing her. It would be interesting to know what was Rufio's brief when Caesar put him in command of the contingents left in Egypt.

There is the question of how far Caesar and Cleopatra trusted one another. For the time being they were in accord about Egypt's future and its place in the Roman world, but times could change. It is certain that just as Caesar would have been totally ruthless about how he dealt with both Egypt and Cleopatra, then vice versa if circumstances changed, Cleopatra would put the interests of Egypt before her private feelings for Caesar as a man and her political perceptions of him as a Roman ally. In the event, Caesar had only three more years to live before he was assassinated, and their political relationship was never seriously tested, nor does it seem that they were ever at odds with each other in their private lives. But even if they did trust each other to any degree, their trust would have always been tempered with stark realism.

In order to underscore their current association, and perhaps also for pleasure and diversion, when the battles were over and Cleopatra was firmly established as Queen, Caesar accompanied her on a grand tour up the Nile. Presumably Caesar attached tremendous importance to this leisurely cruise, since there were many problems facing him in more than one part of the Roman world. Some of Pompey's adherents were entrenched in Africa, preparing to continue the civil war and gaining strength every day. One of Caesar's lieutenants, Domitius Calvinus, left in charge of the province of Asia, was embroiled in a struggle against Pharnaces, king of Pontus, who laid claim to Lesser Armenia and Cappadocia, hoping to gain a foothold while the Romans were pre-occupied in fighting each other. There was much for Caesar to attend to, not least in Rome itself, but he stayed in Egypt apparently enjoying himself. There is very little evidence with which to refute the charge, but it is also highly likely that there was some political motive behind Caesar's Nile cruise.[42]

For Cleopatra, it was highly important. She had already demonstrated that she was more than superficially concerned with the welfare of the Egyptian population as well as the Macedonian, Greek and Jewish inhabitants. The Nile journey would serve several purposes, to create a sense of unity among the entire kingdom, to show herself to the people as no Ptolemy had ever done before, communicating with them on many levels, open and accessible, but never forgetting that she was all-powerful, all-seeing, all-knowing, the personification of the goddess Isis. It would also demonstrate that she could call on Roman support. It was a fortuitous blend of Royal progress, diplomatic mission and show of strength.

When the cruise ended with the return to Alexandria, Caesar finally left Egypt, at some time in mid-summer 47. Despite various suggestions, both ancient and modern, no one knows the precise date when he took his leave, nor when he arrived in Syria to begin the short campaign against Pharnaces.[43] Cleopatra was heavily pregnant by now, giving birth shortly after Caesar departed, to her son nicknamed by the Alexandrians as little Caesar, or Caesarion.[44] His official name given to him by Cleopatra was Ptolemy Caesar, indicating his combined Egyptian and Roman origins. These origins and even the date of birth have been doubted, dismissed and discussed from Cleopatra's times to the present day, without much hope of final resolution.

Caesarion's true paternity is not so important as his political status. Cleopatra intended that Egypt and the world should recognise the boy not only as Caesar's son, but also the heir to the throne of the Ptolemies. She promoted him as such all through his short life, sharing the throne with him after the death of her brother, when Caesarion was only three years old. She was obviously tutoring him for the succession, spreading the same consistent message to the Romans and the Mediterranean world in one direction and to the native Egyptians and the tribes beyond Egypt in the other. Caesarion is depicted as Pharaoh with his mother on the famous reliefs on the outer wall of the temple at Dendera in Upper Egypt. Perhaps more eloquent for the Egyptians was the depiction at the shrine at Hermonthis, where the birth of Caesarion is unmistakably equated with Isis giving birth to Horus, which placed the rulers in a divine context as Pharaohs and gods. Cleopatra played her part with skill and understanding, taking her example from previous Ptolemies who cultivated the loyalty of the Egyptians in the old accustomed manner.

It is equally significant that Caesar is said to have acknowledged Caesarion as his son. The source for this is not Caesar's writings or anything directly associated with him; it derives from the life of Caesar by Suetonius, who says that in a speech to the Senate Mark Antony testified that Caesar had acknowledged Caesarion in front of witnesses, notably his friend Gaius Matius and his secretaries Oppius and Balbus.[45] This public acknowledgement is most likely true. After that it did not matter whether Caesar really was the father of the child or not. Both he and Cleopatra made a declaration to the world and did not care whether the world chose to believe it. Alternative versions would be current as soon as the boy was born, including the possibility that Cleopatra had taken a lover and passed off his offspring as Caesar's, or more preposterously that the twelve year-old Ptolemy was the father of Cleopatra's son. One man who did take the alleged paternity of the young Caesarion extremely seriously was Octavian, Caesar's great nephew and son by adoption.

Cleopatra honoured Caesar, and underlined her association with him, by building the Caesareum, a huge edifice with colonnades, high enough to be visible to sailors as they came into the harbour.[46] Two obelisks, already ancient by Cleopatra's day, but now commonly called Cleopatra's needles, stood outside this building. One of these 'needles', the obelisk of Thutmosis III, is now situated on the Thames embankment in London, England. Keeping Caesar's memory alive in Egypt emphasised his importance, and paved the way for their son Caesarion to fulfil his intended role as descendant of the Ptolemies, supported by Rome. When Caesar left Alexandria[47] Cleopatra could not be sure that she would ever see him again. Although she could remain in contact with him, she could not rely upon his continued presence or even long-standing influence in Egyptian affairs. She had to make the best of the situation and be prepared to meet all challenges alone.

3

A Time in Rome:
Antony and Cleopatra
47–44BC

During his absence from Italy, Caesar placed Antony in charge of affairs as his *magister equitum*, traditionally the deputy of the Dictator. In comparison with the propraetorian office that Antony had held while Caesar fought against the Pompeians in Spain, the powers of his current post were rather less well defined. The most important attribute was that it allowed him to command troops.

It was a distressing time. Opportunists and men with grievances stirred up troubles for their own benefit. As always, debtors were the most easily roused to agitation escalating into violence and could be used to advantage in the programmes of so-called reformers. The first to cause trouble was Marcus Caelius Rufus, whose main cause for unhappiness was that as praetor and a supporter of Caesar he had not been promoted to the more important post of urban praetor, so he bore a grudge which found its expression in his making common cause with the debt-ridden masses of Rome. The consul Servilius removed him from the city, but then he went to Campania to try to join forces with Milo, who had returned illegally from exile in Marseilles. The two rebels eventually met their ends separately in different parts of Italy, Milo in Apulia and Rufus in Bruttium, so the city of Rome was not directly affected, but it was a precedent for worse things to come, in the city itself, where unrest was fomenting.[1]

Ill-advised, but brash as ever, Antony began to display a tendency for self-importance tinged with play-acting. He went about in the costume of a general, especially the purple cloak, and he wore his armour and sword even when calling the Senate together, which upset everyone. He added insult to injury by surrounding himself with a military bodyguard, and six lictors to precede him wherever he went.[2] He took over Pompey's house in Rome without paying for it, though it was to have been sold at auction. Once installed in it he spared no expense in indulging himself and his friends, including Cytheris the actress, who had been waiting to greet him at Brundisium when he returned to Italy. Cicero accused Antony of going through the contents of Pompey's wine cellar in a matter of a few days, and giving away priceless gifts from the furnishings and fittings.[3] Antony's lifestyle, flamboyant, ostentatious, occasionally debauched, naturally attracted opprobrium. His boisterous reputation is probably not simply a product of retrospective vituperation from Cicero's *Philippics*: Antony always knew how to enjoy life to the full. No one could ever accuse him of either abstemiousness or discretion in his private life. He lived as he wished to live, careless about his choice of associates and unruffled by the consequences of his actions – in this he was very different from Caesar, who knew how to be liberal and magnanimous, but at the same time quite decidedly kept his distance from potentially detrimental colleagues. Antony could have learned this much from Caesar, and even more from his rival and eventual enemy, Caesar's great nephew Octavius, who knew that there was no dividing line between public and private life. He understood the importance of acting the part of consummate statesman at all times, and on his death bed he asked his friends if they had enjoyed the performance.

The rift between Antony and the Senate was already crystallising, not helped by Antony's response when Dolabella, emulating Caelius Rufus, began to stir up the debtors in Rome. Antony had obtained from the Senate permission to bring troops into the city, but had not yet done anything positive to restore order. Dolabella announced that he was about to pass a law cancelling all debts and to do this he was going to occupy the Forum with his followers the next day. The Senate in alarm authorised Antony to restore order. Wisely, Antony had waited until he was asked to intervene, but ultimately it did not help him. He brought his troops to the Forum and surrounded the mob, possibly hoping that the very presence of soldiers would bring the rioters to their senses. But serious problems arose when the skirmishing escalated into battle, and deaths followed, estimated at 800 plebeians among the crowd, and more who were rounded up and thrown from the Tarpeian rock on Antony's orders when they would not leave the Forum.[4]

It is not totally fair to blame all this on Antony. He had started, so he had to finish, and once he realised that he would not be able to clear the Forum without a bloody struggle, he could not retire or use half measures. Naturally the Senate reacted with shocked disapproval and would not back him up. It was even speculated that Antony had been driven on by jealousy and personal rivalry with Dolabella, because the latter had seduced his wife, Antonia.[5] The accusation against Dolabella may be true, especially since Antony divorced Antonia at about this time. These are the bare facts, but it is not certain that jealous rage is the correct interpretation of Antony's actions - it is more likely that there was a great deal of speculation and bending of the facts to fit the theory. The supposition that Antony allowed himself to be ruled by his emotions is not substantiated. He was consistently efficient in a crisis, and perhaps in this case he was simply too efficient.

Caesar was not unaware of what had been happening in Rome while he was fighting a rapid campaign against Pharnaces in Syria. His victory was swift, as indicated in Caesar's immortal statement *veni, vidi, vici* – I came, I saw, I conquered. He returned to Rome in October 47, and made it clear to Antony that he did not approve of his actions in quelling the riots.[6] Marcus Aemilius Lepidus was made *magister equitum* in place of Antony, and also consul as Caesar's colleague, and when he left for Africa to pursue the war against the Pompeians, Caesar chose to take Dolabella with him. Antony received no offices or posts for 46. This must have been hard for Antony to contemplate, since it was Dolabella who had caused all the trouble in the first place, and now here he was, being rewarded with a post in Caesar's entourage and taken on campaign, while the man who had put a stop to the riots languished in Rome, without official appointment, and blatantly out of favour.

Caesar acted prudently, conscious of his own reputation. He may have chosen Dolabella simply because it was one way of removing him from Rome and keeping a close eye on him to prevent him from making more trouble. With regard to Antony, Caesar could not afford to condone his heavy handed way of restoring order, even if that had not been Antony's original intention. For political reasons Caesar dropped him for a while. Most of all Antony had to be seen to pay for Pompey's house and treasures, however much he may have contributed to the defeat of the original owner. Pompey was Caesar's enemy, but he had been a great man, the foremost Roman of his day, and it simply would not be fitting to allow the erstwhile lieutenant to take over his property in the city. Spoils of war were all very well on the battlefield, but there must be some higher standard of behaviour in Rome.

While Caesar was absent, fighting the African war that was ended by the victory of Thapsus on 6 April 46, Antony held no office. He remained unemployed throughout the year, and was not asked to participate in September when Caesar celebrated his famous triumphs,[7] four in a row, over Gaul, Egypt, Pharnaces of Pontus and lastly Juba of Mauretania. The final triumph was really over Romans, but Juba had joined the Pompeians, and had lost his life in the conflict, thereby providing the excuse for a more fitting triumph over a foreign enemy. The small son of the king of Mauretania, also called Juba, was paraded through the streets, but then spared the execution that usually followed such a spectacle. He was brought up and educated in Rome, and eventually restored to the throne of Mauretania by Augustus, who married him off to Cleopatra Selene, the daughter of Antony and Cleopatra. The same clemency was extended to Arsinoe, the sister of Cleopatra, and Caesar's enemy in the Alexandrian war. After displaying her to the Roman people, marching in his triumph over Egypt, Caesar sent her to Ephesus to find sanctuary there. She survived until 41, when she was killed on the orders of Antony and Cleopatra.[8]

During the last years of the civil wars against the sons and followers of Pompey, fought in Africa and Spain, Cleopatra was in Rome as the guest of Caesar. There is no surviving contemporary record of her stay in the city, and even Cicero's comments all date from after the assassination of Caesar. It is not even certain when she arrived in Rome. She may not have been able to travel until summer or autumn 46, since she probably gave birth to her son Caesarion in autumn 47, at about the time when Caesar was celebrating his multiple triumphs. She would probably not travel to Rome until the baby was old enough. Though it is known that Caesarion was born after Caesar left to fight the war against Pharnaces, the exact month of his birth is not proven.[9] In his account of the events of 46, Dio places Cleopatra's arrival after the four triumphs and before the Spanish war, so she may have appeared on the scene late in that year, although it has also been suggested that she was not in Rome until 45.

Cleopatra brought with her an entourage about whom practically nothing is known, and the infant Caesarion and her fourteen year-old brother and consort, Ptolemy XIV. One of her motives for accepting Caesar's invitation was no doubt to advertise Caesar's son, and to ensure that the Roman Senate and People of Rome knew that in this child Rome and Egypt were combined. Another pressing need was to achieve recognition from Rome for her rule in Egypt, just as her father had done when Caesar was consul in 59. A formal alliance was arranged by Caesar, and Cleopatra and Ptolemy were enrolled among the friends and allies of Rome.[10]

The Queen was lodged, notoriously, in Caesar's own villa across the Tiber. She and Antony must have met at least on a few occasions, but no tradition has survived of their association during these years. Antony may have noticed her, but since she was clearly attached to Caesar, either emotionally or perhaps merely politically, he may have prudently stood back from what was ostensibly denied to him, especially as he was out of favour with Caesar and would not have risked falling further into disrepute by becoming too closely involved with Caesar's guest. He was free to seduce the rest of the female population of Rome. On the other hand he may have been too distracted to notice Cleopatra at all. He had given up his actress friend Cytheris and at some unknown date become a respectably married man, this time choosing Fulvia, the widow of Clodius and of Curio, and a lady of fearsome reputation.[11] He was devoted to her, as all surviving sources attest, even the hostile ones. Antony's enemies used his indulgent affection for Fulvia as evidence of his undignified and extremely un-Roman behaviour. Fulvia was an intelligent and forceful woman, whose activities were decidedly not confined to spinning, weaving and keeping the keys to the larder. She was ambitious, but being female she was forced to achieve her ambitions through and on behalf of her various husbands, the first of whom were disreputable friends of Antony who did not rise very far in the senatorial hierarchy. Married to Antony, Fulvia found a new lease of life and an outlet for her restless ambitions, which included meddling in politics and military affairs. The fact that she was not brought to heel was construed as a dreadful fault in Antony as her husband. With Clodius and Curio she had not been presented with sufficient opportunity to show her talents, and therefore it may have seemed as though her former husbands had been able to keep her in check. It was said that it was Fulvia who tamed Antony and accustomed him to obey the orders of a woman. His dependence on strong women was retrospectively applied after he and Cleopatra had begun to represent a serious threat to Octavian, who persuaded the Senate and people that the Egyptian Queen was also a serious threat to Rome itself, and Antony was too weak to curb her ambitions.

Before he went off to fight the last of the civil wars, Caesar worked rapidly in Rome, pushing through reforms which he considered necessary, without the attendant freedom of debate that was customary in the Senate. He was made Dictator for the third time, this time for ten years, with specific responsibility for reforming the Republic.[12] One of his most far reaching reforms was the reorganisation of the calendar, which was based on a lunar year requiring constant adjustment. During the civil wars, these adjustments had been neglected, with the result that the seasons no longer matched the months to which they were supposed to belong. Caesar employed Sosigenes, an astronomer from Alexandria, whose calculations were based on a solar year of 365 days, with an extra day to be inserted every fourth year. In order to bring the seasons into line with the relevant months, and start off the new calendar at the right season, Caesar inserted several more days into November 46.

There was little time to attend to the many political affairs that demanded reform, since the sons of Pompey, Gnaeus and Sextus, together with Labienus, had established themselves in Spain and could not be allowed to gain more armed strength or political sympathy. Antony was not given a post with the Caesarian army in the Spanish campaign. Caesar's great nephew Octavius, too ill to accompany the main party, followed on his own initiative with a few of his friends, arriving too late for the decisive battle of Munda which was fought on 17 March 45, but nonetheless risking death and destruction on the way. It required ingenuity and courage to travel to a war zone without an army. His actions impressed Caesar, and may have been influential in persuading the Dictator to include Octavius in his will, which he wrote at one of his villas outside Rome before entering the city in yet another triumph. These details concerning Octavius were added in a codicil, and may not therefore have been part of the original text. The whole problem of Caesar's will is much disputed, but until this time Octavius had not had very much opportunity to demonstrate to his great uncle that he possessed intelligence and staying power. He went everywhere with Caesar while he journeyed through Spain, settling boundaries, adjudicating between various peoples, receiving embassies. One of these embassies, from Saguntum, came to Octavius himself, believing that he could influence Caesar and bring about a favourable result for the Saguntines, which he did, to the great delight of the early biographers of Augustus. Octavius was a discreet youth, astute and level headed, who knew when to talk and when to remain silent. There could be no greater antithesis to Antony, who was full of life, indiscreet, probably noisy when he should have been quiet, silent when he should have been saying something. The normally taciturn youth Octavius travelled in Caesar's carriage on the way back from Spain, and the two would have ample opportunity to converse and to get to know each other.

On Caesar's return from the wars, Antony set off to meet him, but when he reached Narbonne, he heard a rumour that Caesar was dead, so he hurried back to Rome. Cicero said that he had hurried back to prevent his property from being sold off.[13] This is the context of the practical joke that he played on Fulvia when he arrived home. He entered the house in disguise, pretending to be his own messenger with a letter from Antony to his wife, in which he declared his undying love for her. While she read the letter, the false messenger lingered to witness her reaction, which was entirely satisfactory, romantic and tearful, quite contrary to the usual descriptions of Fulvia as a virago with no redeeming features. At this point Antony threw off his disguise, embraced his wife, and presumably lived happily ever after. Plutarch included the anecdote in his biography in order to illustrate Antony's good character.[14] Cicero related it in order to illustrate Antony's spinelessness and dependence.[15] One may be permitted to ask what Antony would have done if Fulvia had tossed the letter aside with disdain.

The rumour that Caesar was dead was unfounded, so Antony set off again with Gaius Trebonius to meet his erstwhile chief. Cicero relates a strange tale that Trebonius tried to bring Antony into a plot to kill Caesar, but Antony neither joined the conspiracy nor did he inform Caesar about it.[16] Various motives have been attributed to him, ranging from loyalty to Trebonius so that he would not betray him, through to disloyalty to Caesar and complete unconcern as to whether he was assassinated or not. This is not quite believable, since he depended on Caesar for advancement and was going to meet him to find out if he was back in favour. He did not hold any position of importance and could not rely upon being given one if the conspirators were successful.

When Caesar finally met up with him, Antony was forgiven for his past transgressions. He travelled back through Italy in Caesar's own carriage, relegating Octavius to a second carriage following behind.[17] No one could be in any doubt that Antony was back in favour. He was promised the consulship with Caesar as colleague for 44. He was thirty-nine years old and his political career, hitherto sporadically advanced and delayed, was just about to start in earnest. He could not possibly have envisaged exactly how, nor how soon, he would be placed in control of the Roman state. He probably dreamed of army commands under Caesar, a second consulship, a proconsular command of his own, perhaps even eventually stepping into Caesar's shoes as virtual head of state. He probably thought it would take a few years and some hard work. He could not have predicted that in less than six months a cataclysmic series of events would cut short his apprenticeship and propel him to the summit in just two days.

In Rome Caesar took up the reins again. Antony's brothers were given offices for 44, Gaius as praetor and Lucius as tribune. It was Lucius who arranged a plebiscite a soon as he entered office in December 45 to empower Caesar to nominate half of all the magistrates and both of the consuls for the following years.[18] Aulus Hirtius and Vibius Pansa were to be consuls for 43, and Decimus Brutus and Lucius Munatius Plancus for 42. These two were to be governors of Gaul before they took up their consular office, Brutus in the Cisalpine province and Plancus in Transalpine Gaul. The other western provinces were also to be handed to Caesarian adherents; Lepidus was to give up office as *magister equitum* and instead to become governor of Nearer Spain and southern Gaul, and Asinius Pollio was to take over command of Further Spain. One man did not receive what he thought his due reward; Gaius Cassius Longinus had been quaestor to Crassus in Parthia, and had done much to re-establish the Roman position in the east after the great disaster. He could normally have expected some important office to mark his political progress, but he was given only a praetorship for 44. He thought he was worth more, and he began to think that unless he became an ardent partisan, all promotion was blocked by Caesar, so his resentment ignited. Such men are dangerous.

Antony did not always bend spinelessly to Caesar's will. As Dictator, Caesar perhaps considered his consulship – it was his fifth – somewhat superfluous, so he resigned it after a short time intending that Dolabella should become consul in his place. It would give him the necessary experience and relieve Caesar of some mundane business, but Antony objected to Dolabella at all times, so he attacked him in a speech in the Senate, precipitating an acrimonious debate. Caesar walked out in disgust. Antony then fell back on his priestly office as augur, declaring the signs unfavourable so that Dolabella could not legally be elected consul. He got his own way, preventing Dolabella from becoming consul for the time being. Caesar seemingly did not bear any grudge against Antony, but Dolabella did.[19]

Grudges were also building up against Caesar as the year progressed. His association with Cleopatra did nothing to help. After Caesar's death, Cicero refers to her arrogance while she lived in the villa across the Tiber, and the disrespectful behaviour of her associates. Nothing of this has survived from any contemporary record; perhaps all the Romans kept their thoughts to themselves while Cleopatra was in Rome and Caesar was there to protect her. He had placed a gold statue of her in the temple of his divine ancestress, Venus Genetrix, and though it did not affect the political life of Rome, socially it meant a great deal. Rumours circulated that he was about to move the capital from Rome to Alexandria, and that he intended to marry Cleopatra.[20] He was already married to Calpurnia, but divorces were not difficult to arrange, and although it was illegal for Roman citizens to marry foreigners, he had shown in the past how he could overcome rules and regulations if necessary. Suetonius reports another rumour that a bill was being prepared to allow Caesar to marry any woman, as many as he wished, in order to beget children.[21] For contemporary Romans, truth would not matter. People were ready to lend credence to these rumours, and would twist the facts to support the gossip.

Cleopatra was accustomed to life in a dangerous climate of intrigue and plotting, and she was also accustomed to dealing with adversaries in a swift and brutal way. To maintain her position as Queen of Egypt, she had to act, or even overact, the part and perhaps this regal attitude affected her association with Caesar. She was probably impatient with the outward forms of senatorial privilege to debate policies which Caesar wanted to implement. In Egypt she was not encumbered with a senate, and was not obliged to listen to her circle of advisers. As Caesar acted in an increasingly high-handed manner in his impatience to effect his reforms, without reference to the Senate, it was probably suspected that Cleopatra had a hand in it all somewhere, coaching Caesar in overweening ambition and kingship every night when they were together in his villa.

Perhaps Caesar knew just who was disaffected, but ignored the signs, since in reality only a fraction of the senators had any serious quarrel with him, and their quarrel was in the main a personal one, however much they dressed it up as a fight for political liberty. It has been pointed out, cynically but accurately, that to most senators, liberty meant freedom to dominate and exploit the lower classes in Rome and the peoples of the provinces. The Roman system of government had to change to accommodate the development of the Empire. Caesar could see only too clearly what was needed, but he was no longer young and felt that he must hurry. It was his lack of time and consequently his lack of patience that led to his downfall. It was not the changes *per se* that caused all the trouble, for many of his measures were beneficial and based on common sense; rather it was the way in which he forced through the changes that he wished to make. It seemed that he had no feeling for the old Roman customs, riding rough shod over them, and sometimes even mocking them. He said that the Republic was just a name, which was eminently true, but anathema to the ears of the patriotically proud Romans who saw no further than the city and the subservient peoples around it whose main purpose was to benefit Rome. Caesar also said that Sulla must have been an idiot to lay down his Dictatorship, which went deep into the consciousness of those who had perhaps hoped that the domination of Caesar would eventually come to an end, and had consequently been prepared to sit it out and wait.

Honours accumulated, granted to him by a Senate that increasingly owed its own status to his power.[22] He had increased the number of senators and filled the House with his own adherents, not all of them of traditional senatorial backgrounds, some of them not even thoroughbred Romans. He enfranchised the Cisalpine Gauls, in an effort to broaden the base of the expanding Roman Empire, extending citizenship to the peoples who formed the Empire and could bring a vital contribution to its growth. There was a joke current in the city that no one would show these new senators the way to the Senate House. The dilution of Roman stock was keenly felt, but what was worse was the knowledge that in his deliberate policy of clemency Caesar held all Rome in his power, literally at his mercy. He even had a shrine set up to himself and his *Clementia* and Antony was appointed as priest of his cult, though he did not take up the office until 39.[23] Much controversy and debate has been worked out on paper as to the precise meaning of Caesar's divinity. Some scholars argue that it was one of the most offensive aspects of Caesar's domination; others more reasonably suggest that the Roman mentality could accommodate divine heroes once they were dead, and that it was never the intention to make Caesar a living god on earth. According to this theory, Caesar was a divinity in waiting, to be included in the Roman panoply once he had died.

If there had been anybody left in Rome who thought that once Caesar had achieved all his aims he would then lay down his powers, these men must have been very disappointed when he accepted the Dictatorship for life on 14 February 44. The fuss about whether he intended to make himself king ought to have receded in importance after this, but it was still a constant theme, which Caesar perhaps decided to bring to a close next day at the festival of the Lupercalia. This was a very ancient and hallowed fertility ritual that dated far back to Rome's past, in which the priests ran around the streets of Rome, clad in loincloths, striking women with leather thongs in the hope that the procedure would aid conception of children in those who were barren. Antony's part in this particular festival in February 44 was politically motivated, but to what specific purpose is not known. The motives of the various participants has been debated ever since the event, with no unequivocal result. No one knows what was in anyone's mind at the time nor why they acted as they did. The festival began, Antony as priest ran the circuit of Rome in the traditional manner, and then approached the chair where Caesar sat to preside over the proceedings. Somewhere on his dash through the city Antony had picked up a diadem which he offered to Caesar, who refused it. The crowd roared approval that he had not accepted it. Antony offered the crown again, Caesar refused it more emphatically, the crowd roared further approval that Caesar had rejected monarchy.

There are several possible interpretations. Antony may have instigated the whole escapade on his own initiative, completely unknown to Caesar, either in the hope that Caesar would accept and become king, or in the hope that Caesar would refuse and thereby convince the people and the Senate that he definitely did not want to be king. This is the interpretation that Dio favours, by inventing or embellishing a speech made by Fufius Calenus in defence of Antony, in reply to Cicero's attack on him. Calenus says that Antony had observed that Caesar's monarchical tendencies had gone too far, so he arranged the Lupercalia events in order to convince the Dictator of the error of his ways. He insists that these noble intentions are proven by the fact that Antony never made the easy excuse that he had been ordered to do it, and after the Lupercalia, Caesar moderated his behaviour. On the other hand, Caesar may have collaborated with Antony, in an effort to put an end to all suspicion that he wanted to be king. There is some mileage in this speculation, especially since the leaders of the Luperci Julii had to be patrician nobles and Antony was from a plebeian noble family. Using the *lex Cassia* passed in 45, allowing him to create patrician families, Caesar converted Antony and his immediate family to patricians in order that he could lead the ancient festival. This is redolent of forward planning and collaboration between Caesar and Antony, rather than a convoluted private scheme on the part of Antony, who, in order to obtain eligibility for the leadership of the Luperci, would have to leak part of his plan by engaging the services of the very man he hoped to surprise with a proposal for kingship.[24]

If it was Caesar's purpose to demonstrate in unforgettably public circumstances that he was not aiming at monarchy, then the plan failed. It simply made matters worse and increased speculation and suspicion, even though Caesar dedicated the crown to Jupiter in the great temple on the Capitol, and ordered the scribes to record the fact that he had refused the kingship to be entered in the *Fasti*, the official journal of the state.

His punctiliousness did not save him. Within a month, the Liberators of the Republic had struck down the man they called tyrant, at a meeting of the Senate on 15 March. The meeting was to be held in Pompey's theatre, not the Senate House in the Forum. There were hints of disaster. A few days earlier a soothsayer warned Caesar to beware the Ides of March, and in the morning as he was to leave the house, his wife Calpurnia tried to prevent him, because of a bad dream she had had the previous night. Decimus Brutus came to his house to accompany him to Pompey's theatre, to allay his suspicions, but primarily to make sure that Caesar did actually attend the Senate that day. It would have been embarrassing and somewhat distressing for the Liberators if their victim did not appear. They would then have been forced to sit through the session with daggers hidden in their clothes, and then go quietly home and start all over again.

It is said that Brutus, idealist that he was, argued against the murder of Antony, so when Caesar arrived, Gaius Trebonius and perhaps Decimus Brutus distracted Antony for a moment and held him back, while Caesar went ahead into the building.[25] The sources are confused as to who did what, but from Antony's point of view outside the meeting house, so far everything was normal. He would be drawn aside for a few meaningless words. He may have noticed a certain nervousness on the part of the men who were addressing him. Then the commotion would be heard from the audience chamber of the theatre, followed by crowds of senators fleeing for their lives, probably shouting about murder or perhaps not shouting at all, grimly intent on finding their attendants and going home. By this time it is highly likely that Decimus Brutus and Trebonius would have prudently left Antony, so he probably had to find out for himself what had gone on. It is not known whether he went inside and found Caesar's body. The sources state that he fled, disguised as a slave, and found refuge in a friend's house. Later he went home and barricaded the doors, prepared for a siege.[26] Caesar was dead. Antony was his closest associate, and also consul, the chief magistrate who only very recently had offered Caesar the crown. It did not matter now whether it was all a ruse, or whether it had been in deadly earnest. The incontrovertible fact was that Antony, of all the men in Rome, could never detach himself from Caesar, and therefore he might have been next on the list for assassination.

After a while he would begin to reason, send out spies to gather information, strengthen his position, and consider what to do. He had not been dragged into Pompey's theatre and struck down with Caesar. He had been deliberately drawn aside, but not trapped in a corner to be killed after Caesar was dead. In fact he had been allowed to get away. That probably meant that he had not been a primary target for the assassins, and the fact that no one was battering his door down some hours after the deadly deed perhaps meant that even in the aftermath of the assassination, he had not been added to the list of victims, if indeed there was such a list. Information was the most urgent need. Gradually Antony would ascertain that the Liberators were a small number of men headed by Brutus and Cassius, and that they had tried to address the crowds in the name of Liberty, but had been driven off and had established themselves on the Capitol Hill, in some confusion that they had not been received with rapturous applause for their act of liberation. They had no military force to speak of, while Lepidus on the Tiber Island had command of several troops. Lepidus was perfectly willing to take orders from Antony as consul, and sent him a message that he was prepared to use his troops as Antony wished. Antony began to rally. He brought legionaries to the Campus Martius and Lepidus blockaded the Capitol.[27]

It is said that only sixty men were party to the plot, which is a very small proportion of the inflated Senate of 900 men that Caesar had created. The Liberators entertained the loftiest ideals but not prepared even the lowliest of plans, save that of killing Caesar. A few months after the assassination, Cicero's judgement was that they had done the deed with the courage of men but with the blind policy of children.[28] Upright and high-minded to the last, the conspirators eschewed the use of force, because that would have been the ultimate paradox, to remove a Dictator they hated and then to replace him with an even more despotic narrow-minded rule based on greater force than ever Caesar had used. Consequently they made no arrangements for the government of Rome or the provinces, imagining that with the tyrant dead, everything would automatically revert to the ideal Republic of old, without a hint of military backing or persuasion of some other kind to encourage law and order. The reaction of the people demonstrated to them the extent to which they were out of touch with reality. Not many Romans had felt the need for Liberty in the idealistic sense that Brutus and Cassius imagined. Caesar had done much to ease the lot of the common people, and the soldiers had little quarrel with him. Only the senators had felt themselves oppressed, but without definite plans for their future they had now delivered themselves to Antony.

Always clear headed and rational in a crisis, Antony acted quickly once he knew the facts. As consul he ordered the Senate to meet on 17 March in the temple of Tellus, which just happened to be near his house and not too far removed from his troops. Before the Senate meeting, Antony worked hard and thoroughly reinforced his position. Control of the Caesarian faction was supremely important, as well as control of the Caesarian troops. He began to find out which members of the Senate and people were his friends and which were real or potential enemies. Lepidus turned out to be an ally, offering the use of his troops, and he and Antony co-operated in restoring order in the city. Antony posted guards all over Rome to make sure there was no gathering of armed forces. There remained men like Oppius and Balbus, Caesar's freedmen secretaries and financiers, and many other Caesarian politicians, military men and equestrian business magnates. Rome was no doubt full of clandestine activity, as slaves and messengers dashed from house to house, putting Antony in touch with as many of Caesar's partisans as possible. Thereafter it was vital to gather all Caesar's papers, which Antony immediately obtained from the great man's widow Calpurnia, ostensibly without any need for persuasion, perhaps because Calpurnia felt that the documents would be safer in the hands of the consul.[29] Along with the papers came Caesar's secretary Faberius, friendly to Antony, compliant, and replete with a great deal of valuable knowledge. Caesar's documents were to feature in Antony's political programme some days later, when he had established himself in control.

Money was just as vital, and here the sources are murky, some of them accusing Antony of robbing the treasury of the temple of Ops to the tune of 700 million sesterces.[30] The main treasury of the state was in the temple of Saturn, which Antony left alone. Another charge made against him was that he confused his own finances with the state's, just as Caesar had done, but in Antony's case it was thought that he had used money that was not legally his own to pay off all his debts. The facts are much too tangled now to make any sense of them. Even at the time it is very likely that there was only an approximate accounting system when Antony accumulated funds, no doubt from every source that was available to him in the circumstances. His expenses would be great; there were soldiers to pay and Caesar's veterans to settle on the land, and some semblance of government had to function even though Rome may have been at a standstill. For a while, Antony *was* the government, and he shouldered the burden extremely well. There was so much to do in a very short time, and he had not wasted a single moment from 15 to 17 March, indeed he had probably scarcely slept since the terrible events in the Theatre of Pompey.

Now on 17 March he faced the Senate, not quite an unknown quantity to him since he cannot have failed to sound out various people during the previous day and night. The debate was stormy, but Antony allowed each to have his say. If he had so wished he could have had all Rome under his thumb, lining the streets with soldiers and dictating terms to all and sundry. Instead he took a calculated risk and endeavoured to bring everything as far as possible back into normal working order. Chaos was only a hair's breadth away, but Antony did not wish to impose rigid control, nor was he ready for open warfare just yet. The restoration of law and order was of paramount importance, and an all embracing amnesty was the only way to bring it about. Cicero proposed such a measure, and it found ready acceptance. There was a tremendous dilemma to be overcome before the state could be put on an even keel. A murder had been committed in full view of Rome, and it was not just a back street skirmish or a drunken brawl. It was a planned assassination, intended to be conspicuous. The vexed question was how to deal with it. If Caesar was innocent, then the Liberators ought to be punished, which would tear the state apart and precipitate another civil war. On the other hand, if Caesar was guilty, deserving of the name of tyrant, then the Liberators ought to be praised to the skies, and consequently all the Dictator's acts could be annulled. That was impossible, as Antony pointed out. Most of the senators owed their positions to Caesar; most of the magistrates both present and future had been appointed by Caesar; most of the current provincial governors were in office because Caesar had put them there. To annul all his acts would be tantamount to abolishing the entire governmental system at one stroke, and elections would have to be arranged to start from scratch. The Senate had no energy for this at the present moment. Then Antony pointed out that the decrees and promises to the soldiers ought not to be annulled, and the provincials and allies likewise stood to lose much if Caesar's acts were suddenly repealed. It followed, therefore, that as Antony proposed, it would be better to confirm all Caesar's acts and intentions, rather than to try to sift through them, confirming some and annulling others.[31] This meeting of the Senate was Antony's finest hour. His measures were sensible and just; they were not revolutionary, not high handed, not purely selfish, and nowhere near dictatorial.

Reconciliation was the order of the day for the time being. There was to be no witch-hunt of the murderers of Caesar, no trials or lynchings or civil war. It was a stupendous achievement, given the circumstances, and most Romans were probably agreeably surprised at Antony's firm but just statesmanship. As guarantee for his good faith, Antony sent his infant son to the Capitol as hostage in the camp of the Liberators, and when the Senate had agreed to the amnesty, he and Lepidus entertained the Liberators to dinner, to demonstrate the new concord that reigned in the city. Brutus dined with Lepidus, and Cassius with Antony. The dinners were probably strained affairs, an interesting amalgam of reconciliation and indigestion in equal measure. But it was the play acting that counted, not real feelings. While they dined, Antony allegedly asked Cassius if he still had a dagger about his person, and Cassius replied that he did, a large one, in case Antony wished to play the tyrant.[32]

Antony's task was an uphill struggle. Personal survival was the first necessity, with sufficient power to ensure that he remained not only alive but in charge. Some modern authors accuse him of aiming at total domination, moving towards it stealthily and slowly, having learned from the reaction to Caesar that the road to total control must not be taken at a gallop. The point is debatable. He scarcely subscribed to the fierce Republicanism of Cato and his party, but he played the game by Republican rules, just as Octavian Augustus did after him, and like Octavian he was still watchful for any opportunities that could be exploited. But Antony as cold and calculating despot plotting an uncompromising course to political and military dominance would have required a consistent patient ruthlessness that he did not possess. That was Octavian's speciality.

Antony ensured his survival by gathering together a bodyguard of 6,000 men, the equivalent of a legion, but mostly as a declaration of intent; he did not put them to any aggressive use to impose his will. He was the legally appointed consul, and in so far as he could, he operated as such. His next task was to reconcile all sorts of disparate entities whose prime motives were alarmingly similar to his own, so he needed to combine precisely balanced amounts of seduction and subjugation, depending on the personages with whom he had to deal at each step of the way. He was no friend of Dolabella, and had blocked his elevation to the rank of consul, but now, instead of remaining without a colleague, Antony allowed him to take up the post that Caesar had intended him to hold.

The general amnesty had been successfully brought about and the Republic shakily preserved without recourse to arms, but the fine balance that Antony had achieved was about to be permanently disrupted. He may not have recognised the fact just yet. On 18 March the Senate agreed to ratify the terms of Caesar's will.[33] The provisions were quite poignant in that Caesar had left money and valuables to some of the men who had killed him. His gardens were to be opened to the public, and he had left money to each Roman citizen. One quarter of his fortune went to his male relatives, Pedius and Pinarius, to be divided equally between them. Antony was mentioned only in the second rank of legatees, so if he had expected to profit from Caesar's will he was disappointed, but his relegation to second rank does at least vouchsafe for his honesty in not tampering with the will or trying to forge parts of it in his own favour. His lack of financial profit was not the hardest blow, nor his most troublesome problem. By far the greatest part of Caesar's wealth went to Gaius Octavius, his great-nephew, the grandson of his sister Julia. Octavius's inheritance embraced more than just money. A codicil attached to the will declared Caesar's adoption of Gaius Octavius as his son, a clause which has caused many problems to ancient and modern scholars alike, and one which Octavius took very seriously. He made strenuous efforts to have the clause ratified by law.

In March 44 Antony knew nothing of the schemes of Caesar's great-nephew. Once he was sure of his own position, Antony was able to take charge of the funeral arrangements for the murdered Dictator. Cicero's friend Atticus had said just after the assassination that if a public funeral was arranged, it would sound the death knell for the Liberators, and he was right. The ceremony took place on 20 March. A pyre had been built in the Campus Martius, but the mob took the body to the Forum and made a pyre of their own by ripping out benches and anything that would burn from nearby buildings. Antony made a speech, to which Cicero refers, but the contents of the speech are unknown. Both Dio and Appian invent noble words which have no basis in fact, and each of them use the speeches to put across their own points of view. Despite this blatant literary device, Dio[34] and Appian[35] possibly adhere quite closely to the spirit of what Antony actually said in much briefer terms. Suetonius says that Antony read out the honours that the Senate had awarded to Caesar, and the oath they had taken to protect him. Then he read the will. Suetonius adds that Antony then said a few words of his own.[36] By the time he had finished with the honours and the terms of the will, he would not need to make any inflammatory remarks, and perhaps never needed to flourish Caesar's blood stained toga as reported in some sources

The important event was the reaction of the people, who made it clearer than they had on the Ides of March that they did not greet the removal of the Dictator with joy. The unknown quantity here is the extent to which Antony intended to stir up these feelings, or alternatively how much of the popular demonstration was spontaneous and beyond his control. It is possible that he engineered it all, in true demagogue fashion, in order to say through other mouths what he probably wanted to say himself. Antony was an emotional man, but when it mattered he kept his emotions under control. If he had given the word, he could have started a war, but he kept his head. He was consul, and responsible for the whole Roman world. But he had been Caesar's friend for a long time. He was closer to the real world than the high minded Brutus and Cassius, and he knew the feelings of the people. Why should he not use those feelings to demonstrate his own at second hand?

The Liberators were in very bad odour. Antony made it possible for Brutus and Cassius to remove themselves from Rome, even though strictly speaking they were in office and should not leave the city. They started to collect bodyguards but Antony ordered them to disband the soldiers, despite the fact that he had formed a bodyguard of his own. The Liberators obeyed. As a political gesture which cost him nothing Antony abolished the dictatorship.[37] This measure brought him considerable support, even though it did nothing to abolish the harsh fact that whoever possessed the political prestige and the troops, and could dispense patronage to large numbers of people, could aspire to a dictatorship no matter what it was actually called. Caesar was dead, but Caesarian politics were still very much alive. A month after the assassination, Cicero expressed it in bitter terms to Atticus, 'the tyrant is dead but the tyranny still lives'.[38]

Antony had managed the state extremely well after the assassination of Caesar.[39] Civil war could have exploded immediately if he had not kept his head, resulting perhaps in the sort of carnage that the struggle between Marius and Sulla had caused. Accusations have been made that Antony had no long term plans and was incapable of making any,[40] but in the first days of extreme tension after Caesar's murder, he could perhaps be forgiven for not being able to see clearly where he wanted to direct the state. His priority was the restoration of order. Shortly afterwards he would have time to think.

At the meeting on 17 March the Senate had decreed that Caesar's acts should be ratified, and that all his unpublished plans and intentions should also have the force of law. By the beginning of April Antony had sifted through Caesar's documents, no doubt with the help of Faberius, and used them to draft out a few ideas. He was naturally suspected of forging new documents and of quietly losing those which did not fit his plans.[41] Cicero wrote testily to Atticus on 19 April that all the acts, notes, words, promises and projects of Caesar now had more validity than they would have had if he were still alive, and a little later he pointed out that they were being governed by Caesar's note books.[42] In another letter he accused Antony of forging documents.[43] Perhaps it is true that Antony fabricated plans and policies which he said he had found among Caesar's jottings, but whatever the origin of his ideas, he acted prudently within the law and did nothing that Republican politicians had not done before.

By the middle of April 44, everything started to change, because of the movements of two people who were to have tremendous influence on Antony's future life. Cleopatra left Rome and Octavius returned. Precisely when Cleopatra returned to Egypt is not known. She no doubt witnessed Caesar's funeral on 20 March, and appreciated Antony's display of respect for Caesar. On 15 April Cicero, studiously remaining away from Rome, wrote to Atticus that he saw nothing to object to in the Queen's flight (*fuga*), implying that she had already left Rome. Perhaps she had even sailed from Italy by then.[44]

The references to Cleopatra in Cicero's letters are tantalisingly unexplained, concerned with rumours, some of which he said were diminishing by mid May, only to flare up again, perhaps about some other scandal, at the end of the month. Whatever it was, Cicero hoped that the story was true,[45] so presumably it was not something beneficial to Cleopatra's interests or well-being. Some authors have used these references to Cleopatra to infer that she remained in Rome until the end of May or even later. Whether she was still in the city or not, there may have been some contact between her and Cicero in the early summer of 44, since after a silence about her lasting several days from the end of May, he launched into a tirade against her in mid-June, writing to Atticus that he detested the Queen and her creatures. He complained that they treated him as though he had no feelings or spirit. In other words he had been insulted, but with Cicero it seemed that it was never very difficult to do that. Consequently he declared that he would have nothing more to do with 'that lot' (*nihil igitur cum istis*).[46] Perhaps Cleopatra had made overtures to him as a senator of considerable standing, whose eloquence could carry the day in a senatorial debate; she may have desired to win him over so as to have an effective mouthpiece in Rome. Caesar had not tried to silence Cicero, and in his turn Cicero was ambivalent and indecisive about Caesar, blowing hot and cold, wanting to like him but deciding that politically he could not allow himself to do so; but for all their mutual respect, it is obvious that they could never have worked together. Perhaps Cleopatra tried to recruit him in an attempt to keep him under control, rather than let him drift into the opposite camp; perhaps she hoped to reconcile him to Antony; or perhaps Cicero had been mortally affronted by what he considered a lack of due respect while Cleopatra was in Rome, and simply could not let the matter drop.

It is not known whether Cleopatra met Antony before she left. They may have discussed the future of Egypt as an ally of Rome, and more immediately important for Cleopatra in April 44 the status of her son Caesarion, now that Caesar was dead. At some unknown date, Antony presented the case before the Senate, declaring that Caesarion was indeed Caesar's son, that Caesar had acknowledged him and there were other witnesses besides Antony himself.[47] This declaration hardly needed Antony's assurance while Caesar was alive, and Antony had no personal interest in the legitimacy or otherwise of Caesarion, so presumably it was part of an agreement made between him and Cleopatra.

Antony may have been relieved when Cleopatra left Rome, removing the need to attend to her needs at a time when he was very preoccupied. Cleopatra may also have been relieved to escape from the city where she had not been welcomed with open arms by everyone, and was decidedly *de trop* now that Caesar was no longer there. Her priorities were to ensure her own survival and that of her country, and she may not have thought of Antony as a permanent fixture in Roman politics.

Shortly after Cleopatra returned to Egypt, Gaius Octavius, now aged nineteen, arrived at Naples on 18 April. He may have seemed insignificant to Antony and everyone else at the time, but he regarded himself as Caesar's successor in every sense of the word. Cicero told Atticus that Octavius had already started to call himself Gaius Julius Caesar, but since the boy's stepfather Philippus did not address him as such, nor did Cicero.[48] The modern world knows him as Octavian, but he never used the name himself. It indicated that he had been adopted into the Julian clan from that of the Octavii.

Although adoption of an heir was a regular practice in Rome, it was nearly always carried out while both parties were still alive. It is very doubtful whether testamentary adoption had any real basis in Roman law. Indeed some modern scholars deny that it was legal at all.[49] This may be why Octavian made every effort to have the adoption formally ratified by a law of the people passed in public assembly. Antony made vague offers of help, but while not actively obstructing him, he worked behind the scenes to prevent the legalisation of the adoption. Octavian had to abandon the scheme, temporarily. He had no intention of forgetting about it. When he became consul it was his first concern, and the law was duly passed. Octavian was careful to start out in properly legalised fashion. He could not afford to leave any loopholes for clever politicians to exploit later on in his career.

Cicero reported to Atticus that 'the boy' was determined to take up his inheritance, and that there would be trouble with Antony if he did.[50] Perhaps Cicero did not realise quite how prophetic his casual phrase would be, since the trouble to which he referred occupied the next fourteen years and turned the Republic that he so adored into the Empire.

4
Separate Ways: Antony and Cleopatra 44–41 BC

In the summer of 44, Cleopatra arrived in Egypt. She perhaps remained in Rome long enough to discover who would emerge at the head of the state, and whether there would be any advantages or dangers to herself and Egypt. Her movements are not recorded in detail, but it is likely that she had already spent some time and effort in planning how to consolidate her position. Her chief Roman ally had disappeared, and so far no one else of the same calibre or empathy had taken his place. Antony was consul and in control of the state for as long as he held the office, but apart from completing the plans that Caesar had set in motion, plus a few of his own which he said he had found in Caesar's notes, he had not displayed any ambition to step into Caesar's shoes. Indeed in the circumstances it would have been somewhat unproductive to try. For the first months at least he was playing by ear, with no long term plans except to remain intact and keep the peace. It was far from certain that he would be able to achieve this, and although Cleopatra may have negotiated with him for the continued independence of Egypt and for recognition of herself as friend and ally of Rome, she would sense that Antony's grasp of supreme power was infinitely more fragile than Caesar's, so she could only watch and wait upon events. If Antony was removed, there was probably no other ally to whom she could appeal if a new leader urged the Senate to revoke Caesar's resolution recognising her as legitimate ruler of Egypt. This was perfectly feasible and would be the first stage on the road towards outright annexation.

The uncertain element in the new situation after Caesar's murder was his great nephew Gaius Octavius, the new Gaius Julius Caesar Octavianus. It was his adoption by Caesar that sealed the future of Octavian, Antony and Cleopatra. As Caesar's son, Octavian represented a potential danger to Cleopatra and Caesarion, especially since there had been no mention of either of them in Caesar's will. Cleopatra's relationship with Octavian up to the assassination of Caesar is not known, but it would be surprising if she had not formed some kind of judgement of him. Vice versa, Octavian had probably formed an opinion of the Queen. In view of their later history it is easy to suppose that there was mutual jealousy and dislike, but there is no contemporary evidence, and both of them were astute enough to mask their feelings in public.

Octavian had travelled to Spain to join Caesar in the last of the civil wars, and had impressed Caesar sufficiently to induce him to adopt him, in the codicil to his will which he wrote just before he entered Rome to celebrate his triumph. Even if he had never spoken of his great nephew to Cleopatra or to Antony, his estimation of him was made clear when he appointed Gaius Octavius his *magister equitum*, and sent him to Apollonia to gain military experience with the legions stationed there in anticipation of the Danubian and Parthian campaigns.

Cleopatra left Rome as Octavian was sailing back to Italy, and their paths did not cross for another fourteen years. Cleopatra devoted herself to home affairs in Egypt. She needed to create a strong government and sound economy before she had to face whichever of the Roman generals or politicians emerged supreme and developed an interest in Egypt. She did not delude herself that Egypt and Rome could exist happily side by side, each going about their separate business. Thinking of the longer term, in order to establish herself and Caesarion as rulers of Egypt, she may have schemed to remove her teenage brother. So far, she had almost ignored the fifteen year-old Ptolemy XIV, and had kept him out of the clutches of influential counsellors who might try to follow the example set by Pothinus and Achillas in favouring and fostering her older brother. As a small boy Ptolemy XIV was perhaps amenable to her direction, but she may have feared that he would grow troublesome as he matured, striving for a greater share in her government and for more independence. Cleopatra could not spare the time for contradictory debate and certainly had no intention of allowing outright opposition to evolve. By September 44 Ptolemy XIV was dead, and Cleopatra shared her throne with her three year-old son Caesarion, named Ptolemy XV Caesar, a declaration of a combined Egyptian and Roman heritage.

The cause of death of Ptolemy XIV is not illuminated in any reliable source, allowing much speculation about it, ranging from a sudden illness to poisoning, but poisoning was a common accusation, often meaningless in an age which observed sensible religious precautions with regard to food, but was at the mercy of a hot climate without the benefit of refrigerators or rigorously enforced government control of food hygiene. Excuses can be advanced in Cleopatra's defence, but the removal of Ptolemy XIV was so fortuitous for her that it is quite natural that she should be accused by contemporaries and later authors of having him killed.[1] She may have agonised over her dilemma for a while. Ptolemy XIV could live for another five or six decades. Since there could be no question of power sharing between her son and her brother, she could not step down in Caesarion's favour, and in any case she would never have entertained that idea for a single moment. If she died before Ptolemy, it was not likely that Caesarion would long survive her. Ptolemy XIV had to be removed, before any faction could promote him and threaten her rule. No public outcry was recorded when

Ptolemy died, which is not the same thing as saying that none ever occurred.

At a later time, when she and Antony were in positions of power in the east, Cleopatra had her sister Arsinoe murdered, so any argument that she might have shrunk from murdering her brother because of sisterly affection falls at the first hurdle. Her motives centered on her own regime and on her son. The fact that Caesarion had not been mentioned in Caesar's will was less relevant than the fact that Octavian was his adoptive heir. For nearly three years Cleopatra had insisted that Caesarion was the son of Caesar and now, as from the Ides of March 44, there was another one, older, more experienced, at the head of a powerful retinue of Caesar's adherents, and assiduously pursuing his inheritance.

While she strengthened her own regime and looked to the welfare of her kingdom, she was keenly aware of what was happening in Rome. She watched as Brutus and Cassius took over territories in the east and raised troops. Willingly or under coercion, neighbouring states all around Egypt went over to Brutus and Cassius, including Cleopatra's own governor of Cyprus, and on two occasions Cassius threatened Egypt itself, making demands for assistance in the form of money, soldiers and ships.[2] In Rome, when it became clear that there was to be no immediate outbreak of war, Antony attended to the measures that Caesar had planned. Settlement of Caesar's veterans was one of the priorities, so in April Antony went to Campania to attend to the distribution of lands, at the same time advertising his presence to the soldiers and selecting some of them for his bodyguard. More land was to be made available as the Pontine marshes were drained, another project of Caesar's that Antony developed. His brother Lucius as tribune passed an agrarian law providing for more land allotments, for veterans and for the poorer classes from the city of Rome, all of which enhanced Antony's reputation.[3]

Cash flowed in from a variety of sources, mostly from foreign rulers who required Roman support. Deiotarus of Galatia had seized various territories and was confirmed as ruler of them in return for ten million sesterces, and the Sicilians paid large sums for Roman citizenship, all in accordance with Caesar's intentions according to Antony. In reality, Caesar had in mind Latin status for the Sicilians, the half-way house to full citizenship, and on his own initiative Antony upgraded it. Accepting money for such favours was not an innovation, since several senators including Pompey and Caesar had always made such cash deals for foreign rulers, and the state profited from their arrangements.[4]

The arrival of Octavian did not at first affect Antony's plans. He did not go to meet him, an omission that was later used against him, but he was consul and Octavian was only lately master of horse, and at the time Antony was preoccupied. According to Appian, Octavian turned Antony's lack of good manners to his advantage and said that he would go to meet Antony instead, as the junior to the senior man. They were said to have met in the gardens of Pompey's house, which Antony had received from Caesar in his will, or more properly his ownership had been confirmed. The speeches invented for them serve as a forum for opposing points of view, with at least some basis in fact. In Appian's account Octavian asks Antony why he did not condemn the assassins to death, and seeks his help in punishing them in the future. He then asks for cash to help to pay the citizens the money promised them in Caesar's will, and in reply Antony points out that Caesar had not actually bequeathed the government to Octavian and so he does not need to apologise for his acts as consul after the assassination. He also explains that he no longer has access to Caesar's funds and in any case the treasury is empty. At the end of his speech, Antony warns that the people are fickle, constantly elevating their favourites and removing them again. After this useful scene-setting device, Appian describes Octavian's next moves to secure his inheritance.[5]

Three of the assassins of Caesar had been removed from Rome. Decimus Brutus had been assigned the province of Cisalpine Gaul, and he left in April to take up the post.[6] Brutus and Cassius also left Rome early in April, and in the summer were given interim tasks, namely the charge of the corn supply in Asia and Sicily. This enabled them to fill in their time profitably before they went to their provinces. Antony assigned them to Crete and Cyrene, where they could not command armies and threaten him or the state unless they left their provinces to do so. Cicero was outraged at the insult to his heroes, and ultimately the scheme failed to avert civil war. Brutus and Cassius eventually left Italy and went to the east to take over provinces illegally, and just as illegally raise armies.[7]

The government of the provinces was one of Antony's major concerns. Caesar had made most of the provincial appointments in advance, and the Senate had confirmed his arrangements, but now some fine tuning was necessary. Dolabella was to be governor of Syria, and Antony was assigned to Macedonia, which arrangement was originally part of Caesar's plans for the Danube campaign and the war with Parthia. Such foreign campaigns were out of the question when the situation at home was so delicate. The struggle would centre on Rome, so Antony needed a different base nearer the scene of action. He chose Cisalpine Gaul. It was an area he knew well, and from his headquarters he could oversee Italy, just as Caesar had done.

On 1 June Antony failed to persuade the Senate to change the provincial assignments, so he had a law passed by the popular assembly to give him the province of Cisalpine Gaul for six years, exchanging for it Macedonia which was now assigned to Decimus Brutus. Octavian assisted Antony, actively canvassing on his behalf to encourage the people to pass the law. He and Antony worked together, but only because the soldiers, who did not want to fight in a war between them, had coerced them. Octavian was more interested in removing Decimus Brutus to Macedonia, than he was in installing Antony as governor of Cisalpine Gaul.[8] Decimus Brutus was not inclined to leave his province without a fight, so Antony required more troops than were currently at his disposal to persuade Decimus to go. He decided to bring back to Italy four of the five legions that had been stationed in Macedonia, and sent his brother Gaius Antonius to organise their transport to Italy.[9]

Antony's plans for his future were sound, but he was hindered at every step by the persistence and determination of Octavian. Whereas Antony had played down the connection with Caesar after all due reverence had been shown at his funeral, and managed to obliterate the name and hopefully some of the memory of the Dictatorship, Octavian blatantly advertised his descent from the Dictator, and seized upon every opportunity to remind people of him. Worse still, he openly vowed revenge for Caesar's death.[10] Octavian tried on two occasions, in May and again in July, to display Caesar's golden chair at the games in honour of Caesar, but Antony blocked him.[11] When it was rumoured that Octavian wanted to become tribune in the place of Helvius Cinna, who had been an unfortunate casualty of the aftermath of Caesar's assassination, Antony used all his influence to prevent that too.[12] Though Octavian was thwarted on these occasions, thereafter nearly everything played into his hands. He put on splendid games in honour of Caesar, during which a comet appeared, visible in the night sky for several days.[13] People said it was a sign that Caesar had indeed become a god. Octavian naturally found it extremely advantageous to claim divine descent, and began to call himself the son of a god, *divi filius*. He advertised Caesar's divinity to great effect. Coins appeared depicting the comet, called *sidus Iulium*, the star of Julius, and decorative stars were placed on the statues of Caesar.

Antony cannot have failed to take note of the power-seeking inclinations of Octavian. He has been accused of failing to take due account of the youth, and of consistently underestimating him. None of this speculation is sufficiently accurate. Antony may have been reckless in some areas of his life but he was not a fool, and he walked with both feet firmly on the ground. When Octavian arrived in Italy in April 44 he was an unknown quantity, so perhaps for the first few days everyone from the consul Antony down to the lowliest senator imagined that he was a nonentity who could be controlled.[14] If Antony initially entertained this misconception, he would not be in error for long.

The fact that Antony tried to curb Octavian's efforts to connect himself with Caesar did not spring from jealousy or churlishness but from a sense of proportion. It demonstrates that Antony realised the political dangers of openly advertising such a connection, but in order to keep reins on Octavian he was scarcely in a position to do more than the law allowed, and he had to second-guess Octavian's next move, constantly manoeuvring to stay one step ahead. The sources imply that Antony brought all his later problems on himself by his cavalier treatment of Octavian, who is depicted as the injured party, dealt with roughly by Antony at their first meeting and cheated out of some part of his inheritance because Antony had squandered it. It must be remembered that apart from Cicero, who was no friend of Antony, the majority of the sources are not contemporary and the account of Antony's behaviour has been revised in the light of the eventual success of Octavian. Much emphasis is placed on the fact that the poor young man was forced to sell his own property and to beg for financial assistance from his relatives Pedius and Pinarius, in order to pay the people of Rome the sums due to them according to the terms of Caesar's will.[15] Antony was cast as the villain who consciously deprived good Roman citizens of their rights, as well as embarrassing the innocent great-nephew of Caesar. This was part of the psychological game that Octavian was intent on winning. He was much more devious than Antony, and on occasion he outwitted him, which lends spurious support to the theory that Antony underestimated him. Antony neither underestimated Octavian nor overestimated his own abilities, but he suffered from the scandalous reputation that had already become embedded in perceptions of him, whereas Octavian, not yet twenty, was an unknown quantity. He was therefore free to establish a carefully scripted reputation for himself, mostly favourable at the time and quite definitely revised and rewritten after the civil wars. When Antony tried his hand at the psychological game, claiming that Octavian had infiltrated his bodyguard with the intention of having him assassinated, he gained no sympathy at all.[16] No one really believed him, and quite a few

men possibly wished that Octavian had succeeded. Antony may
have made it all up to discredit Octavian, but on the other hand the
ruthless young man may well have decided that he really needed to
remove his main rival. It has been pointed out that the two of them
had more to gain by forming an alliance, but that was later, when
other parties had been eliminated.

Gradually, as a result of the devious activities of Octavian, closely
followed by the vituperative speeches and machinations of Cicero,
Antony lost favour. After the Ides of March Cicero had avoided
the political scene, and had made plans to go to Greece and remain
entirely out of the way in case war should break out. He had been
in contact with Octavian since his arrival in Italy. In August, having
stood on the sidelines for several months, he began to think that he
could ally with Octavian and turn him to good use against Antony.
Once again, Cicero saw his chance to save the state. Antony summoned the Senate for 1 September, but Cicero failed to attend.[17] The
meeting was arranged in order to confer upon Caesar religious honours that far exceeded anything yet seen for an ordinary mortal. At
the meeting of the Senate held on the following day, Cicero said that
he had not attended because he could not condone such honours.
Then he launched into the first of the diatribes against Antony now
known as the *Philippics*.

During this first speech, Antony was not present, but naturally he
heard of it and the story presumably lost nothing in the retelling. It
took seventeen days for Antony to respond in kind, but his speech
is not recorded. He was probably quite stunned by this attack on
him. His personal quarrel with Cicero on behalf of his step-father
Lentulus had never coloured his relationship with the orator in any of
his political dealings up to now. The letters that survive from Antony
to Cicero are polite, reasonable, even deferential. The animosity that
sprang up fully fledged is purely Cicero's, not Antony's, so the tirade
presumably came as an unexpected blow to Antony. The Roman
political scene was not one for wilting wallflowers, but Cicero's
speech was, in modern parlance, right over the top, and bewilderingly

inappropriate as well as unfair. After striving to bring concord to the state, and indeed achieving and maintaining an admittedly fragile peace without setting himself up as an autocrat, Antony had been painted in the darkest colours as the greatest enemy of Rome since Hannibal. Like any reasonable politician with a sense of reality, he would have expected opposition, because he had encouraged freedom of speech, but when he heard of the gross accusations of Cicero he may have wished momentarily that he had taken over the city and gagged everyone while he had the chance.

The war of words went on for a short time, while Octavian steadily consolidated his position. He raised troops from among Caesar's veterans, without authority to do so. His excuse for this illegality was that he was protecting himself from Antony. He and Cicero were beginning to sound the same call to arms, each for their own purposes. Cicero desperately wanted to play the part of saviour, and would twist any fact to be able to do so. Octavian wanted legitimate power to enable him to avenge Caesar, and that meant, ultimately, supreme power, and civil war. It was only a matter of time before he and Cicero formed an alliance. The one entity that was lacking was an enemy who posed a serious threat, a deficiency that was soon resolved when it seemed that Antony was intent on emulating Caesar by going to Gaul and from there influencing Roman politics. The senators were sensitive about such things, and now that they allowed themselves to be represented more and more by Cicero, they convinced themselves that they required an army to use against Antony. Octavian had an army but required legal sanction to use it, which only the Senate could give him. What one party lacked, the other could supply. War was now a definite possibility.

Antony went to Brundisium in November to meet his legions arriving from Macedonia.[18] He found that they had been subverted by Octavian, who after all had spent some time with them in Apollonia while waiting for Caesar to arrive for the Danubian campaign. Their loyalty to Antony was now suspect. They had been raised by Caesar and were prepared to fight for him, but after his death their loyalties were divided between the two Caesarian leaders, so it is not surprising that some of the troops wavered. Antony executed about 300 of the ring leaders. It is said that Fulvia was with him, revelling in the bloodshed, but that may be scandalous invention. Antony then paid the loyal troops more than Caesar had left the populace of Rome in his will, but it is said that the soldiers thought it a paltry sum. It is highly likely that Octavian made full use of their vacillation by offering them more money than Antony could afford.

While Antony marched his troops back towards Rome, he was still in control of the government. Octavian and Cicero had not yet concluded their unofficial alliance and Octavian at this juncture was simply an illegal adventurer at the head of troops. Moreover he had just made a serious mistake. Impatient for action, trying to forestall retaliation by Antony, he had marched some of his army to Rome, but had failed to rouse support, so he retreated to the north to lie low for a while. Antony hurried back to Rome, fully intent upon calling the Senate together to declare Octavian a public enemy and outlaw (*hostis*). There was every chance that he might succeed. He had primed his agents, and he had the full weight of the law on his side, because Octavian had acted illegally in raising troops.

Octavian moved faster than Antony, and successfully subverted two of his Macedonian legions, the Fourth and the Martia.[19] This stopped Antony in his tracks. He abandoned the idea of asking the Senate to outlaw Octavian and marched north instead, to ensure the loyalty of the rest of his legionaries. He stayed at Tivoli, where many senators and equestrians came to meet him and swore loyalty to him. The gesture was a spontaneous demonstration, and served to strengthen his resolve, but he did not emulate Sulla and march on Rome. For many reasons, Antony withdrew.[20] His consulship was coming to an end in a month's time. He could gain nothing except accumulating problems with no time to resolve them if he went back to Rome, but at least he knew now that there were some senators and equestrians who would support him while he was absent. It was better to continue while the going was good, take what troops were loyal to him and use them to oust Decimus Brutus from Cisalpine Gaul. Once he was established there, he would be in a better position to build up his influence in Italy.

Antony proceeded to Rimini, on the border between Italy and Cisalpine Gaul. As the legally appointed governor of the province, he cordially invited Decimus Brutus to leave. The Senate, on the other hand, had ordered Decimus to stay where he was.[21] There was every reason for Antony to establish himself rapidly in command. Decimus was quickly bottled up in Mutina (modern Modena), where he prepared for a siege.[22] Antony obliged. He needed quick results if he was to avoid having to fight on two fronts. The new consuls would take up office on 1st January 43, and it was highly probable that the Senate would instruct them to assist Decimus. Already making himself the saviour of the state, Cicero had begun to canvass for support for Octavian. As soon as the new consular year was inaugurated, he set about extracting recognition from the Senate for the young commander and his army, and there could be only one reason for doing so. Very soon Antony would be sandwiched between Decimus' troops blockaded in Mutina, and the relieving armies of the consuls and Octavian.

The alliance with Cicero was profitable for Octavian. He was presented to the Roman world not as a calculating opportunist bent on self-preservation and revenge for Caesar's death, but as the boy-hero whose timely action had saved the state from Antony. Cicero persuaded the Senate to elevate Octavian to senatorial status by granting him the rank of quaestor without having held the post, the important point being that he would therefore be allowed to stand for election to any office that normally followed the quaestorship. With Cicero's assistance he then obtained an appointment as pro-praetor, which would give him the necessary powers and legal basis (*imperium*) to command an army.[23] This was all passed by the Senate in blatant disregard of the age limits placed upon the tenure of such political offices. Cicero pointed out that youth was not necessarily a disadvantage in political and military circles, and finally he vouched for Octavian's good character. He still imagined that he could control the young man, and use him to crush Antony. That one overriding purpose blinded him to the possibility that the young Octavian might have plans of his own. Cicero saw no further than placing the Senate in command of Rome, and restoring the Republic to its ancient glory. When that was achieved, he thought he could discard Octavian.

The new consuls of the year, Hirtius and Pansa, were duly allotted the task of assisting Decimus Brutus, and Octavian was assigned to the same task, his powers somewhat muted because as propraetor he ranked below the consuls.[24] The war of Mutina had almost begun, but Antony still had friends in the Senate. Lucius Calpurnius Piso and Quintus Fufius Calenus spoke for him, trying to avoid war by suggesting that an embassy should be sent to Antony, to ask him to give up Cisalpine Gaul. Antony's reply was perfectly reasonable: he would leave Cisalpine Gaul if he could go to Transalpine Gaul, to hold it for five years. He also requested, quite legitimately, that all his acts as consul should be ratified. He could hardly have expected that these requests would be granted, since he can have had no illusions now about Cicero's implacable hostility and his persuasive oratory in the Senate.[25]

Antony recognised the weaknesses of the unlikely alliance between Octavian, Cicero and the Senate, and saw through the divergent ambitions of each of the participants. His reply to a letter from Octavian and Hirtius is preserved in part in the Thirteenth *Philippic*, where Cicero cites passages from it and answers the points raised. It shows that Antony had a firmer grasp of reality than many of the senators who were swayed by Cicero's oratory.

The senatorial army did not unite until spring. Octavian and the consul Hirtius made camp near Bononia (modern Bologna) where they waited for the other consul Pansa to bring up more troops from Rome. They moved closer to Mutina in March, and as they did so Antony abandoned Bononia, strengthened the blockade of Mutina and decided to launch an attack on one army before the two consuls could join forces. His intelligence networks were accurate, and it was a sound strategy to take advantage of the enemy's split forces. It nearly paid off. On 14 April Antony laid an ambush and fell upon Pansa's troops, mostly inexperienced recruits, and routed them. Pansa was wounded, and several days later died of his wound. Unfortunately Antony had no time to consolidate the victory or regroup his army. While the soldiers were still scattered, Hirtius came up to rescue his colleague, putting Antony into a dangerous situation. It is to Antony's great credit that as the evening progressed into night he withdrew in reasonable order. These bloody skirmishes were collectively known as the battle of Forum Gallorum.[26] Octavian's part in it was to defend the camp near Mutina. He shared in the honours granted by the Senate, and along with the two consuls was hailed by the soldiers as Imperator, which was to become the most important title of the Emperors of Rome.

The next battle followed within a few days, near Mutina. The consul Hirtius was killed, but Antony had to acknowledge defeat. He wasted no time in coming to a decision; he abandoned the siege of Mutina, rounded up what was left of his army, and set off towards Gaul.[27] He was not certain of his reception there. During the previous month, it seemed that the other Caesarian governors, Munatius Plancus in Transalpine Gaul, Lepidus in southern Gaul and Nearer Spain, and Pollio in Further Spain, might join him, or at best remain neutral, but times had changed. Antony's defeat had been greeted with near delirium in Rome. In his previous speeches Cicero had tried unsuccessfully to have Antony declared an enemy of the state and an outlaw (*hostis*), but the senators had not dared to take matters that far. Now that they thought it was safe they did so with alacrity, overwhelming anyone who tried to speak up for Antony. His defeat was considered decisive. It was thought that Rome had seen the last of him. Thanksgiving to last for fifty days was decreed.[28] Antony was declared an enemy of the state, and Decimus Brutus was ordered to pursue and annihilate him.

It was time for Antony to take stock of the possibilities open to him. Retreating to Gaul from the eastern to the western coasts of northern Italy, over the mountains in the cold winds of April, surrounded by a defeated and starving army whose loyalty was sorely tested, cut off from his family who were now outlaws because of senatorial hostility to him, Antony perhaps came to grim terms with fate. After all he had done after the Ides of March to keep the state on an even keel, punishing none of the Liberators and exercising every restraint, Rome had rejected him. Very well. There were other places, other armies. He was not beaten yet.

Crossing the Apennines and southern Alps is not an easy task without modern roads and vehicles, and in April 43 it was particularly difficult.[29] The snows had not melted in the passes and there were no supplies. Antony had not had time to gather rations before he raised the siege of Mutina and withdrew. He could not afford to delay progress by wandering around in search of supplies, so the army had to live hand to mouth, content with what it could find on the march, which was precious little. Plutarch tells of Antony drinking brackish water without flinching in order to encourage the men. In a crisis he was always brilliant, sustaining hardships that might have broken other leaders even if there was hope of salvation at the end of the hardships, but in this case there was none. Antony was faced with the possibility of having to go to war just to stay alive in Gaul, and there was the possibility that some of his own men might decide that they had had quite enough of following a loser and suddenly turn against him. He probably reflected that loyalty is a tenuous commodity, usually proportionately related to the benefits that ensue from it. He was an outlaw, beyond state protection. He had no legal status and no right to command troops. His death would be welcomed by many, and the person who despatched him would be regarded as a hero. Apart from his own safety he had to consider that of his family in Rome; he perhaps did not know at this stage that Fulvia had found protection with Cicero's great friend and correspondent Atticus, who kept out of politics, did not take sides, extended kindness to all and sundry regardless of their associations, and survived to old age.[30]

It was not all doom and gloom on the march into Gaul. On 3 May Antony was joined by three new legions raised and led by his friend Ventidius Bassus, who had skilfully avoided any military encounter on his way northwards, and evaded Decimus Brutus' troops which were in pursuit of Antony. Ventidius[31] was an adventurous character who had started life in difficult and humble circumstances. His family had been on the wrong side in the Social War of 91–87. As a child, Ventidius was taken prisoner and led through the streets of Rome as one of the human trophies in the triumphal procession of Pompeius Strabo, the father of Pompey the Great. Ventidius rose via the army and attracted the notice of Caesar, whose loyal follower he had been for many years. From Caesar's side he progressed to Antony's, joining him with fresh troops as he retreated into Gaul – more mouths to feed, but heartening because Antony was about to enter the province of Gallia Narbonensis and he now had enough troops to counter anything that the legitimate governor, Marcus Aemilius Lepidus, might do to stop him. But in fact nobody seemed able or willing to stop him, perhaps because Antony's reputation as a soldier went before him, and because potential opponents would reason that here was a man leading troops who, like himself, were experienced, battle-hardened, hungry, angry, with very little to lose. Lepidus posted a guard at the mouths of the passes, under the command of an officer called Culleo, but when Antony's brother Lucius approached with the advance guard on 7 May, Culleo made no effort to block him.[32] By the middle of May Antony and the whole army were in Gaul.

Marcus Aemilius Lepidus faced the most important cross-roads of his life. He was one of Caesar's generals, a respected patrician, and Antony had made him Pontifex Maximus in Caesar's place, in return for his co-operation in the aftermath of the Ides of March. He was a close associate if not a friend of Antony, and probably had no desire at all to fight against him. On the other hand he wished to retain the high regard of the Senate, with which he was in regular correspondence, writing lots of words but saying very little until he knew how matters would turn out. Lepidus no doubt reasoned that to throw in his lot with an outlaw who might be defeated in the end would finish his career and probably his life. He also knew that whatever he did would reflect on his family.

The Senate, led by Cicero, tried to win Lepidus to their cause. Cicero flattered him by voting him a golden statue for his work in coming to an agreement with Sextus Pompey, who was now operating on behalf of the Senate, using his fleet to secure the Mediterranean. The honour of having a statue in the Forum rendered no help to Lepidus in his present circumstances. He stalled for as long as he could, writing anodyne reports, and finally moving his legions to block Antony's progress. Antony was camped on the banks of the river Argenteus, so Lepidus camped on the opposite bank. The soldiers began to fraternise. One day Antony, long haired and bearded, walked casually into Lepidus' camp.[33] The tale has been questioned, but it has a definite Antonian panache about it that found ready acceptance in ancient times. The disregard for personal safety, the all-or-nothing gamble was typical of Antony. It took courage to confront Lepidus' troops, ignoring the risk that one of Lepidus' officers might take it upon himself to be a hero and do his commander a favour. It would be small comfort to him to know that his potential assassin probably would not survive the next few seconds.

An alliance was forged. Lepidus wrote to the Senate to say that his hand had been forced by his soldiers. The Senate promptly declared Lepidus an outlaw. His own brother Aemilius Paullus instigated the proceedings, possibly to remove himself from all suspicion. Perhaps the senators did not stop to reflect that their actions had just united two of the foremost Caesarian leaders, whose desperate position gave them common cause to use the ten legions which they had at their joint disposal.

Theoretically, Lepidus and Antony were threatened on two fronts. In Transalpine Gaul there was Munatius Plancus with three legions, backed up by Asinius Pollio in Further Spain with two more legions. From Italy, Decimus Brutus pursued Antony with weary troops who had been severely weakened during the siege and blockade of

Mutina. Octavian was ordered to help Decimus,[34] but he stayed put, holding onto his own troops and also those of the dead consul Pansa. Here was a rift to be exploited. Octavian had received no rewards after the Mutina battles, and although he had been solemnly assured that the rewards that he had promised his soldiers would be paid, nothing was forthcoming from the Senate. A committee had been formed to look into the question of the settlement of veterans, but Octavian had not been asked to sit on it, so he could not person- ally represent his own troops, nor could he protect their interests. On a more personal level, Octavian had been informed that Cicero had spoken about him in public, saying that the young commander should be praised, rewarded, and immortalised. The phrase sounds innocuous enough in English translation, but in Latin it is a clever pun. The word used for 'immortalised' (*tollere*) has two meanings, one denoting elevation to fame, and the other elimination by death.[35] Cicero was a master of words, and could never resist the urge to be clever, especially when he had an audience. He still thought that he was in control of Octavian. He never seemed to grasp the fact that Octavian would never co-operate fully with Decimus Brutus, who had helped to murder Caesar. In truth, all that Octavian required at first was legal command of an army. Now he had set his sights somewhat higher. The two consuls were dead, and Octavian was determined to be appointed in the place of one of them. With unassailable political power he would be able to obtain all he wanted, namely legalisation of his adoption as Caesar's son,[36] condemnation of Caesar's murderers, and sufficient status to face Antony on equal terms.

For about a month, Octavian laid low, pretending that he could not control his troops and that they would not march with Decimus Brutus against Antony. In June he sent a deputation of centurions and soldiers to the Senate, to ask for the consulship for their com- mander. The Senate refused. Octavian no doubt expected this, but it was all part of the elaborate game to do everything as properly as he could. There was a small chance that he might have obtained the consulship after his soldiers had asked politely for it, in which case he could have taken it up legally without the expenditure of too much effort. After the polite questions, there remained the last resort of force. When it was clear that the Senate would not co-operate with him, Octavian wasted no time in marching on Rome. Only now beginning to panic, the Senate summoned two legions from Africa, and called out the legion of recruits that Pansa had left near Rome, but the senators had left it too late to take any effective action. Just short of his twentieth birthday, Octavian was elected consul and took up office on 19 August, with his kinsman Pedius as colleague.[37]

Watching from the sidelines in Gaul and Spain, Plancus and Pollio decided that their best policy was to do nothing and await the outcome. They knew Antony, and perhaps did not consider him so easy to defeat as the Senate did. Pollio came over to Antony in July, but Plancus wavered a little longer, writing reports to Cicero, expressing surprise and then dismay that Octavian had not marched to help Decimus.[38] Plancus and Decimus joined forces in August, but then Octavian became consul, and so Plancus yielded to the inevitable. He and Pollio were after all Caesar's men, more comfortable with Antony than with the assassins. Decimus' troops guessed correctly what was happening and went over to Antony. Decimus was out on a limb, deserted except for a few officers. He went north to the Rhine, but was killed by a Gallic chief, who did as Antony told him.[39]

The way was now open for an alliance between Antony and Octavian. Correspondence may have been winging its way northwards to Antony from Octavian long before he obtained the consulship.[40] This is one of history's imponderables, but it can be assumed that Octavian would cautiously sound out Antony's mood and strength before he acted. He fortified his own position before he embarked on the alliance with Antony. Once installed in office, Octavian first brought about the legalisation of his adoption by a law of the people. As Caesar's legitimate heir he could claim all the property left to him, and more important he could place himself at the head of Caesar's considerable band of dependants and followers, or *clientelae*, without which following no Roman politician could hope to maintain any influence. Next, Octavian set up a special court to bring Caesar's murderers to trial.[41] The fact that they were absent from Rome and not able to speak for themselves did not deter him, indeed it facilitated the proceedings, which were initiated and concluded in a single day. All the so-called Liberators were found guilty. They were outlawed and their property was confiscated. Octavian's revenge was not confined to the actual murderers. He condemned several men who knew about the conspiracy but had not revealed it; they were treated as assassins even though they had had nothing to do with the actual killing.

The first stage on the road that led to civil war had been prepared. Other steps towards war were being made in the east. Brutus and Cassius had refused the tasks assigned to them and gone on to carve out provincial commands for themselves, collecting troops on the way. Cicero finally persuaded the Senate to make them the legally appointed governors of the territories that they had seized.[42] This meant that they could legitimately command the troops that they had gathered, but now that they had been outlawed by Octavian they were converted into armed opponents of the state, thus providing Octavian with the excuse to make war on them. This he fully intended to do but he was not strong enough on his own account to carry out his plans. For full scale warfare in the east he needed Antony and Lepidus, and the twenty-two legions they had assembled in the west. It was necessary, therefore, to revoke the laws declaring them enemies, and then to reinstate them as military commanders in the eyes of the law. The consul Pedius repealed the laws making them *hostes* while Octavian marched north to meet Antony, with Lepidus as ballast.

On an island in a river, probably near to Bononia (Bologna), where Antony had a large following of *clientes*, the three generals met, conferring for two days to thrash out the details of one of the most infamous alliances of the Roman world.[43] Modern scholars label it the second Triumvirate. Technically, as outlined in a previous chapter, there had never been a first Triumvirate. The agreement between Antony, Octavian and Lepidus was legally sanctioned as *Tresviri rei publicae constituendae*, literally 'three men appointed to reconstitute the Republic'. On 27 November 43 the necessary law to create the new magistracy was passed by the tribune Publius Titius.[44]

Each of the *Tresviri*, who are called in synthetic modern parlance Triumvirs, was to have powers equal to the consuls, so that they could co-exist with the two supreme magistrates without being overshadowed by them. It was a fiction, of course, since in reality the Triumvirs were much more than the equals of the consuls, and in any case there was scarcely any danger of conflict between them and the elected consuls, because all holders of the consulship in the immediate future would be Caesarian or Triumviral sympathisers. The Triumvirs were to empowered to make laws, to nominate magistrates and provincial governors, and above all to assume provincial commands themselves. Pompey and Caesar had shown that the way to gain and hold power was to maintain an influence or even a personal presence in Rome while at the same time commanding troops in one or more of the provinces. On the other hand Caesar's dictatorship for life had revealed that it was unwise to rob people of the hope of freedom in the future, so the Triumvirs put a five-year limit on their powers, giving the impression that they had merely adopted stringent emergency measures to restore law and order, and once that had been achieved, they would step down.[45]

Their provincial commands provided the power base for the Triumvirs.[46] Antony was the senior partner, and he knew it. Moreover the others knew it, and acquiesced in his demands for the provinces of Cisalpine and Transalpine Gaul. From this power base Italy could be watched and controlled. Lepidus was confirmed as governor of Gallia Narbonensis and the Spanish provinces; Octavian was to govern Sardinia, Sicily and Africa. The areas assigned to Octavian were not pacified and in some cases not even accessible, but if he could subdue them, he would then be able to control the corn supply of Rome. The major thorn in his flesh would be Sextus

Pompey, who had taken to the seas and now commanded an entire fleet with which he terrorised coastal areas and threatened all shipping. Octavian would have to deal with him before he could hope to control his provinces. All the Triumvirs would govern their provinces via legates, while they attended to business elsewhere, not least to the major problem of a full scale war against the Liberators.

Marriage ties were proposed to bind the three men together.[47] Lepidus' son was already betrothed to Antony's daughter, an arrangement made when Antony obtained the post of Pontifex Maximus for Lepidus after the Ides of March. It was suggested that Octavian should marry Antony's step-daughter Clodia, the daughter of Fulvia and Clodius. Probably the marriage ties meant very little to each of the participants, but it was a public demonstration of unity for the edification of the rest of the Roman world. The pivot was Antony, who bound each of the other Triumvirs to him personally by the offers of marriage with members of his family, illustrating his supremacy.

The main business of the Triumvirate concerned vengeance for the death of Caesar. The Liberators had already been condemned by Octavian. Not only the assassins of Caesar, but also their entire circles of supporters and clients were targeted. This ultimate aim necessitated thorough and ruthless preparation. There would be a war in the east with Brutus and Cassius and their followers,[48] but there was much to do in Rome before the Triumvirs could embark on a campaign. They could not hope to achieve anything at all without the support and unquestioning loyalty of their troops, so the generation of that loyalty became the foremost concern of each of the Triumvirs. Their joint armies were in need of rewards and revitalisation; there were veterans to discharge and settle on the land, and new recruits to be found to make up numbers. Eighteen Italian cities were earmarked as the areas where veterans would be given lands.[49] It would not be a very easy or peaceful operation, since it involved the eviction of existing landowners and tenants, but the Triumvirs would deal with that problem when the time came.

Recruitment was largely dependent upon ready cash and promises of glory, so that would have to wait for a while. The soldiers were informed of the measures concerning them and the main features of the triple alliance between the Caesarian leaders. Octavian as consul read out to them what had been agreed.

He did not read out to them any details concerning the planned proscriptions of many of the most eminent men in Rome.[50] A preliminary list of seventeen names was drawn up and sent to the consul Pedius in Rome, where organised mayhem resulted in the removal of these men. The city was closed off and guarded in order to prevent the escape of the intended victims. Pedius may have thought that the horrors were all over after this grisly episode was concluded, but it was merely the beginning. Many more names were subsequently added to the lists of the proscribed, when the Triumvirs arrived in Rome.

It has been suggested that the prime motive for the proscriptions was the appropriation of wealth, since the proscribed men forfeited all their property even if they escaped with their lives. Without doubt, the Triumvirs needed a great deal of money, for all sorts of purposes, and they were not particularly squeamish about how or where they obtained it, but as far as the proscriptions were concerned the acquisition of property and money was a fortuitous by-product. The deaths or expulsion from Italy of enemies, real or potential, was the prime concern. No faction could be allowed to gain control of Rome and Italy while the war was in progress in the east. Antony could not know how long it would take to bring Brutus and Cassius to battle, nor how long the campaign might be protracted. Caesar had defeated Pompey in the east, but that had not ended the war. He had fought in Egypt, Africa and Spain before most of the followers of Pompey had been defeated. Sextus Pompey was still at large, with a powerful fleet which he could use to assist the Liberators. He could blockade Italian ports, disrupting transport and food supplies for the Triumvirs, while at the same time he could carry supplies and troops for Brutus and Cassius. If necessary he could transport their entire armies, so it might happen that even if the first battles were victories for the Triumvirs, the Liberators could regroup and take the war into another theatre altogether. There were endless possibilities, all of which would prolong the war. If the Triumvirs were absent from Rome for any length of time, there would be an opportunity for their enemies to regain power, and then there would be more battles for the control of the city and provinces. The proscriptions provided a foolproof insurance policy for the future survival of the Triumvirs.

Rome had seen wholesale murder and rapine before, but that does not excuse the proscriptions of 43. The episode is a stain on all the Triumvirs, equalling anything that Sulla or Marius had done in the civil strife of the recent past. There were some cold blooded actions, by which the Triumvirs perhaps hoped to demonstrate their ruth-less impartiality. They included in the lists of the proscribed certain members of their own families. Lepidus was not averse to naming his brother Aemilius Paullus, who had helped to have him outlawed; Antony put his uncle Lucius Julius Caesar on the list.

The most famous casualty was Cicero.[51] He was named along with his brother and nephew. All three met their ends quite quickly, though it is feasible that they could have escaped. They set off to join the Liberators, but vacillated. Cicero's brother and nephew went back to Rome to collect money and property, and were killed. On his way to the coast, Cicero himself was caught by a party of soldiers and died bravely. His head and hands were nailed to the Rostra, after Fulvia had driven pins through his tongue, in revenge for his having spoken the words of the *Philippics* against Antony. The ghastly tales of mutilation may be true, and if so, they do not redound to Antony's credit. It is true that Cicero had ruthlessly put Antony's step-father to death, and that much later he had singled out Antony as an enemy of the state, using his own particular brand of extremely hostile polemic to stir up the Senate and the people against him. Cicero had made all sorts of gross accusations against Antony, but the treatment of Cicero's corpse cannot be defended. It is not sufficient excuse to throw all the blame onto Fulvia, since ultimately Antony would have had the final word. Once his mortal enemy was dead Antony could have allowed him a proper funeral despite his proscribed status, but instead he chose to despatch Cicero to the next world in separate pieces.

The ancient historians and many modern scholars have sought to exonerate Octavian for his part in the murder of Cicero, usually at the expense of Antony.[52] Lepidus escapes blame for the most part, but ought to take his full share. Cicero had voted him a gold statue and tried very hard to win him over to the Senate, but if Lepidus protested about the proscription of Cicero it has escaped the record. It is said that Octavian argued strenuously to save Cicero, but was overwhelmed by his colleagues. The truth is probably very different. It would have been quite impossible to leave Cicero active and hostile in Rome. He had signed his own death warrant with his eloquence. It is highly probable that the very first name on the list of seventeen proscribed men was Marcus Tullius Cicero, chorused in joyous unison by all three Triumvirs.

When the two-day meeting at Bononia was ended, each of the Triumvirs came into Rome separately, on three different days,[53] each with their entourage and many soldiers, who were lodged in the city, contrary to all custom. Octavian as consul was the first to enter the city. When Antony arrived, Fulvia presumably left the safety of Atticus' house to rejoin her husband. The details of their reunion must remain conjectural. Antony's state of mind can only be imagined. Almost two years had elapsed since the murder of Caesar, when suddenly Antony had been deprived of his friend and patron, and had become head of state. From his point of view, he had been dealt with very roughly. The reward for his efforts to keep the peace had been distrust, hostility, and ultimately exile. It was exactly one year since he had departed for Cisalpine Gaul, not really knowing what his fate would be. During that year he had fought battles against fellow Romans, suffered defeat, frozen almost to death in the mountains, eaten roots and bark to survive and then staked everything, his reputation and even his life, on walking unprotected into the camp of a former ally. It could not have been the same Antony who now came back to Rome. Some characteristic points of reference were probably still in evidence in his personality, but he could be forgiven if his sense of humour had been somewhat stifled. The man who had left in 44 was still the old Antony, full of daring, light-hearted optimism and tolerant bonhomie. The man who came back was icily thorough, narrowly focused, and murderous. If the war that he had tried very hard to avoid was now to be fought after all, so be it. But it had to be done properly. No prisoners. *Clementia* was merely a half-measure, and the fate of Caesar demonstrated its ineffectiveness. The new lists of proscribed men were posted up on 28 November, the day after the act was passed confirming the Triumvirs in power. The killing began immediately, throughout Italy. The consul Pedius died, of stress or a broken heart, or both. Living among carnage, Antony cannot have been other than grim and determined. His thoughts of the future would probably have been confined to the immediate aim of eliminating the enemy. Beyond that he could not make specific plans.

Their chronic lack of money was a serious problem for the Triumvirs, especially as the resources of the whole of the east had been appropriated by the Liberators as Brutus and Cassius took over provinces and allied states, denying the Triumvirs access to the normal taxes from these areas. Antony and Octavian were forced to resort to extraordinary means to raise cash. Robbing temple treasuries was not so lucrative as it had been, since too many men had already done it, Julius Caesar included. One supposedly sacrosanct source of wealth was the private deposits in the care of the Vestals, hitherto untouched. The Triumvirs appropriated all the savings, no matter to whom they belonged.

The sums raised by various means were not sufficient. The Triumvirs therefore resurrected antiquated taxes which had lain dormant for years, and invented new ones to fill their coffers. The consuls for 42, Lepidus and Plancus, instituted a wealth tax, which even extended to women, hitherto exempt from taxation. The system had a curiously modern flavour – that of self-assessment – which led to charges of attempted fraud.[54] Perhaps the Triumvirs considered that a chronic fear of reprisals would turn everyone into scrupulously honest men, so that self-assessment would yield sufficient funds, without the tedious administration that tax-collection normally requires. But they met unexpected resistance from the women of Rome. Fulvia would not countenance such resistance, but Octavian's sister and Antony's mother Julia joined the ranks of the protesters. Hortensia, the daughter of Cicero's great rival in the law courts, led a deputation to the Triumvirs to point out that since women were allowed no voice in the government they ought therefore to remain exempt from taxation. The women declared themselves ready to make any sacrifice if Rome itself should be threatened, but a civil war for which they were unable to vote was not construed as a threat to Rome.[55] Reluctantly the Triumvirs backed down. The number of women obliged to relinquish a percentage of their wealth to meet the taxes was reduced from 1,400 to 400.

Since their avowed purpose was vengeance for Caesar's death, the Triumvirs had a vested interest in elevating him to the highest level, for many reasons, one of which was to ensure that the cause for which they fought was a just one. The Romans had always been adept at finding just reasons for their wars, even those which they had begun themselves without much provocation. The Triumvirs brought to completion the original plans for deification of Caesar that had been mooted while he still lived.[56] He was now officially a god. Antony was to be a priest of his cult but did not take up the office for several years.

Octavian benefited even more, since he was now the son of a god. The date of his first use of the new title *divi filius* is disputed. There is evidence to show that he was using it by 40, but the better context for it is somewhat earlier in 43–42 when Caesar was formally deified. When he first arrived in Rome in the spring of 44 and was in need of recognition, Octavian may already have adopted the title for its immediate usefulness in self-promotion. At the beginning of 42 he could make much use of the deification to advertise himself as well as his pursuit of vengeance for his adoptive father. He reminded people of the divine Caesar at every opportunity, employing *Divus Julius* as the watchword of the army, and later inscribing sling bullets with the name at the siege of Perusia.[57] Antony equated himself with divinity when he was hailed as the new Dionysus in the east, and Caesar claimed descent from Venus. But these associations were mythical and symbolic; Octavian's association was with a living, memorable person, who combined symbol with reality.

On a more practical level, all Caesar's acts as Dictator were confirmed. Each of the remaining senators and magistrates took an oath to observe and maintain them.[58] Antony had attempted to bring this about in 44, but now he made certain of it. It was not simply a demonstration of loyalty to Caesar; it was the foundation for the future. Antony's past achievements and the basis upon which he fought the coming war, indeed his whole destiny, were linked to Caesar, just as much as Octavian's future goals were rooted in Caesar's groundwork. If Antony had chosen to fight on his own account without reference to Caesar, his cause may have been a just one in his own mind but not necessarily in the minds of the Roman people. Thus it was as a lieutenant of a dead commander that he fought the Liberators, no matter that he was a consular and a Triumvir in his own right.

The Roman world was about to witness another civil war. Polarisation into separate halves was almost complete, Caesarians in the west and the Liberators in the east. In Rome and the west, Antony and his colleagues reassigned the magistracies and provincial commands to fill the gaps as the original postholders fled to Sextus Pompey, or to the Liberators, or were killed. The consulship was obviously the most important magistracy, and must be secured for the next few years. The consuls for 42, Lepidus and Plancus, had already entered office. For 41, Publius Servilius Isauricus and Lucius Antonius were designated, and for 40, Asinius Pollio and Gnaeus Domitius Calvinus. These were preponderantly Antonius' men, inherited from Caesar. For the consulship of 39, when hopefully the

wars would be concluded, Antony and Octavian designated themselves. As for the other magistracies, the Triumvirs were accused of
handing out commands as rewards for their friends, but whilst there
was more than a grain of truth in this it is highly improbable that
unsuitable or incompetent characters would have been placed in
important positions, however much the Triumvirs may have owed
these people some sort of favour. When they left Rome, Antony and
Octavian required firm control of the western provinces via their
chosen men, whom they could trust. The entire western world was
thoroughly Caesarian and it was intended that it should remain so
for some time to come.

The east was almost exclusively in the hands of the
Liberators. Brutus recruited troops in Macedonia, where he arrested the
provincial governor, Antony's brother Gaius. Cicero had advised
Brutus to kill Gaius. For a while the noble Brutus refused, but since
Gaius repeatedly stirred up trouble he finally gave in, probably after
he had heard of the death of Cicero. Gaius Antonius was executed.[59]
Antony therefore began the war against the Liberators with more
than one death to avenge. The capture and then the death of Gaius
reduced the Caesarian foothold in the east to almost nil.

The Caesarian Dolabella ultimately fared no better. As his consulship ended he went to take up his governorship of Syria, travelling
via Macedonia and Thrace. He defeated and killed Trebonius, the
Senate's legally appointed proconsular governor of Asia. The contest
for Syria began. Cassius travelled by sea and arrived first. He was
already a respected figure in the east, having fought with Crassus in
the disastrous Parthian campaign, and he had rendered good service
in Syria in the aftermath of the retreat. He had built up a secure
following and established himself in a secure base.

While the Liberators set themselves up in the eastern provinces
and recruited their armies, Cleopatra had been threatened twice but
left unmolested. She was acutely aware of their movements at all
times in case they developed an interest in her kingdom as a base,
or for the extraction of tribute. She assembled four legions and sent

them to aid Dolabella, but Cassius diverted them and took them over.[60] The Egyptian troops were outnumbered and there would have been no point in fighting it out, so they submitted to Cassius. These four legions, added to the eight he had already raised, brought his force to a total of twelve legions, reasonably loyal to his cause.

Dolabella made no headway against Cassius and was blockaded in Laodicea, where he could hope for no rescue or means of escape.[61] In despair he committed suicide. The Liberators now had most of the eastern provinces under their sway, and also control of the sea. They possessed ships of their own and had a potential ally in Sextus Pompey, who was spiritually associated with the Liberators by dint of his long-standing quarrel with the Caesarians. Fortunately for the Triumvirs, neither Sextus nor the Liberators actively pursued the idea of an alliance, each preferring to act independently. Despite the lack of unity among their enemies, the perceived threat to the Triumvirs remained just as strong, since they could not know that Sextus and the Liberators would remain aloof from each other.

Men, money, and ships were assembled to begin the wars against both the Liberators and Sextus Pompey. Lepidus was to remain in Rome with some troops to enable him to keep order. He surrendered seven legions to Antony and Octavian to help them with the campaign. As a preliminary move, Octavian sent his friend Salvidienus Rufus to Sicily in an attempt to wrest the island from Sextus Pompey, and to clear the Mediterranean of his fleet.[62] Much depended on the success of this venture. The transport of troops from Italy to Greece to begin the campaign would be far less hazardous if Pompey's ships were removed from the scene, and if he had been forced to relinquish Sicily, the Triumvirs would immediately gain control of the lucrative corn supply, and also a naval base. Unfortunately the attempt was a disaster. Sextus Pompey's sailors were much more experienced than those of Salvidienus, and easily drove him off. War was largely a seasonal occupation, and crossing the Mediterranean was inadvisable except in summer, so Antony needed to start without delay. Every moment spent lingering in Italy cost more in supplies and soldiers' pay, and lessened the chances of starting the campaign that year, while at the same time the Liberators would gather strength, supplies and money, and perhaps even bring in the Parthians on their side. This was a very dangerous prospect, since Brutus sent Quintus Labienus, the son of Caesar's bitter personal enemy Titus Labienus, to Orodes of Parthia to ask for help, but this news only emerged later, after the Caesarian victory at Philippi. Quintus Labienus stayed in Parthia when he heard that Brutus and Cassius were dead.[63]

At the outset of the war, Antony had only a few ships, and like Caesar before Pharsalus he could not carry the whole army across the sea in one magnificent invasion. At this point Queen Cleopatra made efforts to help the Triumvirs. She assembled an Egyptian fleet to aid Antony and Octavian. Unfortunately, before the fleet could be put to use, it was caught in one of the sudden Mediterranean storms and was wrecked. According to Appian, Cleopatra sailed with the fleet, and returned with the remnants of it to Alexandria.[64] The episode demonstrates her courage, as well as her determination to play some part in the war against the assassins of Caesar and publicise her solidarity with Antony and Octavian.

Although her fleet was of no help in transporting troops and equipment, and took no part in any naval battles, the service that Cleopatra rendered to Antony was considerable, since the reported progress of her ships troubled the Liberators sufficiently to send out their own fleet under the command of Staius Murcus and Domitius Ahenobarbus, to search for them and to destroy them.[65] In this brief respite, with the enemy fleet drawn off from Brundisium in search of the Egyptian fleet, Antony rapidly ferried eight legions across the Adriatic under Decidius Saxa and Norbanus Flaccus, who landed on the unguarded coast of Macedonia, then moved rapidly eastwards along the Via Egnatia to Thessalonika. From there they proceeded to Thrace to guard the passes controlling the route from Europe to Asia. The speed of the operation took Brutus and Cassius by surprise, and forced them to move to meet the threat. They brought their armies into Thrace and moved westwards along the Via Egnatia to block Norbanus and Saxa, who withdrew to Amphipolis and dug in. With sure connections to their coastal supply base at Neapolis, Brutus and Cassius camped to the west of a place called Philippi.[66] The scene was set for the decisive battle.

In order to ferry the rest of the army across the Adriatic, Antony required favourable westerly winds, over which he had no control, and more ships to combat the blockading forces under Staius Murcus and Domitius Ahenobarbus. He was hampered by his lack of oared ships, but even so he sometimes succeeded in extricating his cumbersome sailing transports, keeping the enemy fleet at a safe distance by artillery fire from engines mounted on barges. But it was a slow business, not much improved until he finally obtained oared ships from Octavian, who for the time being relinquished the attempt to take control of Sicily so that the Triumvirs could combine their forces against the Liberators.[67] For a brief moment Staius Murcus drew off from Brundisium, and once again Antony seized his chance. He and Octavian ferried the bulk of the army to Dyrrachium. Next Antony had to find the armies of Brutus and Cassius, and bring them to battle as rapidly as possible. Delays would only increase his difficulties over supplies. It was like Pharsalus all over again, but that meant that Antony would have no illusions about what he was up against, and could draw on considerable experience to guide him when the time came.

Octavian was too ill to march after he had reached Dyrrachium, so Antony started out eastwards along the Via Egnatia without him. He knew that Norbanus and Saxa were entrenched in Amphipolis, and by now he would know where Brutus and Cassius were camped. Antony marched rapidly to join his eight legions in Amphipolis. He left one legion to hold the city, and took the rest of the army towards Philippi. He sent out a small party to reconnoitre the strength of the Liberators' camp. Brutus and Cassius had utilised every advantage of the ground. They had camped across the road, Brutus in the northern camp with mountains to protect his flank, and Cassius in the southern camp with his flank protected by a marsh. They had also entrenched themselves behind well-guarded earthworks. Antony kept up an outward display of confidence that he perhaps did not feel, made camp, and decided that the Liberators must be cut off from their supplies. The only way to do that was to make a causeway across the marsh and try to come round to the rear of Cassius' camp. He began the work in secret and was not discovered for some time.[68]

By this time Octavian had joined him, travelling in a litter from Dyrrachium, still very ill, but determined to play his part in avenging Caesar, and more than likely very anxious not to allow all the credit for any victory go to Antony alone. He could possibly have dealt quite easily with a defeated Antony limping back to Dyrrachium, or even with the news that Antony had been annihilated and was dead. In either case, Octavian would take some of the blame for the disaster, then he would regroup and launch another campaign, in a desperate last bid for vengeance. But if Octavian did nothing except lie in bed at Dyrrachium while a victorious Antony won the war, he would be eclipsed for ever. Antony would be the sole avenger of Caesar, sole champion of the soldiers, sole political conqueror. Octavian had to be there, wherever the battle was to be fought.

As a distraction to divert enemy attention from the causeway that he was building across the marsh, Antony drew up his forces to offer battle each day, but eventually Cassius realised what was happening to threaten his rear, and began to build counter works. It was here that the first battle of Philippi began, in a skirmish over the defences.[69] Antony passed a few cohorts across the causeway, and Cassius attacked them, so Antony committed more troops to rescue them. Brutus' men could see the fighting to the south and began an attack of their own, imagining, possibly, that they would be able to finish Antony by a swift flank attack. In the confusion, Antony took Cassius' camp, but Brutus took Octavian's. The two armies swivelled round to end up at a ninety degree angle to their original positions, but neither side could hold onto what they had gained, and had to return to their bases. Octavian had prudently hidden in a bog, so he fortunately evaded capture. Later he said that he had been warned in a dream not to stand in the battle line. The most important result of the first battle was that Cassius, driven from his camp, gave up much too soon, thinking erroneously that Brutus had been defeated and killed. Instead of waiting for properly authenticated news, he assumed the worst and committed suicide.

Brutus was now alone, but still in a fairly strong position. He entrenched, and began the waiting game, knowing that the supply problem would eventually weaken Antony. There was no need to offer battle in these circumstances, but it is probable that Brutus's officers and even some of the soldiers thought that Antony would be quickly defeated. Their blood was up, and they wanted action. They may have worn Brutus down, demanding battle. At any rate, for some inexplicable reason, several days after the first battle, Brutus drew up his army. Antony probably could not believe his eyes. He accepted the challenge straight away. This time Octavian's men held firm, though they were pushed back. Antony tried to outflank Brutus, which may have been a feint, because when Brutus plugged the gap by sending out his reserve, Antony switched to an attack on the centre. It may have been a carefully arranged trap, or perhaps Antony simply watched carefully, seizing the chance once he recognised where the weakest spot was, and then throwing in everything he could spare to exploit it. Either scenario reflects great credit on him for ingenuity and promptness of execution.[70]

Brutus escaped with four legions, pursued by Antony. One of Brutus's officers, Lucilius, delayed the pursuers by impersonating Brutus and allowing himself to be captured. He demanded to be taken to Antony, who knew immediately that he had been duped. He did not display any anger, excusing the soldiers who had made the mistake by saying that he was rather glad that it was not Brutus, because he would not have known what to do with him. He and Brutus had been acquaintances, if not friends, and had been drawn together in the political arena. Antony probably was genuinely glad not to have to give the order to execute him. There was no deeply personal animosity between them, unlike the rancour between Antony and Cicero, even though Brutus had been directly responsible for the death of Gaius Antonius. In the end Brutus helpfully committed suicide, and his followers split up, some joining Sextus Pompey or Domitius Ahenobarbus, while others came over to Antony and Octavian. One of the most famous converts was the poet Quintus Horatius Flaccus, who remained in Octavian's circle until his death, and is known to us as Horace. The rest were killed, and it is said that Octavian delighted in cruelty, exacting the last ounce of vengeance from the deaths of some of the conspirators. He made a father and son throw dice to decide who should be spared, and laughed as the one chosen to survive committed suicide over the body of the other. The legend states that the soldiers hailed Antony as the victor, but reviled Octavian; the tale is usually connected to those of Octavian's cruelty, but if there is any truth in the revulsion felt by the troops, it probably stemmed from the fact that Antony had done all the hard work while Octavian was ill. Perhaps Antony himself did not stop to reflect that courage takes many forms, one of which is the ability to overcome illness and take at least some part in the fighting. There is no need to doubt that Octavian was genuinely ill, but from Antony's point of view, the activity of the past months with Octavian in tow had probably been comparable to wearing a ball and chain.

After the victory, Brutus' body was brought to Antony's camp. He covered the corpse with his own cloak and ordered an honourable funeral for him. Octavian demanded that Brutus's head should be cut off and thrown down at the foot of Caesar's statue in Rome.[71] In view of his treatment of Cicero, Antony was hardly in a position to refuse on ethical grounds, so Octavian had his wish. At the same time, Antony exacted revenge on Hortensius, the officer who had killed Gaius Antonius. Appropriately, Antony had him put to death near Gaius's tomb.

There may have been an overriding sense of anti-climax. The Liberators were dead or dispersed. The battle fields were to be cleared up. There were hundreds of troops to be reorganised, paid off and settled on the land. The provinces were to be reassigned, the whole of the east required delicate restructuring, the government of Rome and Italy was to be set on a firm foundation, friends were to be sifted from enemies, financial affairs were in chaos, the food supply was threatened, Sextus Pompey was still at large. The list was endless. Most important, the Triumvirs, now for all practical purposes whittled down to two men, since Lepidus was marginalised, had to protect and prolong their powers. They could not disband their armies entirely, and therefore had to find a legitimate excuse for keeping them. From the combined troops of their own armies and those of the Liberators, the Triumvirs formed eleven legions, five of them for Octavian and six for Antony, but since they were already in the east, where Antony would need troops, Octavian was to lend two of his to Antony, and then reclaim two legions from those stationed in the western provinces.

Octavian's task was to settle the veterans on lands in Italy and to pursue the war against Sextus Pompey. His provinces were to be Spain, Sardinia, Corsica, Sicily if he could win it from Sextus, and Africa. If Lepidus was to be trusted, he was to be assigned to Africa in Octavian's place, but if it proved to be true that he had been making overtures to Sextus Pompey and might have allied with him, then he would be deleted from the Triumvirate, and Octavian would keep Africa. It sounds like a plot to discredit Lepidus, but on this occasion it did not pay off. Lepidus remained part of the Triumvirate for a few years longer, though not as a decisive element in the wars or decision making.

Antony took the lion's share, reflecting the seniority of his position. He was to govern the two Gauls, through his legates Calenus, Plancus and Ventidius, with about seventeen legions. Cisalpine Gaul would be governed by Pollio, pending its integration with Italy, which was to be common ground for both Antony and Octavian. With a preponderant influence in the west, unassailable at the head of large armies, Antony himself would remain in the east, taking up in due course the great Caesarian project of war against Parthia.

Octavian returned to Italy, where his main task would be to settle the veterans on lands promised to them at the meeting at Bononia, at the beginning of the Triumvirate.[72] Antony began to reorganise the eastern provinces and client states, in chaos after the upheavals caused by Brutus and Cassius. Some states had sympathised with the Liberators, some had resisted, others had tried to remain neutral but had been forced to contribute money or supplies. The result was the same whichever side they had chosen. Many of them were impoverished or damaged in some way, and it could not be assumed that every city or state would welcome Mark Antony with open arms. Antony travelled far and wide, repairing damage, hearing cases, exacting tribute, meting out punishments where necessary. The chronology is difficult to establish, since most sources merely tell us that Antony went to Athens for the winter, as though that was all he did, oblivious to all else. Common sense dictates that he could not simply leave the huge army that was reassembled after Philippi, nor could he ignore the immediate needs of the eastern territories. Stability in the east was the prime necessity, which entailed placing the troops at strategic locations under reliable commanders, and tactful handling of Roman governors, client kings and rulers of free states. That was not something that he could achieve in a few months.

When all was reasonably quiet, in the winter of 42–41, Antony did go to Athens, the city of his student days.[73] The years since the death of Caesar had been strenuous and nerve wracking, so after he had toured the eastern provinces and safely quartered the troops, Antony cast off his role as soldier and became a leisured tourist. Generous and open handed, he also became a benefactor of Athens. He liked to be seen at the theatre and the games, dressed in the Greek style. He went to lectures, and joined in debates. His voluntary return to Athens suggests that as a student he had appreciated all that the city had to offer, and appreciated it now for different reasons. It had the advantage of being not too far from Rome but conveniently placed so that he could keep in touch with the eastern territories. Athens satisfied several criteria at once. Communications were good, the winter climate was mild, the pleasures were numerous, and Antony was no doubt glad to indulge himself in culture and learning as an escape from the carnage of the past few years.

The Greek way of life appealed to him, because it liberated him from the strict but frenetic atmosphere of Rome, where even as Triumvir and conquering hero he would have to be watchful at all times for anything his enemies might use to bring about his downfall. In Athens he could be himself in a way that he could never be in Rome. When spring came he had to attend to business once again.[74] The Roman provinces of the east included Asia and Bithynia (occupying western and northern Turkey), and Syria. Their larger neighbouring territories were ruled by kings supposedly favourable to Rome, and there was a host of lesser kingdoms and territories under a variety of rulers. All these lands required much fine tuning, especially if Antony was to persuade them to disgorge the funds he needed to finance his various ventures and pay the troops. Reparations had to be made to those states which had suffered at the hands of Brutus and Cassius, and those that had sided with the Liberators would have to be handled delicately. He left Lucius Censorinus with six legions to look after the Greek states, and took two legions with him to Ephesus.[75] There he was hailed as the new Dionysus, an appropriate divinity for Antony, the god of wine and beneficence. To a stern Roman, full of *dignitas* and *gravitas*, this was highly suspect, but it was the eastern custom, so Antony played the game according to the eastern rules. Pompey had received the same treatment when his eastern conquests had brought him fame. Earthly divinity lent Antony power in the east, and to protest that he was a mere mortal would only undermine it. Besides, his new-found status as a living god provided a counterweight to Octavian's claim to be the son of a god.

Antony based himself at Pergamum, and summoned representatives from the eastern states to meet him there. His first demand for ten years taxes payable in one year was greeted with disbelief. Brutus and Cassius had made similar demands to finance their war and consequently had stripped most of the east already. Now the victor wanted even more. One of the spokesmen pointed out that since Antony was powerful enough to ask for a second levy of taxes after the Liberators had already levied the first one, then perhaps he would be good enough to arrange for a second summer and a second harvest. Antony liked frankness, especially when it was combined with wit, so he arrived at a partial compromise, settling for nine years taxes payable in two years.[76] Having secured his cash and supplies, Antony could be magnanimous. Several cities which had supported Brutus and Cassius were pardoned. They had for the most part been coerced and in any case it was preferable to forget the past and make a new start. There was more to be gained from a slightly damaged but extant economy than an annihilated one, however much the desire for revenge might have dominated Antony's thoughts. He tried to make amends for the more serious depredations of the Liberators, and readjusted some boundaries here and there. Athens and Rhodes were given or restored to the overlordship of some neighbouring islands, not solely for the political power that this would bring them but for economic reasons.

Cassius had taken some Jewish prisoners on his tour of the east, and now Hyrcanus of Judaea arrived at Antony's headquarters to ask for their release, which Antony readily granted. He also heard another deputation from Judaea making accusations against Herod, son of Antipater, but when Antony met Herod personally in Bithynia, he found in his favour. The sources do not preserve much of the detail of Antony's administrative arrangements in the eastern territories. From the few known facts, it seems that Antony merely reacted to requests rather than taking the initiative himself, so he stands accused of dilatoriness in sorting out the complicated affairs of the east, as though he had no real political interests and was merely determined to take advantage of anything that might be beneficial to him, allowing the rest to follow its own course. On the other hand, if he had gone about his tasks in typically Roman fashion, coldly logical and brutally efficient, he would have earned a reputation for arbitrary arrogance and high handedness.

That was not the way to deal with the east. It was probably simple enough to survey the scene from afar with an unemotional attitude, to analyse the problems and then to suggest what had to be done, where boundaries should lie and who should be subordinate to whom. But to apply such neat schemes would have been disastrous. The eastern cities had a long history and a complex and intricately entwined structure. Their relationships were volatile and changeable, so it was easy to upset the delicate balance of power but difficult to repair the damage once that had been done. Antony probably reasoned that there was no need to redefine all the eastern territories, uprooting the ruling houses which had lent aid to the Liberators. He dealt with each case on its own merits, provided always that his interests and those of Rome were not compromised. It may seem that he put his own interests first, but it was not megalomaniac tendencies that motivated him. Personal power brought with it the capacity for patronage, which would be very beneficial to him in Rome. That was also what the east generally understood. The concept of the strong, semi-divine leader and protector took precedence over any sense of corporate identity. A treaty made with Rome was perfectly understandable in a context where some of the city states had a longer history than Rome herself, but in some parts of the east the personal representative of Rome was always regarded as the more important factor, no doubt because it was more practical to contact an individual whose habits and characteristics were known, rather than an anonymous and possibly arbitrary body such as the Senate. Pompey had made sound administrative arrangements for the east for which he made every effort to obtain ratification from the Senate, but nonetheless he did not relinquish his position as influential personal liaison between the various eastern cities and Rome, nor did he give up the potential source of wealth that this position automatically conferred on him. Antony simply followed suit, especially since his financial needs outweighed any

1 *Left*: Head of Julius Caesar from Egypt, carved in green slate. Courtesy of Berlin Museen.

2 *Below*: The siege works surrounding the Gallic citadel of Alesia, the context of the first mention of Mark Antony by name in Caesar's *Gallic War*. Antony and Gaius Trebonius rushed troops to threatened points during a night attack, and repulsed the Gauls. Drawn by Jan Shearsmith.

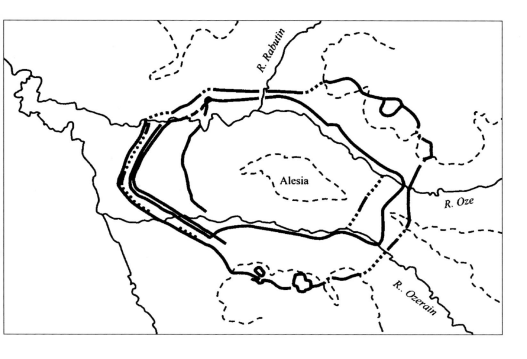

3 Head of Mark
Antony from Rome.
This damaged sculpture
is probably securely
identified as Antony
since it bears more than
a passing resemblance to
his coin portraits, with
his square jaw, thickset
neck, and his fleshy face
wearing a determined
stare. Courtesy Capitoline
Museum, Rome.

4 *Below, left*: Coin in the Macedonian Ptolemaic style representing Cleopatra's father, Ptolemy XII Auletes. Drawn by Jaqui Taylor.

5 *Below, right*: Silver coin from Alexandria with an unflattering portrait of Cleopatra. Her prominent hooked nose was inherited from her father. Drawn by Jacqui Taylor.

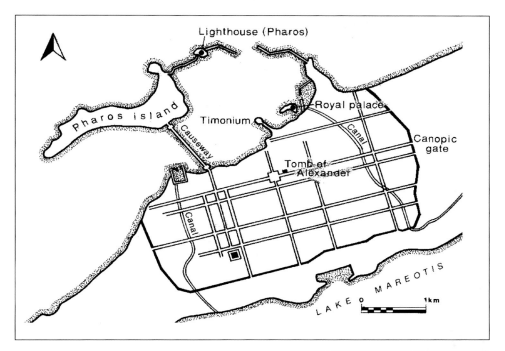

6 *Above*: Plan of Alexandria. Drawn by Graeme Stobbs.

7 *Right*: On this relief from the temple at Dendera in Upper Egypt, Cleopatra is portrayed as the goddess Isis, the supreme deity of the east, with whom the Ptolemaic Queen is strongly identified. The cartouche at the top left displays Cleopatra's name in Egyptian hieroglyphics. Photograph courtesy of David Brearley.

8 *Below*: Silver denarius of Caesar Imperator. Although portraits of individuals regularly appeared on coins in the east, the Romans usually restricted their coin portraits to gods. In the final months before his assassination Caesar started to issue coins bearing his own image, setting the precedent for the Imperial coinage. Drawn by Jaqui Taylor.

9 Caesar as dictator for the fourth time on this silver denarius issued in 44. Drawn by Jaqui Taylor.

10 Silver denarius of 44, showing the earliest coin portrait of Mark Antony. He is bearded and veiled, as augur. A *lituus*, one of the symbols of the augurs, is shown under his chin. On the reverse, the two galloping horses and the rider wearing a cap are associated with the Games of Apollo, but the full meaning of this representation is not understood. The design is very similar to one of Caesar's coins, issued shortly before this one, showing him also veiled and looking to the right. Drawn by Jaqui Taylor.

11 This silver denarius of 43 shows the head of Antony's younger brother Gaius Antonius, in Macedonian dress with a cap and a Greek style chlamys, or cloak. Gaius Antonius was sent to Macedonia as governor in 44. The legend proclaims him *C. ANTONIUS.M.F. PRO. COS.* (Gaius Antonius, son of Marcus, Proconsul). The reverse shows religious symbols and the word *pontifex*, an office which Gaius held from 45 until his execution by Marcus Junius Brutus before the battle of Philippi. Drawn by Jaqui Taylor.

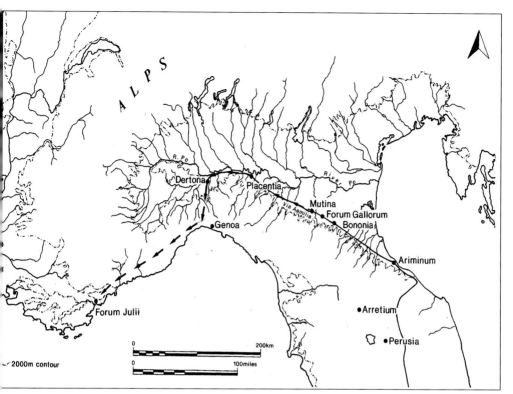

12 Map of northern Italy. After the battles of Mutina in April 43, Antony retreated into Gaul over the Apennines, joining up with Ventidius Bassus about thirty miles west of Genoa, and arriving in Gaul at Forum Julii (Frejus) in May. Drawn by Graeme Stobbs.

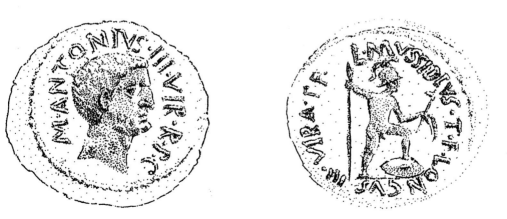

13 Obverse of a gold aureus of 42. Antony is styled as *IIIVIR. R.P.C.* or *Tresvir Rei Publicae Constituendae*. On the reverse the god Mars is depicted, with the name of Lucius Mussidius Longus, who was one of the officials who issued gold coinage with portraits of the Triumvirs from 42 to 40. Drawn by Jaqui Taylor.

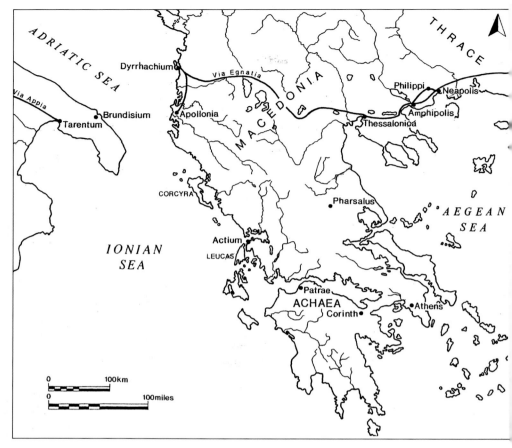

14 Map of Macedonia and Greece where Antony fought several battles. He was with Caesar at Dyrrachium and Pharsalus; he fought and defeated Brutus and Cassius at Philippi, and he met disaster at Actium. Drawn by Graeme Stobbs.

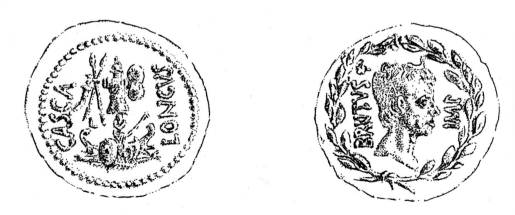

15 The head of Marcus Junius Brutus on the obverse of a gold aureus of 42. Casca Longus, named on the reverse, was one of Brutus' legates, and the military trophies celebrate the raising of troops in the east. Drawn by Jaqui Taylor.

Plans of the two battles of Philippi showing the various stages of the main episodes.

16a *top*: Philippi First Battle, October 42. Antony builds a causeway across the marsh to cut the communications of Brutus and Cassius, and get behind Cassius' camp.

16b *Bottom*: Antony defeats Cassius and drives him from his camp. Cassius withdraws to the north east, and later commits suicide. At the same time Brutus defeats Octavian and captures his camp, but Octavian survives by hiding in the marsh.

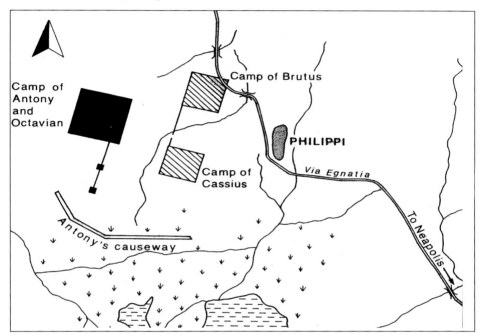

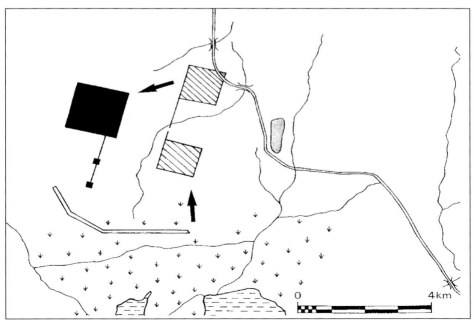

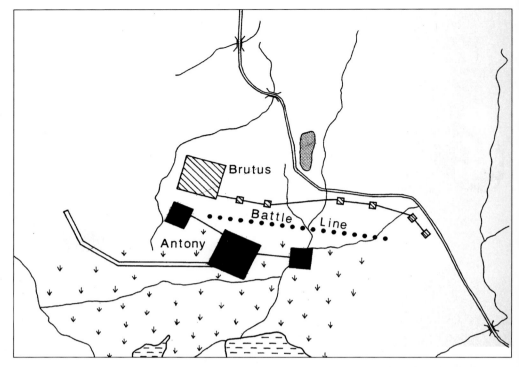

16c Philippi Second Battle, November 42. Brutus moves into Cassius' camp, and Antony continues his outflanking movement. Brutus builds small posts to keep pace with him, but offers battle in mid-November. Antony and Octavian eventually encircle him and drive him off. Drawn by Graeme Stobbs.

17 A gold aureus dated to 41, issued by Gnaeus Domitius Ahenobarbus, with a portrait perhaps of himself. The temple of Neptune on the reverse epitomises Ahenobarbus' career, first as a naval officer of Brutus, and then an independent admiral after Philippi. He made an alliance with Antony in 40, adding his naval power to Antony's forces. Drawn by Jaqui Taylor.

18 *Above, left and right*: Full face and profile of a head of Cleopatra in classical Greek style, and reminiscent of portraits of Alexander. Cleopatra combined her Egyptian heritage with her Macedonian Greek ancestry, and portrayed herself in both styles. From the Berlin Anitkensammlung, courtesy of Berlin Museen.

19 *Below, left*: Head of Mark Antony, older and more rugged and experienced, with double chin and worry lines between his eyebrows. Courtesy Musée Archéologique, Narbonne.

20 *Below, right*: Portrait of Antony on an intaglio, showing marked resemblance to the images on his coins. Drawn by Jaqui Taylor.

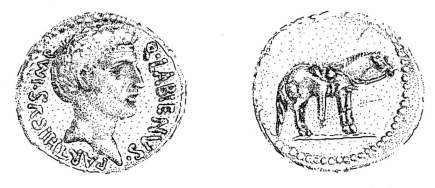

21 Quintus Labienus, the son of Caesar's general Titus Labienus, was sent to Parthia by Brutus, to try to organise an alliance with the Parthian king Orodes. After Philippi Labienus remained with the Parthians and was instrumental in instigating the invasion of Syria. His title Parthicus proclaims his alliance with king Orodes. When Antony's general Ventidius Bassus drove the Parthians out, Labienus disappeared and his ultimate fate is unknown. Drawn by Jaqui Taylor.

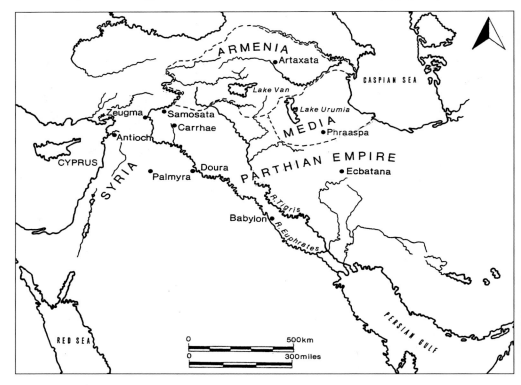

22 Antony's eastern campaigns. The Parthians invaded Syria in 40–39, but were driven out by Ventidius, who besieged the last remaining fugitives in Samosata. During the offensive against Parthia in 36, Antony assembled his troops at Zeugma as though he wished to invade Mesopotamia from the west, but then he marched rapidly north eastwards then south into Media, finally arriving at Phraaspa, to which he laid siege. If he had been successful, he would probably have marched on Ecbatana, the Parthian capital, but with the loss of his siege engines he had little chance of bringing the war to such a rapid close. When he prepared for the abortive campaign of 33, he had overrun Armenia and converted it into a Roman province, and forged an alliance with Media, so he perhaps planned to invade eastwards from Syria and southwards from Media. Drawn by Graeme Stobbs.

23 Gold aureus issued *c.*40, when Antony and Octavian settled their differences and Antony married Octavian's sister. On the obverse, the legend proclaims Antony as Imperator and Triumvir (*M. ANTONIUS IMP.IIIVIR. R. P. C.*), and the reverse bears the unlabelled portrait of his wife Octavia. Drawn by Jaqui Taylor.

24 Antony and Octavia are shown together on this silver coin, with the legend, partly worn away in this example, *M. ANTONIUS. IMP. COS DESIG. ITER. ET. TERT.* referring to his military command as Imperator, and the fact that he was consul designate for 38. The reverse shows Bacchus flanked by two intertwined serpents. Drawn by Jaqui Taylor.

25 On this gold aureus issued *c.*37 Octavian proclaims himself *CAESAR DIVI.F. IIIVIR. ITER. R.P.C.*, son of the divine Caesar, and Triumvir for the second time, after the extension of the triumvirate for another term of five years. Drawn by Jaqui Taylor.

26 Cleopatra and her son Caesarion from the temple at Dendera. They are depicted as Isis and Horus, in the ancient regalia and pose of the Pharaohs, and firmly embedded in Egyptian tradition. Photograph David Brearly.

27 One example among many of a series of coins issued in the east *c.*37–33. The dates of issue and the particular mints are hard to identify. The Greek legend proclaiming Cleopatra Queen, and the younger Thea (transliterated from the Greek: *BASILISSA CLEOPATRA THEA NOTERA*. These coins predate and postdate the Donations of Alexandria, but the legend makes Cleopatra's territorial ambitions quite clear. Her title 'the younger Thea' makes reference to the earlier Cleopatra Thea, daughter of Ptolemy VI. She married three successive Seleucid rulers of Syria, and was widely known in the east. The message on these coins indicates that Cleopatra VII portrayed herself as ruler of Egypt and Syria. Drawn by Jaqui Taylor.

28 Antony and Cleopatra on opposite sides of a silver denarius of 32. Antony celebrates the conquest of Armenia by the legend *ANTONI ARMENIA DEVICTA*. He garrisoned the country and opened Armenia to Roman traders, but Octavian dismissed the conquest as worthless. The portrait of Cleopatra and the accompanying legend forms one of the most important icons of her history. She is proclaimed Queen of Kings and of her sons who are kings (*CLEOPATRAE REGINAE REGUM FILIORUM REGUM*), referring to the territorial arrangements made by Antony in the ceremony of the Donations of Alexandria. Drawn by Jaqui Taylor.

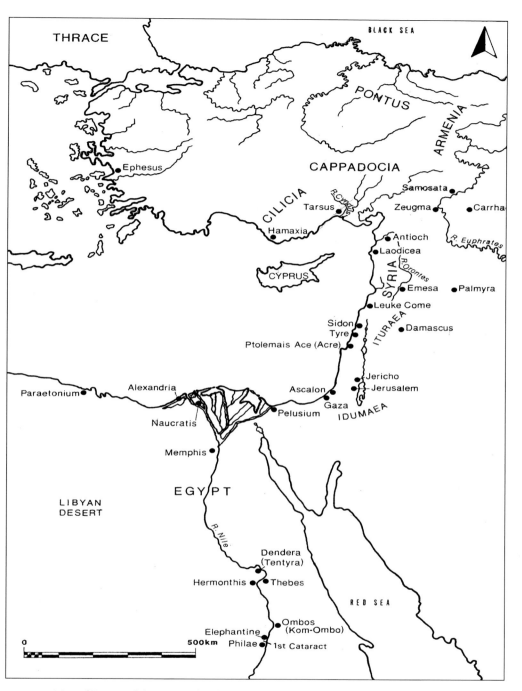

THRACE

BLACK SEA

PONTUS

ARMENIA

CAPPADOCIA

Ephesus

CILICIA

Samosata

Tarsus

R. Cydnus

Zeugma

Carrha

Hamaxia

Antioch

Laodicea

SYRIA

R. Euphrates

CYPRUS

Orontes

Emesa

Palmyra

Leuke Come

ITURAEA

Sidon

Damascus

Tyre

Ptolemais Ace (Acre)

Jericho

Ascalon

Jerusalem

Paraetonium

Alexandria

Gaza

Naucratis

Pelusium

IDUMAEA

Memphis

EGYPT

LIBYAN
DESERT

R. Nile

Dendera
(Tentyra)

Hermonthis

Thebes

RED SEA

Ombos
(Kom-Ombo)

Elephantine

Philae

0

500km

1st Cataract

29 Map of Egypt and the surrounding kingdoms and provinces. Cleopatra's interest in acquiring control of certain territories was most probably driven by economic considerations rather than pure and simple imperialistic urges. When she succeeded to an impoverished throne her aim was to reconstitute the Ptolemaic Empire and its trading potential. With Antony's help, in his capacity as Triumvir with legally approved control of the eastern half of the growing Roman Empire, she achieved much, but not all, of what she desired in order to revive and sustain the economy of Egypt. Drawn by Graeme Stobbs.

30 Another of the series of coins proclaiming Cleopatra Queen and the younger Thea, though in this example the second part of the legend has worn away. On the reverse of these coins, Antony is shown with the Greek version of his titles Imperator and Triumvir (transliterated from the Greek it reads *ANTONIOS AUTOKRATOR TRION ANDRON*). Drawn by Jaqui Taylor.

31 *Left*: Portrait from Alexandria identified as Cleopatra. The features such as the nose and the shape of the face support the identification as the Queen. Photograph David Brearly

32 *Below*: On the obverse of this silver denarius of Antony depicts one of his war galleys, and proclaims himself Triumvir, in contrast to Octavian who ceased to use this title. The standards of the Seventh Legion (*Legio VII*) are depicted on the reverse, just one example of Antony's numerous coin issues naming his legions. Drawn by Jaqui Taylor.

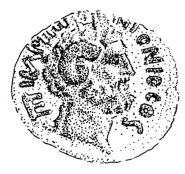

33 Silver denarius issued by Antony and his general Scarpus in 31. The legend round the head of Jupiter Ammon, an amalgamation of the chief Roman and eastern deities, runs *M. ANTONIO. COS. III. IMP.IIII*, naming Antony as consul for the third time in 31, but Octavian had deprived him of the office. The abbreviated *IMP.IIII* indicates that Antony had been hailed as Imperator for the fourth time. It is not established which particular event gave rise to the proclamation by the troops, but the context must be one of his battles fought in 31. An optimistic portrait of the goddess Victory is shown on the reverse. Drawn by Jaqui Taylor.

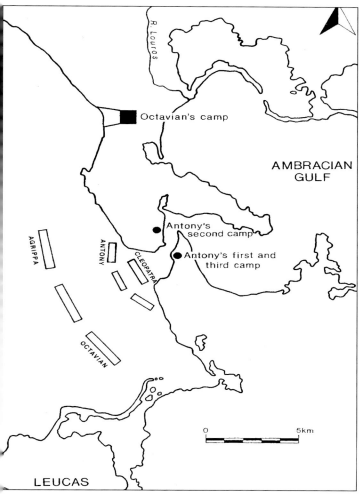

34 The battle of Actium, 2 September 31. Before the naval battle was fought, there was a prolonged series of skirmishes on land, which cannot be documented in detail. Antony crossed the entrance to the Gulf of Ambracia to try to cut off Octavian's water supply, but he had to withdraw as his allies deserted him. Octavian built protective walls from his camp to the sea to ensure his supplies, and meanwhile Agrippa captured several ports and harbours, including the island of Leucas to the south of Actium. As the stranglehold on Antony grew more serious, he was forced to try to break out. Instead of retreating into Macedonia as Canidius advised, he chose to fight at sea. He burnt the ships that he could not man, and shortly after the battle started, many of his ships turned back into harbour, while he and Cleopatra sailed away to Egypt. Drawn by Graeme Stobbs.

35 Silver denarius of uncertain date, c.31 or perhaps slightly earlier, issued by Octavian, with a fine portrait of himself. The reverse (not shown) bears the legend *CAESAR DIVI F.* and a depiction of Venus Victrix, the divine ancestress of the Julii. Octavian probably began to use the title *Divi Filius* as soon as he claimed his inheritance, but the earliest coin examples date from the period after Philippi when he was settling the veterans in Italy. Drawn by Jaqui Taylor.

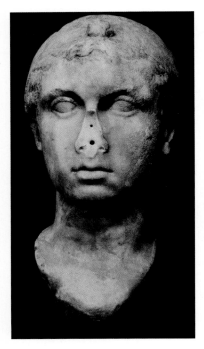

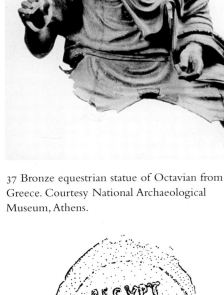

36 Plain and unadorned head of Cleopatra, showing her severe hairstyle as depicted on coins. Courtesy Vatican Museums, Vatican City.

37 Bronze equestrian statue of Octavian from Greece. Courtesy National Archaeological Museum, Athens.

38 On this gold aureus of 27 issued three years after the fall of Alexandria, Octavian reminded the Roman world that he had captured Egypt (*AEGVPT CAPTA*). He styled himself *CAESAR. DIVI.F. COS. VII*, (Caesar, son of the divine Caesar, consul for the seventh time). Drawn by Jaqui Taylor.

other consideration, and probably always would. Apart from his own personal needs, he had a large army to pay and feed, and an equally large administrative personnel to organise.

The states bordering on the Parthian Empire required subtle wooing. Even when there were no hostilities with Parthia, the Romans needed to maintain good relations with these border states in order to keep open the major routes through them, and to obtain reliable intelligence about Parthian intentions. In wartime, the border territories would be in the front line if the Parthians attacked, and consequently in a good position to cut off any Roman forces which might invade Parthia. It was prudent to be on good terms with rulers of those territories through which one needed to march home, either as confident victors or in abject retreat. The loyalty of the border cities and states had to be earned or bought, and then assiduously cultivated.

The territory of Galatia in modern central Turkey was ruled by Deiotarus, who had sided with Brutus and Cassius during the civil wars. Antony did not supplant him. It was better to rely on a king who knew his people and terrain than to try to find a suitable substitute who might change allegiance or be ejected as soon as the Romans were removed to a safe distance. The kingdom of Cappadocia (eastern Turkey) was in turmoil because there were two rival claimants, Archelaus (also called Sisina) and Ariarathes, both of whom were fighting for the throne. Antony made a tour of inspection and installed Ariarathes as king. It is said that he had a brief affair with Glaphyra, the mother of Archelaus, but in this instance he may not have initiated the proceedings himself.[77] It was more likely an effort on Glaphyra's part to influence Antony, and a shameless exploitation on Antony's part of whatever came his way. It also demonstrates that he made decisions quite independently of attempts to seduce him. His choice of Ariarathes may have suited the needs of the moment, but he had to revise his opinion later. Ariarathes did not prove loyal, and in the end Glaphyra's son Archelaus was given the kingdom of Cappadocia.

Between them, Deiotarus of Galatia and Ariarathes of Cappadocia watched large areas of the east in close proximity to Parthia. There remained Armenia, the continual source of tension in Roman and Parthian politics, but before attempting to solve that particular problem, Antony turned his attentions to Egypt. He needed vast quantities of money and also a fleet, and though he had already set about obtaining the former and building the latter, the resources of Egypt would further his projects considerably. He decided to ask Cleopatra to come to meet him.

Secure as possible in her regime, with the undoubted opposition almost muzzled, Cleopatra continued to strengthen Egypt, with eyes and ears constantly alert for what was happening in Rome. The fact that as Caesar's guest in Rome she was able to spend so much time away from Egypt seemingly without precipitating rebellions or riots attests to the fact that her ministers, officials and administrators operated efficiently, possibly even ruthlessly, but above all loyally, otherwise she may have had no kingdom to return to after Caesar's death. She will have built up a following of loyal adherents, whose names are not known to us. Details of her administration are sketchy, and have to be extrapolated from general knowledge about Egypt under its Macedonian rulers. Perennial concerns were the food supply, religious observance, and for Alexandria, the control of trade. The Nile was not always dependable and was watched anxiously each year for signs of the likely flood levels and the consequent irrigation. There was an optimum level, within certain parameters; too much water was problematic; too little was disastrous. Cleopatra ensured that all her subjects witnessed that she was scrupulous in attending to all aspects of ceremonial and sacrifice. She could not command the Nile to rise to optimum levels, but when all was well she could be seen to be effective, and when there were problems, explanations could be found, the gods could be propitiated, and hopes could be focused on the following year.

In religious terms Cleopatra was identified with Isis, wife of Osiris, and Caesarion was equated with their son Horus. This was a particularly fortuitous circumstance since Horus was the avenger of his father, and Caesarion was named Philopator, lover of his father, so the parallel between Osiris-Horus and Caesar-Caesarion was crystal clear. When Caesarion was born, Cleopatra issued coins with a representation of herself suckling the infant, which was equated with the many representations of Isis suckling Horus. On the walls of the temple at Hermonthis, where some years earlier Cleopatra attended the inauguration ceremony of Buchis, the sacred bull, sculptures show Cleopatra and Caesarion once again equated with Isis and Horus. The birth of Caesarion and that of Horus are shown side by side. Egyptian gods and goddesses surround Cleopatra and her son, placing them among the panoply of deities and proclaiming their divine rulership.

Cleopatra's concern for religion also embraced the Greek population, for whom Osiris, Isis and Horus were the Egyptian counterparts of Dionysus, Aphrodite and Eros. Alexander the Great had identified himself with Dionysus, and Cleopatra's father Ptolemy Auletes had proclaimed himself to be the new Dionysus. When Antony took charge of the eastern provinces, he too identified himself with Dionysus, who was held in great esteem by the peoples of the east. His association with Cleopatra as Isis-Aphrodite elevated them both to a higher plane than the merely mortal. In the east, people were comfortable with the divinity of their kings and queens. In Rome, living individuals were solidly earthbound, but they could claim divine descent if their ancestors hailed from the distant and mythical past. Exceptional people could become divine, but only after death.

Central control of food production had always been the responsibility of the rulers of Egypt. The Ptolemies assumed the powers of the Pharaohs, and like their predecessors they owned all the land and administered much of it directly; a vast bureaucracy monitored all aspects of leases to tenants, planting, harvesting, and taxation. Warehouses were under Ptolemaic control, so that when famine threatened, the issue and rationing of food was so much simpler. Egypt was more or less self-sufficient in food production, but also required imports, especially of timber in a virtually treeless land. No useful commodity was ignored, especially since all imports could be taxed. There were different rates for different items, all of it under Royal control. Cleopatra fostered trade and business deals outside Egypt, always aware of advantageous opportunities. She invested time, effort and money only where it would bring profit.

Issuing coins in her own name, Cleopatra profited from her attention to the coinage, lowering the precious metal content but insisting upon assessing the coins at their old values. To make certain that merchants accepted them for what she said they were worth, she had the denominations marked on the coins. It seems such a common-sense, practical procedure, but it had not been done before. Cleopatra possessed sufficient power to enforce her regulations, and could watch her coffers filling every day.

This accumulating wealth was one of the primary attractions for Antony, but perhaps not the only one. He summoned Cleopatra to meet him at Tarsus in southern Cilicia (modern Turkey), ostensibly to answer the charge that she had aided the conspirators. It seems an unlikely story, but if the accusation was in fact made against her, both accuser and accused knew that it was grossly unfair. She had done all that she could to help the Triumvirs, and it was not her fault that her efforts had been unsuccessful. The accusation was an excuse to get her to come to Tarsus because Antony wanted something; the fact that she went means that she had something to gain. Antony and Cleopatra had much to offer each other. She did not acquiesce without some preliminary wrangling. Letters were sent to her, which she no doubt answered charmingly without committing herself, then Antony sent Quintus Dellius in person to persuade her.[78] His reputation was worse than Antony's for improper behaviour and non-Roman activities. Cleopatra probably found him great fun. She said she would come to Tarsus.

5

Reunion:
Antony and Cleopatra
41–35BC

The meeting of Antony and Cleopatra at Tarsus removes them both from the mundane sphere of history into the fabulous realm of legend. For them, it also marked a turning point leading directly to their ultimate fate. Their association was continuous from then onwards, and Cleopatra used Antony's power and influence to gain what she wanted for Egypt. Her ambitions were later portrayed by Octavian as nothing short of world domination, but her primary concerns were for a secure throne in a secure territory, and after that a secure future for her son Caesarion, who represented a challenge if not a direct threat to Octavian.

Antony was currently the most important figure in Roman politics, and was also one of Caesar's immediate associates. That made it all the more acceptable to go to meet him. If Brutus or Cassius had emerged victorious from the battle of Philippi, Cleopatra would have still required diplomatic contact with them and the Roman Senate to keep Egypt intact and as free of Roman control as she could make it. Alternatively if it had been Octavian who remained

in the east, sooner or later he and Cleopatra would have come face
to face. Octavian was younger, more calculating and colder than
Antony, more narrowly focused and less scrupulous about the means
that he used to achieve his ends. He was not averse to sexual affairs,
but if he had enagaged in an affair with Cleopatra he would have
kept her firmly in her place as Queen of Egypt, and his own position
in Rome unassailable. The wealth of Egypt would have bound him
to her, and he would have taken it all in the end, but the final act
would probably have constituted merely a footnote in history, and
literature, plays and films would have been the poorer for it. With
Antony, loyal to Caesar but no threat to Caesarion because he was
not Caesar's natural heir, Cleopatra would find bargaining to secure
the autonomy of Egypt a more palatable task. Her own security and
the future of Egypt depended upon the favour of Rome, or at least
upon the absence of hostilities. Sailing to Tarsus, she obviously hoped
for something far better than that.

   She prepared well and dressed for the occasion, intending to make
an unforgettable impression, and from all accounts she succeeded.
She was the Queen of Egypt coming to meet the Roman Triumvir,
but she was also Aphrodite coming to meet Antony as the New
Dionysus, and in Egyptian terms she was Isis and Antony–Dionysus
was Osiris. This was not just play acting. The Queens of Egypt had
always been equated with Isis, whose supreme importance in the east
cannot be too strongly emphasised.[1]

   Cleopatra's Royal barge, with its purple sail that always signified
Ptolemaic Royal ships, was not an innovation, created especially for
the purpose of impressing Antony and his officers. It followed in the
Ptolemaic tradition of such splendid ships, large enough to entertain
many guests in several different rooms, and also seaworthy enough
to make long voyages. During excavations at the Royal port of the
Ptolemies at Alexandria, archaeologists found the remains of a ship,
30m long, in the private harbour of the Palace. This ship was sunk,
probably by deliberate ramming; at any rate it somehow acquired
a large hole in the hull. On board were remains of rigging, fine

pottery, glassware, and jewellery. Radio carbon dating techniques reveal that the timbers were used sometime between 90BC and AD 130, so while this particular ship cannot be linked unequivocally with Cleopatra, it does demonstrate what it may have been like.

The legendary, splendid Royal ship conveyed Cleopatra up the river Cnydus, according to Plutarch,[2] in swathes of precious perfumes, with handmaidens on each side and boys costumed as Cupids wafting fans over her, as she reclined under a canopy of cloth of gold. The description could go on and on, mounting superlative upon superlative. Magnificence was expected of the Ptolemies, or of any eastern kings who wished to retain credibility, and Cleopatra understood the value of showmanship.

Cleopatra entertained Antony to dinner onboard ship. Plutarch says that it was brilliantly lit with an extraordinary number of lights. It was lavishly equipped and decorated, with rich hangings and tapestries, rose petals on the floor, jewelled drinking cups, dazzling silver and gold everywhere. The effect was probably completely over-whelming. Antony tried to match her hospitality on the following night, but failed miserably. Plutarch describes how Cleopatra quickly assessed his character, full of bluff soldier's humour, and accordingly she adapted her own behaviour to suit his. If she met him while she was in Rome, she would have made an estimate of him and his main attributes, his strengths and weaknesses, talents and deficien-cies, and most of all his usefulness. At Tarsus, she may have remained cautious, sounding him out before she allowed him to set foot in Egypt, leaving herself with the option of keeping him at arm's length. The Romans had such a happy knack of ultimately annexing territories that they first entered casually.

As for Antony, he was probably swept off his feet on the spot. Appian says that from that moment he was ready to obey Cleopatra's slightest whim, gradually becoming quite oblivious to Rome and all it stood for.[3] This is part of the Augustan repertoire, where Antony is depicted as weak, spineless, bewitched by the evil Queen. The por-trayal condemns Antony and provides the excuse for reviling him, but at the same time it excuses him because it presupposes that he was in the grip of a power stronger than himself, more evil and infinitely more to be feared. Octavian built up Cleopatra into the supreme enemy of Rome and then defeated her, converting himself into a hero and making the Romans grateful for what he had achieved, so grateful that they did not seem to mind that one of the direct results of his achievement was that he took over the whole of Egypt, together with its vast Treasury, and kept it as his personal preserve.

Later authors have modified or embellished the legend of Antony and Cleopatra after the meeting at Tarsus. Romantics cling to the love story. Cynics opt for the theory of bald political expediency and nothing more. Moderates try to blend the two extremes. At Tarsus Cleopatra obtained from Antony the removal of her sister Arsinoe, who was killed at Ephesus on Antony's orders. Similarly, a pretender to the Egyptian throne claiming to be Ptolemy XIII was executed. In return Antony obtained help for his Parthian campaign.[4] Political and economic considerations predominated at Tarsus, but these were not the sum total of the association between the Egyptian Queen and the Roman general. If there had been no personal considerations, contact may have ended at Tarsus and continued via correspondence and envoys. When Cleopatra returned to Egypt, Antony promised to follow her to Alexandria as soon as he had attended to the administration and settlement of the provinces.

There was some trouble in Syria, where the populace was restive because of the heavy tribute imposed by Rome, and there was no lack of aspiring leaders, some of them backed by Parthia, eager to exploit the unrest. Antony's response was to launch a raid on Palmyra, poised between the two great Empires of Rome and Parthia but free from direct Roman or Parthian control. He wished to make a demonstration of his potential power, but the reasons for his actions are obscure, perhaps even deliberately deleted from the record to make him seem irresponsible. There was little to show from the raid, because the Palmyrenes simply decamped and abandoned their city, taking their belongings with them across the Euphrates and waiting until Antony's soldiers went away. Appian accuses Antony of creating a terrible mess in Syria by this unprovoked attack, and then imposing further tribute.[5] Before he had sorted out the problems, so the story goes, he went off to Egypt because he was so besotted with the Queen. The accusations are unlikely to be true, but lack of evidence in Antony's favour makes it impossible to refute them entirely. Antony had first hand knowledge of Syria, its problems, and its advantages, and he also knew that it was feasible to invade Egypt from Syria because he had been there, done it, and survived. He would not turn his back on Syria until he had settled affairs there. He placed Decidius Saxa in command, one of the generals who had led his advance guard into Macedonia before the battle of Philippi, and one of the most trustworthy of Antony's lieutenants. With the province settled and Saxa in charge, Antony went to Egypt.

The Alexandrians liked Antony and his sense of fun. They said that in Rome he wore his tragic mask, but for them he exchanged it for his comic mask. He formed a club called 'The Inimitable Livers' dedicated to pleasures of all kinds. Various anecdotes about his behaviour have passed into legend, but are perhaps not too far from the truth, and reveal something of the man and his relationship with Cleopatra.[6] On a fishing trip where he caught nothing, he sent his slaves underwater to attach some newly-dead fish to his line, and then he hauled them in, pretending to have caught them all at once. The next day Cleopatra sent some of her own slaves underwater to attach a salted fish to his line, surpassing his ruse of the previous day. Such fun and games, if not true in their specific details, are probably representative of Antony's Alexandrian adventures. It may have been politically expedient for the foremost Roman general in the east to woo the Queen of Egypt to ensure her allegiance to Rome, and it may have been shrewd manoeuvring on Cleopatra's part to entertain the Roman Triumvir to keep her country intact, but their relationship certainly went beyond that. In the following year Cleopatra gave birth to twins, a boy and a girl, and Antony acknowledged them as his own.

While Antony enjoyed the company of Cleopatra in Alexandria, Octavian was faced with very difficult problems. His main concerns after Philippi were centred on Italy and the settlement of the time-expired veterans.[7] This was a thankless task because it involved an enormous redistribution of lands and the eviction of farmers already settled on them. Octavian no doubt anticipated trouble but perhaps had not foreseen the tremendous complications that arose. He smoothed the path at first by tact and diplomacy, but then met with active opposition, aroused and fostered by Antony's wife Fulvia, and his brother Lucius Antonius, who was consul. The other consul was Servilius Isauricus, but as Dio says, the real consuls for that year were Lucius and Fulvia.[8] Lucius had two potential levers to use against Octavian. First he espoused the cause of Antony's veterans, implying that Octavian had not treated them fairly. Octavian removed the difficulty by allowing Antonian representatives to supervise the settlement of Antonian veterans. Thwarted of serious trouble-making in that direction, Lucius changed tactics and began to stir up the displaced farmers. Whichever way Octavian turned he was certain to be wrong-footed. It seemed that Lucius and Fulvia were determined to bring him down.[9]

The soldiers could see clearly that war was looming, and since they would be directly involved in any fighting they tried to avert it by arranging a conference between Lucius and Octavian at Teanum. The two men met as planned and discussed the problems, but without result. Things went from bad to worse. Lucius and Fulvia fled to Praeneste, making great play of their fear of Octavian, who recruited troops from any and every source, and placed his friend Marcus Vipsanius Agrippa in command of them. He recalled his legate Salvidienus Rufus who was marching to Spain with six legions to take over as governor there. While Octavian was engaged in this desperate recruitment drive, Lucius marched on Rome, where he made politically correct noises about dismantling the Triumvirate and restoring the Republic. He was given a legitimate command by the Senate and set out to meet Octavian's troops, but Agrippa moved quickly around him and managed to cut him off from Rome. Panicking, Lucius marched north to Perusia, where Octavian lost no time in besieging him. It was a short lived affair, which ended in February 40 with the town's destruction by fire, perhaps the result of an unfortunate accident. Octavian put to death anyone who had had the remotest connection with the death of Caesar. Lucius was allowed to go free, since he was Antony's brother and it would cause tremendous problems to kill him. He was sent to Spain, ostensibly as governor, but in reality a sort of prisoner, closely watched by Octavian's men.[10]

Antony's part in all this is shrouded in mystery. No one knows for certain whether Lucius and Fulvia had taken it upon themselves to foster Antony's interests without his knowledge, or whether they acted on his secret instructions. When Lucius talked of restoring the Republic, presumably Antony was to feature as the senior statesman in this new scheme of things, no longer the anomalous Triumvir but as traditional and lawful consul. Blood ties do not guarantee loyalty, but it is difficult to believe that Lucius was about to undermine his brother and install himself as supreme magistrate. It is even more difficult to believe that it was part of Fulvia's plans to supplant her husband and deprive him of political power.[11] The question is, how much did Antony know of the escalating war? Plutarch exonerates him, but Dio, on the other hand, is certain that Antony had engineered the whole incident, but sat on the fence while it was played out, pretending that he did not know about it.[12] Between these two extremes there are several possible permutations of the facts, without a hope of resolution.

It stretches credulity somewhat to suggest that Antony knew nothing of what was going on in Italy. Despite the difficulties of travelling in winter, friends who wanted to help him and enemies who wanted to discredit him would fall over themselves to inform him. The case for the defence has to prove that Antony was a victim of misplaced zeal exercised unwisely on his behalf. The case for the prosecution has to find evidence that Antony wanted to be recalled to quell disorder, as the first stage on the route to supreme power. Appian was clearly aware of these implications, when he says that Antony's henchman Manius reminded Fulvia that as long as there was peace in Italy, Antony would stay with Cleopatra, but if there was serious disruption, he would be the one man who could restore peace.[13]

Events did not unfold in that way in the end. Antony left Egypt for Athens with problems erupting all around him. The Parthians overran Syria, perhaps towards the end of 41, or early in 40, undoing all that Antony had achieved there. The instigator of these attacks on Roman and independent eastern territories was Quintus Labienus, the son of Titus, who had been sent by Brutus and Cassius on a mission to the Parthian court and was consequently isolated after the battle of Philippi. Having nowhere to go, he threw in his lot with the Parthians and worked in conjunction with Pacorus to overrun the eastern cities and place them under Parthian control. Labienus advertised his exploits by means of his coinage, displaying his portrait and his newly adopted titles celebrating his military successes. He called himself Imperator, and also 'Parthicus', which to a Roman would normally have meant that he had conquered Parthia, but to Labienus, the title signified his change of allegiance from Rome to the camp of Rome's traditional enemy.[14]

Trying to repel the Parthians, Antony's governor Decidius Saxa was killed.[15] Herod fled from Judaea to Egypt, and the Parthians installed Antigonus as ruler in Jerusalem. Although Cleopatra did not look favourably on a strengthened Judaea on her borders, a Parthian controlled state was even worse. She treated Herod kindly and lent him a ship to convey him to Rhodes, and from there he went to Rome to appeal to the Senate. Antony's supporters Lucius Sempronius Atratinus and Marcus Valerius Messalla Corvinus spoke in his favour. The Triumvirs recognised him as king, a title that had not been used in Judaea for a long time.[16] Roman recognition was not the end of the story, however, since Herod faced many difficulties before he could claim his kingdom.

Though the greater part of the east was in ferment, Antony could do little to restore the balance, unless he was prepared to ignore events in the west and perhaps suffer a total eclipse there. Octavian had emerged from the Perusine war more successful and stronger than ever. Civil war cast its shadow once again. Most of Antony's associates and his immediate family had fled after Perusia fell. Ventidius Bassus rounded up the Antonian troops and remained in Italy, until the autumn of 40, or the spring of the following year, when Antony sent him to the east to re-establish the situation there, while he attended in person to the degenerating relationship with Octavian. Fulvia, together with the Antonian general Munatius Plancus, whose legions had gone over to Octavian, decamped to Greece.[17] Whether Fulvia had acted independently in her husband's best interests, or whether she was his willing agent acting under his orders, Antony was not grateful. There may have been an irrevocable split between them on account of the highly emotional issue of Cleopatra. Fulvia may have understood that political needs outweighed personal concerns, but it was evident that Antony had mixed business with pleasure on a grand scale. No one knows what passed between Antony and Fulvia, or whether they parted as friends or enemies. Antony could not afford to waste time in meeting Octavian, so he left Fulvia behind in Greece, even though she was very ill. Perhaps he did not know that it was to be a fatal illness. He never saw her again.[18]

Antony's mother Julia also fled from Italy, and found refuge with Sextus Pompey, who at some point made friendly overtures to Antony, suggesting an alliance.[19] The exact chronology is not established, but if Julia was confident of a friendly reception it suggests strongly that negotiations had already begun before Perusia fell. Antony replied to Sextus in favourable terms, but did not commit himself. He promised that if he could not come to terms with his rivals he would ally with Sextus, but if he succeeded in making peace with Octavian, then he would endeavour to reconcile Sextus and his followers with the Senate and people of Rome. This reply was no doubt made for public consumption. It was an honourable and reasonable decision, with just enough of a threat of strong action if negotiations with Octavian failed.

Control of a fleet in the Mediterranean was an important consideration, one which Antony could not afford to ignore. Instead of entering an immediate alliance with Sextus, Antony chose the less inflammatory alliance with Domitius Ahenobarbus, who had kept his fleet together after Pharsalus and had been a free agent ever since. Domitius was a Republican and therefore less repugnant to the Senate than Sextus, especially since he had not harried the coastal ports or disrupted the food supply as Sextus had done. For Antony he was a politically correct associate and a useful assistant in helping to patrol the seaways.[20] Together Antony and Domitius approached Brundisium, only to find that there were large numbers of Octavian's troops there, and the town had closed its gates against them.[21]

Antony concluded that Octavian had ordered his troops to guard the town and not to let him land there. Grimly he set about besieging the place. His troops captured the nearby town of Sipontum, and Octavian's response was to send Agrippa to retake it. He also despatched Publius Servilius Rullus to drive Antony off from Brundisium but Antony attacked before Servilius was ready for him, and drove him off instead. He killed many of Servilius's men, which encouraged many of the remaining soldiers to change sides and join Antony. The troops saved the situation at this point.[22] The men had no desire to fight each other, having for the most part known each other when Caesar was in command of them all. Their loyalties were divided now between the two successors of Caesar, and besides they were tired of war, especially the kind of war which brought them no lasting glory, no rich booty from foreign lands and only the prospect of more war until eventually one man emerged as sole victor, or the antagonists came to some agreement.

The outbreak of another civil war was averted by diplomacy and compromise, in September 40. Octavian's equestrian and non-military friend Maecenas became his spokesman, and Pollio was intermediary for Antony. Also present at the initial talks was Lucius Cocceius Nerva,

who was not a partisan of either party. By the time that the negotiations began, the balance had tilted in Octavian's favour. He had
ended his marriage to Fulvia's daughter, Clodia. She was very young,
and the marriage had probably not been consummated. Now he
married Scribonia, the sister of Lucius Scribonius Libo, whose
daughter was married to Sextus Pompey. Octavian's intention was
transparently obvious. He did not marry for reasons of affection,
but for political expedience, as a preliminary to a political alliance
with Sextus. Antony probably felt himself completely upstaged, and
may have regretted not having allied with Sextus early in the year,
when he had the chance. Octavian was now in a strong bargaining
position, and a fortuitous event made him even stronger. In the summer of 40 Antony's legate in Gaul, Fufius Calenus, suddenly died.
Octavian immediately took over Calenus' legions without even the
hint of a struggle. He declared that he did so to protect Antony's
interests, but his own interests were hardly neglected when he took
over the troops.[23] It was a tremendous advantage to him to be able to
control Gaul and also to be able to call upon so many extra soldiers.
His main concern was no doubt to pre-empt the considerable problems that would have arisen if Calenus' legions had fallen into the
hands of someone else, especially if that someone were to pick up
the threads that Lucius Antonius and Fulvia had dropped when they
were defeated at Perusia. The inevitability of it all, and the supremely
fortunate timing of events from Octavian's point of view, probably
made Antony think that his luck had deserted him. He acquiesced
in the loss of his command of Gaul and of his legions, though he
received some compensation by way of extra troops for his later
eastern campaign.

The agreement reached in the autumn of 40 is known as the
Treaty of Brundisium. Its terms redefined the division of the Roman
world and determined Antony's future.[24] From now on he would
focus exclusively on the east. The division between east and west
was tidier than the previous arrangements that had been made after
Pharsalus. The new dividing line was placed in Illyria at a town called

Scodra, now in northern Albania. Octavian received all the western provinces. His main tasks were to win back Sicily and Sardinia from Sextus. Lepidus was left in command of Africa, out of harm's way. Antony was to control all of the east, and was to have greater powers to reorganise and restructure it. Then he was to deal with the Parthian problem. For a short while there seemed to be an optimistic accord between the two Triumvirs, celebrated probably throughout the Roman world, but the evidence for the celebrations is limited. All that is left is a trace element of the response to the Treaty of Brundisium. 'Concord' was the catchphrase of the day. Coins were struck with the legend *M. Anton. C. Caesar Imp.* referring to the two men as military commanders, with a representation of the goddess Concordia prominently displayed.[25]

Despite the optimistic outlook and celebratory adulation, Antony had lost pre-eminence in the west and was never to regain it. Although it was intended that Italy should be common recruiting ground for both Triumvirs, Antony's influence waned for the principle reason that after 39 he was permanently absent and therefore unable to sustain the personal contacts that were necessary for the maintenance of client relationships, and for the nurturing of loyalty among the troops and potential recruits.

The two Triumvirs went to Rome in the late autumn, to demonstrate their solidarity and to organise the government to their joint satisfaction. Antony at last became *flamen divi Julii*, the priest of the cult of the divine Caesar. Octavian gave his elder sister Octavia to Antony in marriage. Both were recently bereaved, Fulvia having died in Greece, and Octavia's husband Marcellus had died, too recently for her to marry according to Roman custom. Formalities such as those never stood in the way of men like Octavian and Antony, but since they had to be seen to do things correctly according to the social rules, they persuaded the Senate to give the necessary permission for Octavia to remarry before the end of the proper ten month mourning period.[26]

There were also some punishments. Antony's associate Manius had been one of the prime movers in the build up to the Perusine war, suggesting to Fulvia that in the disorder her husband would be recalled to save the state. Antony was obliged to demonstrate that he would not tolerate such revolutionary talk implying that turmoil in Italy could be stirred up and then used for personal reasons. It was of no consequence whether Manius had expressed an opinion of his own, or whether he had acted under the orders of Antony himself. What counted was the elimination of suspicion, so that Antony emerged whiter than white. Manius had to go.[27]

More puzzling is the removal of Salvidienus Rufus, who was one of Octavian's closest and long-standing friends. They had been together in Macedonia just before Caesar was murdered, and they had sailed back to Italy together, along with Marcus Vipsanius Agrippa. Antony declared that while he was preparing for the siege of Brundisium, Salvidienus had sent word to him that he was prepared to desert Octavian and join him. The tale may be as simple as that. Perhaps Salvidienus had grown tired of Octavian's single minded pursuit of supremacy, which entailed the subordination of all his friends to that one purpose. There are many more sinister permutations of the facts, but there is no available information to support any specific theory. Octavian was careful to dispose of Salvidienus by fully documented legal means. The Senate obligingly passed the last decree (*senatus consultum ultimum*) to recall Salvidienus from Gaul and condemn him to death.[28]

The air was now cleared. All the machinery was in place for the Triumvirs to take charge, but the path to power was never smooth. Sextus Pompey had obtained very little from his efforts to negotiate with either of the Triumvirs, who were plainly more concerned with their own immediate needs than they were with his. His immediate response to his lack of positive gain was to attack the coastal towns of Italy yet again and to disrupt the food supply of Rome to such a degree that famine became a real threat. His strategy worked. The people of Rome rioted. Octavian had to be rescued by Antony's troops when he attempted to speak to the mob, who pelted him with stones.[29] The situation could not be tolerated, but neither Octavian nor Antony were properly prepared or adequately equipped to go to war against such an experienced adversary as Sextus. They had not developed sufficient naval expertise and possessed neither the ships nor the sailors to attempt a battle at sea. Fortunately Octavian was still married to Scribonia, and was therefore one of Sextus' relations by marriage. Antony suggested that the relationship should be made to work for them, and that Octavian's brother-in-law Scribonius Libo should be asked to act as intermediary with Sextus. In negotiation, the Triumvirs had to concede that Sextus would retain control of Sicily, Sardinia, and Corsica. They were primarily interested in restoring the food supply of Rome so that the rioting would cease and so that their own credibility would be revived. They could do nothing to wrest from Sextus his absolute command of the islands and the predominance it afforded him over the coastal areas of the whole Mediterranean. They undermined his support by offering his soldiers the same rewards as their own, but that was a hollow victory, and not even an immediate one. All else would come in good time. Sextus perhaps understood all this when he entertained the two Triumvirs on board his flagship, after they had signed the Treaty of Misenum in summer 39. His admiral Menodorus suggested to him that he could solve his problems all at once if he simply cut the cables and sailed off with his guests, tipping them overboard somewhere in the open sea. Sextus nobly refused.[30] He would have gained little, and would have merely ostracised himself more than ever. Rome would not automatically accept him because he had disposed of the Triumvirs. He took a chance with the Treaty of Misenum, which restored the status quo and did him no harm. He was made an augur, and promised the consulship for 33. He was also promised control of the Peloponnese for five years, which was to be handed over to him from the eastern territories under Antony's control.[31] If it had actually come about, it would have meant that Sextus had a foot in both camps, and a presence in each of the Triumvirs' territories.

Peace was restored among the Romans for the time being. Octavian had emerged in a much stronger position now that he controlled the western provinces, but there was much to do in Italy. Security still depended on the goodwill of Sextus. Octavian's ability and political shrewdness were not in doubt, but Antony was his equal in political matters and his superior in the military sphere. There was perhaps no need for Antony to worry about the loss of the western provinces, and the encroachments made by Octavian. After all the youth was frail, always ailing, and perhaps might even die, then Antony could come back to Rome to take charge, preferably after a victorious campaign against the Parthians. A victory would bring him considerable kudos and enhance his standing in Rome. It would enable him to reorganise the east and stabilise it, making it secure for the future, with each provincial governor and each carefully chosen client ruler owing his or her supremacy to Mark Antony. Such a vast range of wealthy clients in his entourage could do him nothing but good. The avenger of Crassus would enjoy considerable prestige even among those Romans who were not his clients. He would be a potent force, and equal to anything that Octavian could achieve.

Antony is so inextricably associated with the east, and his reputation for having 'gone native' is so indelible that in the autumn of 39 when he set out for Athens with his new wife Octavia it is tempting to assume that Antony had turned his back on Rome totally and irrevocably. It was more a result of circumstance than intention that he never returned to Rome. At the end of 39 he was looking towards Parthia, and he was all powerful in the east, but he was still a Roman official, brought up with a Roman philosophy, and with a Roman perspective on the world. He was a soldier with ambitions of conquest, but that did not mean that once he had con-quered he would forget Rome. His command was sanctioned by the Senate and he had taken the precaution of obtaining ratification of all his acts, past and future.[32] He thought ahead to the time when he would return to Rome, and like Pompey the Great would require ratification of his arrangements for the provinces, treaties with client kings, and land allotments for his soldiers. He had no intention of being thwarted and delayed as Pompey had been.

Antony spent the winter of 39 in Athens with his new wife, and prepared for the Parthian campaign. He dressed as a Greek civilian, freely enjoying the Greek way of life, but his leisurely appearance did not preclude activity. Appian depicts the tremendous contrast between his household in winter, when it was peaceful, unhurried, and uncluttered, and the sudden burst of energy in spring, when his house became a military headquarters in all its noisy splendour, with couriers coming and going, queues of officers at the door, and Antony himself dashing about clad in Roman military dress.[33] Appearances can be deceptive, and in this instance have been used to imply that Antony did nothing for a few months and then burst into ill-planned action at the last minute. But he could scarcely have forgotten the east for a single instant while he was in Athens.

At the end of 40 or the spring of 39, while he negotiated with Octavian, Antony sent Ventidius Bassus to restore order in Syria and Asia Minor. This able lieutenant concentrated all his energies on the renegade Labienus, who was soon driven into unseemly flight. He was last heard of in Cilicia, and then disappeared. Next Ventidius drove the Parthians out of Syria.[34] There will have been a great deal still to do after the fighting was over, but Ventidius' arrangements for consolidation are not recorded in detail. He would need to distribute his troops for the winter to guard routes and strategic points, especially those on the frontiers with Parthia, and most important of all he would need regular and dependable food supplies. He levied tribute from various cities, especially those which had either assisted Labienus and the Parthian Pacorus, or at least not put up a very determined resistance to them.

All through the winter of 39 and during the early part of 38, Ventidius will have been in communication with Antony, keeping him informed of events. Once he had reached Athens, Antony could communicate with Ventidius much more easily and much more rapidly than he was able to do while he was in Rome. Indeed in Athens he was in the best position to keep in touch with both the east and the west. If he expected further trouble from the eastern cities and the Parthians, he would certainly need to know what Octavian was doing. After the loss of his Gallic legions and his western provinces to Octavian it is extremely unlikely that Antony trusted his Triumviral colleague in the slightest degree.

For this reason, his house in Athens will have witnessed many a coming and going from both halves of the Roman world, but while his despatches to and from the east were official, as part of his eastern command sanctioned by the Senate, his agents in the west would need to be more circumspect. Octavian would definitely be watching him just as closely, so the leisured life in Athens, in conjugal bliss with Octavian's sister, may have been a deliberate screen to declare to the Roman world in general and to Octavian in particular that their political relationship was progressing smoothly. If such it was, his plan backfired on him, because Octavian was able to use it to disseminate a portrait of Antony as an ineffective and even disreputable general and politician. There are few contemporary literary sources that can be said to depict Antony in his true colours. What survives is a thoroughly reworked record, moulded to suit Octavian's purpose. Occasionally a fortuitous discovery of an inscription or a fragment of one can serve to set part of the record straight. The famous series of inscriptions from the city of Aphrodisias have been dated to the Triumviral period and throw some light on the state of affairs pertaining in the east.[35] One of the inscriptions refers to a man called Stephanos, who was authorised to act in Antony's name in the east, but the text of the inscription reveals that Octavian also sent instructions to Stephanos directly, without going through Antony's offices first. There is insufficient evidence on which to base any firm or wide ranging conclusion, but it would seem that there was a potential source of conflict in this system, since it implies that Antony's command of the east was not quite as exclusive as he had been given to understand. It is not known if Antony enjoyed the same rights in the west that Octavian seemed to be able to exercise in the east. To be sure, Antony would have some say in what happened to his clients in the Italian cities, but the case just outlined in the east is not comparable. Octavian's monarchical tendencies revealed themselves long before he restored the Republic and became Augustus.

In spring 38, Antony began to move. There was much preparatory work to do. The eastern cities and states required more adjustment and fine tuning, which could be done successfully only on a basis of sound local knowledge and careful balancing of immediate needs against long term plans. Two things happened which delayed Antony, almost a repeat performance of the events of 40 and 39. The Parthians launched another attack on Syria, and at the same time Octavian summoned Antony to the west, where the situation in Italy was deteriorating rapidly. Ventidius was once again put in charge of operations against the Parthians and Antony sailed to Italy. Octavian was in deep trouble. The peace treaty with Sextus Pompey had lasted barely a year. Very shortly after it been concluded, Octavian divorced his wife Scribonia, on the very day that she gave birth to his only child, his daughter Julia. Sextus Pompey took the hint that their relationship was ended, and recommenced his raids on the Italian ports and harbours, disrupting the food supply all over again. In consequence Octavian was in very bad odour in Rome, though his situation improved somewhat when Sextus' admiral Menodorus deserted to him, bringing men, money and ships, and relinquishing control of Sardinia and Corsica to him. From then on Sextus Pompey and Octavian were at war. Sextus was the better admiral and strategist, and easily defeated Octavian in two separate encounters. Antony wasted valuable time and expense in coming to Brundisium to meet Octavian, only to find that Octavian was not there. Antony went off in a justifiable rage and made his sentiments known in an open letter to Octavian.[36] He then dashed to Syria, arriving in midsummer. Ventidius had succeeded in stabilising the situation once again, so all was not lost. He had brought Pacorus to battle in north eastern Syria, at Gindarus, and there he had defeated him utterly. The Parthian leader's head was brought to Ventidius as a trophy, and he sent it on a tour of the eastern cities as proof that he had defeated the enemy decisively.[37]

As soon as he was able to spare the troops, Ventidius sent a contingent to assist Herod, while he himself marched to Samosata on the right bank of the Euphrates, where Antiochus, king of Commagene, was sheltering Parthian refugees. Ventidius besieged the place. It was quite outside Roman control, so Ventidius' siege was designed to be construed as an aggressive punitive act to restore Roman supremacy. Antony arrived at Samosata in late summer and took over from Ventidius, who went back to Rome to hold a well-deserved triumph in November 38. The Triumvirs allowed their legates to celebrate this supreme honour, but later on when Octavian had gathered all power to himself, the triumphal procession through the streets of Rome became a rarity, a jealously guarded reward, restricted to members of the Imperial family.

A rumour circulated that Ventidius had accepted bribes from Antiochus to put an end to the siege, and in consequence Antony cashiered his former friend, and sent him home in disgrace.[38] Another story maintained that Antony was jealous of his legate's successes, and that the death of Ventidius some short time later was not altogether a natural occurrence. This is nonsense. It is a contradiction in terms for a disgraced general to celebrate a triumph. As for the possibility that Ventidius' death was suspicious, Antony had much to gain with Ventidius alive and well and working for him in Rome. Besides, if he had wanted him dead, he did not need to wait until after Ventidius' triumph to dispose of him. It would have been quicker, more economical, and far more credible to arrange a little accident in Syria. Nonetheless, Antony may have had an ulterior motive of a far different kind in sending Ventidius home to make a great display in the city. Octavian had enjoyed very little success in the battles against Sextus Pompey, but Antony's lieutenant had twice prevailed against that most dangerous of enemies, the Parthians. The celebrations proclaimed Antony as much as Ventidius, and plunged Octavian into the background. It was a war of words and attitudes, posturing and upstaging.

After the departure of Ventidius, the siege of Samosata slipped into impasse quite quickly. Antony negotiated a settlement and

returned to Athens for the winter of 38–37. There was nothing more
to be done in the east until the next campaigning season started
in the spring of 37. Meanwhile the west had not escaped turmoil
in 38. Agrippa had won notable victories in Gaul, where there had
been serious problems in Aquitania. Octavian had battled on against
Sextus Pompey but had gained nothing. In fact his record was
abysmal. Tactfully, Agrippa refused a triumph for his Gallic
campaigns, because the contrast between his successes and Octavian's
failures would have been too great. As the year was drawing to a close,
Antony received a visit from Octavian's friend Maecenas, who had
come to ask for assistance against Sextus Pompey. Since it would have
been unwise to march into Parthia with such a potential flashpoint
behind him, Antony agreed to meet Octavian once again to come
to some arrangement. Either Sextus must be defeated decisively, or
integrated fully into the Triumviral government, but the latter choice
was unlikely, since neither Antony nor Octavian wanted Sextus as an
ally in the Mediterranean, and they certainly did not want him in
Rome. Antony had either to assist Octavian and hope for his success,
or take on the war himself. In the spring of 37, he got together a fleet
of 300 ships, and sailed to Brundisium. For the third time, he met
with difficulties when he arrived. Brundisium was closed to him,
and the town authorities would not allow the fleet to sail into the
harbour. There is some disagreement in the sources about this event,
where perhaps the previous debacles have been confused with this
one. At any rate, for some reason Antony sailed on to Tarentum, and
that was where Octavian came to meet him.

Octavia played an important part in reconciling her husband and
her brother. The agreement made at Tarentum in 37 embraced more
than just the immediate needs of the two Triumvirs.[39] Octavian was
to receive 120 ships from Antony, to replace those that had been
destroyed by Sextus, or wrecked in storms. These Antony gave him
straight away. The deal was supposed to benefit Antony too. In his
Parthian campaign he would have more need for soldiers than ships
and sailors, so Octavian agreed to give him 20,000 men. One may

be permitted to wonder if Antony really believed that he would ever receive them, or if Octavian ever intended to do more than promise the men to Antony. He never relinquished them all. What Antony finally received was too little, and too late.

After the exchange of ships and men had been agreed, the Triumvirs turned to their joint needs. Technically, they held no legal power because the Triumvirate had been set up for a fixed term of five years in November 43, which meant that at the end of 38 it had run its term. For the time being it was highly unlikely that either of them would be challenged, and no one had yet begun to shout the name of Lepidus as a candidate for sole government. Antony and Octavian were still in power because they held most of the armed forces of the Roman world, and besides they were the two men most able to put an end to the depredations of Sextus Pompey and thus restore freedom of the seas and the food supply of Rome. The Roman mob for the most part had enough sense not to bite the hands that fed them, and the Senate was muzzled after the savage proscriptions of 43. But there remained the problem of political correctness. Neither Antony nor Octavian could hope to continue on this nebulous basis for too long. At the present time of emergencies and disasters, there was not much danger of legal wrangling, but a close examination of the Triumvirate would reveal so many loopholes that the Triumvirs would not risk having their powers placed under scrutiny. Questions as to whether there was a fixed legal term or whether the Triumvirate was open-ended until the Triumvirs resigned were probably being asked in many a private household, but no one had asked them in the Senate, and probably never would. But it was a risk that could not be allowed. Being in a hurry, Antony and Octavian did not bother with too many time-consuming formalities. They renewed their powers for another five years, and shortly afterwards the position was legalised by a law of the people of Rome. Theoretically the new terminal date was to be the end of 33, but in 38 probably neither of the Triumvirs lost any sleep over that particular dilemma.[40] Their present predicament probably absorbed their whole attention. Octavian and Agrippa had to build up a new fleet and train their crews, and Antony had to reorganise and stabilise the east. Neither task was a sinecure.

The negotiations at Tarentum were prolonged until the late summer or early autumn, which meant that for Antony the prospect of beginning a campaign in the east was now very remote. It was therefore relegated to the following spring of 36. During the intervening months, there would be plenty of time for Antony to make an assessment of where he stood. Octavian had gone from strength to strength, and had declared for all to see the direction that he was following. His marriage to Livia Drusilla in January 38 was an important political step, no matter how much he may have been bowled over by her charms and however much he may have loved her. He had married her in unseemly haste, manipulating the laws in order to do so.[41] Livia had to be divorced from her first husband Tiberius Claudius Nero, by whom she already had one son, and was pregnant for the second time. Since the paternity of the second child was not in doubt, and there was no hint of previous relations with Octavian, Livia was duly divorced and remarried according to Octavian's wishes. Her two children by her previous marriage were the future Emperor Tiberius and his ill-fated younger brother Drusus. Octavian had a daughter by Scribonia, and no doubt he hoped for more children by his new wife, to ensure that he would have male heirs and could pass on whatever he possessed to reliable successors of his own blood. It was not to be, but his marriage brought him other benefits. Livia Drusilla was the daughter of Marcus Livius Drusus Claudianus. Her background was impeccable and she was well connected with the noblest families of Rome. She would play an important role in bringing over to Octavian powerful allies from the senatorial body, men whose sense of their own dignity might have been affronted by an alliance with an Octavius, but not by an alliance with a scion of the Claudian house.

There was still the problem of Sextus Pompey for Octavian to overcome, and there was every possibility that he would find the task too difficult, but whatever the outcome of that particular struggle, by now Antony would be aware that Italy and the west were closed to him unless he asserted himself. Despite his marriage to Octavia, Antony was not exactly a close associate and trusted friend of Octavian, and would have to work very hard to remain one step ahead. It did not matter that Antony's agents were working for him in Rome, nor that he himself could perhaps look forward to future consulships and high offices. His absence from Italy had gradually given the advantage to Octavian, who was continually in the public eye, and continually exploited every political expedient that he could muster to advertise himself, putting himself into the best possible light. He did not do so in a vacuum, because it was so much more pertinent to present himself as a perfect Roman hero if he had something against which to contrast himself. Antony was to provide him with an ideal antithesis. Octavian deliberately chose to adopt sober Roman attitudes and behaviour, and sober gods such as Apollo and Mars. He referred to ancient Roman custom all the time, and as an additional insurance policy he began to imbue all his actions with glory, not for himself but for the people of Rome, whose saviour he was determined to become. The comparison with Antony played into his hands at every turn. In 37 Antony was the strongest of the Triumvirs, his military reputation was unsullied, and he had done nothing to incense the people against him. He had not descended on Italy to put himself at the head of the state, and he had not forcefully evicted Italian landowners and tenants in order to settle his veterans. He had assisted Octavian whenever he was asked to do so, and he was preparing for an eastern campaign which promised to bring wealth, booty and vengeance for Rome. But there were already several loopholes for Octavian to exploit. Antony espoused eastern rather than Roman customs. His name was linked with the dangerous and scheming Queen of Egypt. He had always been far from sober himself, and he adopted far from sober gods such as Dionysus and Hercules to promote his cause. The rot had already set in as far as the Romans were concerned, and though it may have been subtle at first, easily remedied if only Antony could achieve a great victory against the Parthians, the fact that all these characteristics were deeply embedded and of long duration made it so much easier for Octavian to discredit him properly when the time came.

Antony spent the winter of 37–36 in Antioch in Syria, where he could gather information, issue orders rapidly, and make preparations for the next spring. He left his family in Italy, preferring not to expose them to the dangers of the war zone. There was every excuse, since Octavia and Antony already had an infant daughter, the elder Antonia born in 39, and Octavia was pregnant for the second time; this child would be another daughter, Antonia *minor*, to distinguish her from her elder sister. Octavia had also taken under her wing Antony's two sons by Fulvia, Antyllus and Iullus Antonius. In order to keep them safe, and perhaps to remind the people of Rome that he was still a force to be reckoned with, Antony insisted that the whole family should wait for him in Rome. Once he was free of them, he lost no time in inviting Cleopatra to Antioch to stay there with him until the campaign began. She brought with her the twins born to him in 40, Alexander Helios named for the sun (Helios), and Cleopatra Selene, named for the moon (Selene). The names were not given to the children as the result of a whim or a fortuitous accident. They were meant to convey regal authority.[42] Antony acknowledged paternity of these two children. It may be that he married Cleopatra according to Egyptian rites, while they were at Antioch. The date and even the existence of any form of marriage between Antony and Cleopatra is disputed, and all the possible permutations have been proposed. Whatever the truth of the affair, Octavian was able to make it seem that Antony had married Cleopatra illegally, since marriage with foreigners was forbidden by Roman law. Perhaps there was some form of ceremony at some time, either in Antioch or in Egypt, that could be construed as a marriage by eastern witnesses.[43] There was the ready comparison of a marriage between Osiris and Isis, or Dionysus and Aphrodite, which appealed to both Egyptian and Greek populations of the east. The symbolic marriage was more readily accepted in the east than in the Roman world, so the contrivance of posing as Osiris and Isis, and naming the children for the sun and moon, was double edged; in the east Antony's actions in acknowledging these two children by Cleopatra would strengthen their joint authority, but in Rome it condemned him.

During their stay in Antioch, Cleopatra became pregnant again, and when the baby was born and named Ptolemy Philadelphus, Antony acknowledged him as his son. Despite their obviously close relationship, Cleopatra was not simply a personal guest, brought to Antioch for Antony's amusement for the months before he went to war. Politics and economics were never far from Cleopatra's thoughts, and her ambition was to reconstitute the once extensive Egyptian Empire. She was granted lucrative territories to add to her already wealthy domains. She ruled Crete, Cyrene and Cilicia, Phoenicia, and Nabataean Arabia. These areas yielded profitable resources that had once been controlled by Egypt, among them large wooded areas, providing timber for ships that Cleopatra was to build for Antony's fleet. She also gained several important coastal cities of Syria, with the exception of Tyre and Sidon, which remained independent. In this latter case Antony gave away territory that belonged to Rome, but he was not entirely under her sway, since he refused to give her complete control of Judaea.[44] She did obtain the balsam groves of Jericho, part of the kingdom that Herod was winning back for himself. As a business woman, Cleopatra was shrewd and ruthless. Herod was in no position to argue, having only just asserted his authority over Judaea. Cleopatra leased the balsam groves back to him at a vast annual rent.

To Cleopatra a strong Judaea was anathema, but to Antony it represented security behind him when he invaded Parthia, so he prevented Cleopatra from supplanting Herod as king. He reorganised the other eastern kingdoms to the advantage of Rome and himself. He adjusted some boundaries and refashioned some of the lesser kingdoms, choosing men whom he trusted to rule the larger territories. Galatia was entrusted to Amyntas, Polemo was installed as king of Pontus, and Archelaus was given Cappadocia in place of Antony's previously mistaken choice of Ariarathes.[45] Before he embarked on his Parthian war, he ensured that he was surrounded by capable men who were as reliable as any man could be in the circumstances.

There remained the kingdoms outside his immediate control. During the period of preparation for the war, Antony sent Canidius Crassus to Armenia, to secure the territory for Rome.[46] It was vital to neutralise this kingdom before marching into Parthia, so that the Roman army would not be faced with the possibility of an attack on their rear while they marched, or being cut off from their retreat. Canidius defeated Artavasdes, who obligingly severed his long-standing alliance with Parthia, and became the ally of Rome. But the victory brought further complications, since it rendered the neighbouring kingdom of Media nervous and hostile to Rome. It was nigh impossible to be the friend and ally of both these mutually inimical kingdoms of Armenia and Media, so a choice had to be made between them. The king of Media, also called Artavasdes, strengthened his alliance with Parthia, but that was only to be expected. Military conquest was the only solution, but that would be left until the following year. Satisfied with the results in Armenia, Canidius went on to campaign against the peoples of the Caucasus. The first stage of the project was in operation, and so far it looked like standard Roman procedure for protecting the rear and flank of the invading army.

The timing of the Parthian war was only slightly faulty. If Antony could have started a year earlier he might have caught the enemy off guard. There had been a revolution in the ruling house, which had lasting consequences. The Parthian king Orodes was supposedly devastated by the death of his son Pacorus at the hands of Ventidius' army, so he abdicated in favour of one of his many other sons, Phraates. Shortly afterwards, Orodes died, or perhaps more likely he was killed on the orders of Phraates.[47] All the many sons of Orodes and any other close relatives who might have posed a threat to Phraates also disappeared, including Phraates' own son. The eradication of opposition was not limited to the ruling house. Phraates went on to weed out suspect members of the nobility as well, much as the Triumvirs had rooted out opposition in Rome. Unfortunately for Antony, by the time he invaded Parthia, Phraates had consolidated his position, and the comparative weakness of the Parthian high command could not now be exploited.

Antony's choice of Antioch as his winter quarters made it quite clear that his next project would be to invade Parthia. It would have been almost impossible to keep the invasion secret, since at some point Antony would have to assemble troops and supplies somewhere near the border, and Parthian spies would observe and report. Instead of preparing with the greatest secrecy, Antony made a noise about the forthcoming campaign. He sent an embassy to Phraates to ask for the return of the Roman standards lost in 53 at Carrhae. Presumably he did not expect that the request would be answered by the meek delivery of a bundle of Roman eagles accompanied by a note saying sorry. It was a declaration of intent, outlining the purpose of the coming war. Antony's request for the return of the eagles would have deep significance for Augustan and later audiences, who would know perfectly well that where Antony had failed in war, Augustus succeeded in diplomacy. In 20, after a tense interlude of negotiating, the standards were returned to Rome by the Parthians. The contrast would render Antony that much more pathetic, all bluster, armed force and failure as against Augustus's cool, rational patience. The point is worth labouring, because Augustus laboured it himself. Literary references to the achievement leave no doubt as to its importance, and artistic representations on coins and statues were used to impress contemporaries and keep the tradition alive for posterity. Where Antony could not prevail, Augustus triumphed.

Antony assembled his troops at Zeugma on the north eastern border of Syria, which served to draw the Parthian army into the plains of Mesopotamia to await his invasion.[48] This was all very plausible, because to the east of Zeugma lay Carrhae, where Crassus had met defeat, so it would seem likely that the Romans were about to launch a grand campaign to avenge Crassus in the very place where he had died. But Antony did not enter Mesopotamia from Syria. Instead he marched north to Samosata and then by way of Armenia to Media, where he laid siege to the Median capital Phraaspa (sometimes rendered as Phraapa, and Plutarch calls it Phraata). The exact location is not known for certain. It may have been situated south east of Lake Urmia. Antony arrived there, despite the extremely long journey, before the Parthians did. Antony declared that he was following a plan that Caesar had outlined long before.[49] There would have been plenty of opportunity for Antony to discuss with Caesar where Crassus had gone wrong, in mistakenly fighting in the open plain against an enemy who excelled in combat in such terrain. There is no absolute proof that Caesar had made any plans, and it could be said that it was highly unlikely that he had revealed them to anyone. But the elaborate ruse to lure the enemy to a false battle ground and then the rapid dash to come down behind the Parthians was a typically Caesarian manoeuvre, risking all on speed and expertise.

Antony dashed to Phraaspa without his siege train, which lumbered on behind him, protected by two legions under Oppius Statianus, together with some Pontic troops under their king Polemo, and contingents of Armenian troops under their king Artavasdes, who fled when the Parthians attacked. Polemo was captured, but ransomed later, and Statianus was killed.[50] The siege train was destroyed. In itself it did not necessarily presage disaster. If Antony could reduce Phraaspa very quickly by blockade, he would be able to spend the winter there and go on to attack Parthia itself in the next year. He may have intended to do so all along, but no one knows what his plans were. It would make sense to reduce Media first, garrison it securely, and then make for Ecbatana, or Ctesiphon. Whatever Antony had planned, Phraaspa did not fall to him. The delay was fatal because the Parthians arrived in force, and lingered just out of reach, harassing Antony's army, but not giving battle. Despite all Antony's attempts to bring them to battle, and despite his considerable successes in repulsing the Parthian attacks, final victory eluded him.[51]

When he was forced to the realisation that he had failed, he had to begin to think of retreat. With winter approaching, he could not continue the siege, and if he could not inflict a decisive defeat on the Parthian army before winter came, it was very likely that his troops would be picked off little by little. The allies who marched confidently with him at the outset of the campaign would have no reason to remain with him, and could prove his undoing if they joined the Parthians. Phraates had every reason to encourage Antony to retreat.[52] He was worried that his allies might desert him, because if the siege went on too long, they would go home to gather their crops. Phraates offered a truce; Antony asked for the return of the Roman standards; Phraates destroyed some of Antony's siege works, then offered a safe passage back to Armenia. If Antony believed that, he deserved no credit at all.

The soldiers for the most part understood why they were marching away, and followed Antony loyally. As in any famous retreat, there were desperate heroics and tragedies. The Armenian contingents, whose heart was not in the campaign anyway, went home. Antony was left with an ever reducing army, retreating over ground that had already been stripped of supplies, with the winter already advanced. He had been in this desperate position before, when he left Mutina to march into Gaul, and in these difficult circumstances he once again showed himself capable, brave and resourceful.[53] He used every stratagem that he had learned, so that Plutarch's account reads like a military manual on what to do when retreating, hard pressed by the enemy in difficult terrain.[54] Discipline had to be enforced when the Romans wavered, so five days into the retreat, Antony decimated cowardly troops and put the survivors on punishment rations of barley instead of wheat. Unfortunately Plutarch does not enlighten his readers on where the supplies were obtained. At this point food was perhaps not in quite such short supply; later, the position would become desperate, so that the men ate roots of all descriptions, including one which caused madness. The victims started to turn over stones as though they had no other purpose in life, then eventually vomited and died. The antidote to the poisonous roots was said to be wine, but the Romans had long since run out of wine.

Training and expertise still existed in Antony's army, so that he was able to march in square formation, escorted by clouds of scouts and flanked by skirmishers. Even so, he lost many men, especially during an attack on the rearguard when Antony lost 3,000 dead and 5,000 wounded.[55] Progress was no doubt very slow. Even when the army reached Armenia, the problems were not over. Antony was not capable of making any demonstration of strength, though he was urged by the soldiers to take revenge on Artavasdes for deserting them. There was nothing to be gained from engaging in another war at the moment, but Antony would not forget.[56]

It was time to act decisively to save what he could of his army. Domitius Ahenobarbus and Canidius were charged with bringing it out of the snows of Armenia, while Antony went on ahead to make arrangements for supplies of food and clothing. He made for the coast of Syria, and camped at Leuke Come, between Berytus and Sidon. He had sent messages to Cleopatra to bring food, clothing and money. Loyally, she set sail, risking a winter voyage, bringing with her the necessary supplies. It was probably in January 35 that she arrived there, but the date is not known. Her detractors accused her of being very slow to set out, as though she deliberately chose to delay taking assistance to Antony, though no one advanced any theory as to what she might have gained from such deliberate dilatory behaviour. The problem may have been predominantly logistical. Antony's message will have taken some time to reach her, and having received it she then had to gather clothing, food and money and have it loaded onto the ships, which cannot have happened overnight. Another delay may have been caused by the birth of Ptolemy Philadelphus, her son by Antony conceived while they were in Alexandria before the Parthian campaign began. There is no reason to imagine that Cleopatra delayed any longer than she needed.[57] The focus should be on why she sailed with the fleet herself, in winter, not long after giving birth. Any other allied king, on being asked for assistance, would have sent a convoy under the command of a trusted subordinate, perhaps grudgingly at that, but Cleopatra left her kingdom to go to Antony in Syria.

While waiting for her, Antony took heavily to drink, more so than usual, if the reports are correct. Having nothing much to do, he kept leaping up from half eaten meals to go outside, gazing wistfully seawards, hoping that her ships would appear on the horizon. It must have been a relief to everyone when they did. Antony set about distributing money, food and clothing to his soldiers, and after doing all that he could for their comfort, he went back with Cleopatra to Alexandria.[58]

It was much more of a relief that the Parthian army did not follow him to Syria. He was not yet in a position to repel an invasion. Fortunately for Antony, new dissensions in the Parthian royal house prevented Phraates from mounting an aggressive campaign, and he was further restricted by the defection of Media. The two kings had quarrelled initially about the distribution of the Roman booty after Antony had retreated. The Median Artavasdes, recently Antony's enemy, made friendly overtures to him in 35, proposing dynastic marriage ties, and releasing from captivity Antony's ally Polemo, king of Pontus. It was evident that there was more to the quarrel than the division of the spoils of war, and that here was an opportunity to exploit the differences of opinion to attack Parthia again. Instead of having to fight for and win a base, Antony could march into Media and pick up where he left off in winter 36. If he had grasped the opportunity there and then, he might have been able to achieve his aims, humble Parthia, retrieve the lost Roman standards, return them to Rome triumphant, and perhaps regain some of his lost supremacy in the west. But Artavasdes of Media was more interested in gaining Roman assistance to attack his namesake Artavasdes of Armenia. Although Antony set out on the campaign, pretending that his goal was Parthia but in reality aiming for Armenia, but no campaign took place.[59] Antony had another problem in the west.

News reached Antony while he was in Syria that Octavian and Agrippa had finally defeated Sextus Pompey at the battle of Naulochus in early September 36. Sextus had escaped with his life and very little else. Agrippa had prepared thoroughly, building new ships to add to the depleted fleet, and training the crews for months on a lake, artificially deepened for the purpose, until they were more practised than Sextus's sailors. This naval expertise of Agrippa's was to have great import for Antony and Cleopatra a few years later. The victory at Naulochus, fought on land and sea, gave Octavian control of Sicily. It was an important province, because it yielded much of the corn that fed Rome. At this stage the corn supplies of Egypt were not under direct Roman control. The province had not fallen into Octavian's hands without a struggle, however. The forgotten Triumvir Lepidus had brought troops from Africa to help Octavian in the final land battles, and at their conclusion he had decided to assert himself, declaring Sicily his province and trying to hold it by force. His attempted resistance crumbled instantaneously. The result was that Octavian also gained control of Africa, another lucrative corn-producing area. Lepidus was sent back to Italy and kept under surveillance for the rest of his life.[60] He was allowed to retain his priestly office as Pontifex Maximus, and when he died in 12BC, Augustus, as he then was, quietly assumed the priesthood for himself. Patience was one of Octavian's enduring talents.

After his defeat at Naulochus, Sextus fled to the east, hoping for an alliance with Antony, which might have been arranged but for the fact that when he thought Antony had been defeated and possibly killed, Sextus did not wait to find out if the rumours were true, but began to intrigue with the Parthians. In all his dealings with Antony Sextus showed himself to be thoroughly untrustworthy. Antony sent his general Titius against Sextus with orders to spare him if he submitted. The final encounter took place in Bithynia. Sextus began to recruit an army after landing at Nicomedia, drawing down on his own head the charge of outlawry. Some of Sextus's officers left him and joined Titius, intending to submit to Antony.

Sextus promised to negotiate with Titius's colleague Furnius and king Amyntas of Galatia, not with Titius himself, then immediately tried to burn some of Titius's fleet. He was, to use an anachronistic phrase, a loose cannon. In the end Amyntas captured him, and not wishing to compromise himself, he handed the renegade over to Titius, who executed him, perhaps on his own initiative, or possibly on the orders of Plancus, Antony's legate commanding Asia Minor and Syria. Thus the last surviving son of Pompey the Great met his end.[61] It was the only logical conclusion.

This minor civil war with Sextus, and perhaps sheer exhaustion, prevented Antony from taking any further action against Parthia in 35. He did not intend to remain entirely inactive, since he offered help to Octavian, who began a campaign against the tribes of Illyricum in that same year. More than ever, Octavian needed military renown and experience if he was ever to have full standing in Rome. Until now his victories had always depended on someone else, Antony at Philippi, Agrippa in Gaul and at Naulochus. As Caesar's son, he wanted to show that he too could wage successful wars and bring glory to Rome. More important still was the need for a legitimate excuse to keep an army together under his personal command. After his victory at Naulochus and the defeat of Lepidus, he had more than forty legions at his disposal, far too many for the tasks in hand. He settled many of the veterans in the provinces, but he still could not afford to disband all the troops. Antony had more than one reason to command a large army because without troops he could not administer and defend the eastern provinces, but once Sextus and Lepidus had been eliminated, Octavian could only reasonably command the armies in Gaul and Spain. If a future conflict were to develop with Antony or even with the Senate, Octavian required access to troops more rapidly than those in Gaul. He conducted a campaign in Illyricum, close enough to Rome for a rapid return and far enough away to justify the command of an army. The war was not strictly necessary for Rome's safety, and brought very little tribute into the coffers. But the campaign did bring Octavian some credit, which he was quick to seize upon and enlarge. Antony's so-called Parthian victory was beginning to tarnish a little in the light of Octavian's more tangible successes.

This was the time when Antony should have gone to Rome to promote himself, while Octavian was engaged on his campaigns in Illyricum. He either chose not to go, or did not see the necessity of doing so. Even when his wife Octavia came to Athens with money, extra troops and supplies, he did not go to meet her, but directed her to send on the troops and to go back to Rome. Octavian had sent only 2,000 soldiers and seventy ships, 18,000 men and fifty ships short of what had been promised.[62] Antony can be forgiven for his anger at the shortfall and the way in which Octavian dismissed him, but he must have realised that in turn he had just insulted a virtuous woman who had never done him any harm. Octavia dutifully returned to Rome, where she remained in his house looking after his children. She gained more credit than she would have done if she had wailed and protested. Antony's son Marcus Antonius Antyllus went to join his father in Alexandria, not necessarily as a result of any dispute with his step-mother, though there may have been some definite parting of the ways. Antony must have known that Octavian would eventually use his churlish behaviour against him. Perhaps he intended to demonstrate to his colleague that he was now following an independent course. The ancient authors concluded that Antony was so besotted with Cleopatra that he no longer cared. The Queen of Egypt is blamed for the downfall of a once mighty Roman general, using her wiles to enslave him each time he threatened to leave her. Plutarch even includes a ridiculous tale about her deliberate playacting to convince him that she was madly in love with him, greeting him with joy each time he appeared and not quite controlling her tears when he was absent. Not knowing what was in his mind, it is difficult to explain why Antony acted as he did. He is open to charges of stupidity, naivety, arrogance, misplaced confidence in his own abilities, or even madness. The incontrovertible fact is that when he repudiated Octavia so decisively in 35, he had burnt his boats.[63] He had not renounced Rome, but he had broken with Octavian. The seeds of the final conflict had been sown.

6

Caesar's Heir: Antony, Cleopatra and Octavian 35–30BC

Antony was consul in 34, but *in absentia* and only for one day. He laid down his powers and installed Lucius Sempronius Atratinus in his place.[1] After a delay of one year, he intended now to settle accounts with Artavasdes of Armenia. An alliance had been proposed by Artavasdes of Media, and Antony accepted. The Median king agreed to return the captured standards of the two legions which had escorted the siege train during the invasion of 36. The daughter of Artavasdes was to be betrothed to Alexander Helios, and was brought to Alexandria in fulfilment of the alliance. Dio says that Antony and the Median Artavasdes united against the Parthians and Octavian, but Antony's aims even at this late stage perhaps did not include war with Octavian. When the civil war did start, the alliance with Artavasdes could be brought into play, but the original terms perhaps did not include a pact that specifically targeted Octavian. The Median king was more interested in a war against Armenia than with the Parthians or Octavian.[2]

As a preliminary, observing the rules of political correctness, Antony opened diplomatic exchanges with Artavasdes of Armenia, but the overtures yielded nothing.[3] Artavasdes refused family marriage ties with Antony and Cleopatra. Antony invited the

Armenian king to join him in an expedition against Parthia. An ideal opportunity for a Parthian expedition had presented itself, since Phraates was deeply involved with his own dynastic squabbles with his family and his nobles, or what was left of them after his judicious disposal of the most troublesome elements. This was known to the Romans and to the Armenian court, but Artavasdes declined the invitation to join Antony's legions in another foray into Parthia.

Antony's response was to march to Nicopolis, a city founded by Pompey after his victories over Mithradates. Cleopatra, and Antony's son Marcus Antonius Antyllus, accompanied him for part of the march, then Cleopatra travelled back to Egypt through the eastern states, visiting a few cities such as Emesa and Damascus, finally dropping in on Herod as highly unwelcome but well-treated guest. She would survey all the territories that she travelled through with an eye to whatever economic gains might present themselves, but nowhere more avidly than in Judaea. Josephus relates how Herod wrestled with his conscience as to whether to have her assassinated while he had the chance, but to kill her would bring the wrath of Antony tumbling down on Judaea, so he refrained.[4] A good story, but untrue except for Herod's wishful thinking. He was a realist, like Cleopatra. He had to engage in friendly political relations with her, but he did not have to like it.

The facts about Antony's Armenian campaign are sparse. In order to persuade Artavasdes to come to terms, Antony marched to Artaxata, where he invited the king to a conference, but when the royal guest arrived Antony arrested him along with most of his family, and sent them all to Alexandria as prisoners, at first under house arrest but later put in chains, albeit made of silver. Shortly afterwards Antony returned to Alexandria, and issued coins bearing the legend *Armenia devicta*, or Armenia conquered.[5] The conquest of Armenia made little impact in Rome, perhaps by design of Octavian. The surviving account is suspect. Antony is made to appear slipshod, disorderly, and devious. The whole episode is construed as a desire for revenge with no strategic purpose behind it, but it was much more than a punitive campaign. The territory was annexed and converted into a Roman province, complete with military garrison and the rapid infiltration of Roman settlers and traders. Antony's claim to have conquered Armenia was perfectly correct, so Octavian could not deny it, but chose instead to cast doubt on the motives and methods that Antony used to achieve it. The reason why Antony's campaign was depicted as useless and rather comic was probably because, far from being ill-advised, it promised to bring him success.[6] In retrospect, the conquest of Armenia seemed irrelevant because it was very short-lived. During the civil war between Antony and Octavian, the Parthian king Phraates was driven out by Tiridates, one of his own generals, and in the same year that Alexandria fell to Octavian, Phraates won his kingdom back again. Stronger than ever now, Phraates also overran both Media and Armenia. There was no one to stop his progress, so he installed Artaxes on the Armenian throne and probably rejoiced when his puppet king massacred all the Roman settlers and traders. Octavian, the victor of Actium and Alexandria, could not repair the damage by restoring Roman rule in Armenia.[7] It would have entailed a full scale war with Parthia, so Octavian acquiesced in the loss of the territory, and Armenia reverted to an independent state sandwiched between the Parthian and Roman Empires. In order to save face for not settling accounts with the Parthians and not putting a garrison back into Armenia, Octavian was constrained to prevent any credit for the initial conquest from attaching itself to the name of Antony. He could not redress the balance, so what he could not obtain was represented as unworthy and unprofitable, and its original conqueror was depicted in the same light.

While Antony garrisoned Armenia, Octavian was fighting in Illyricum, making a name for himself as a general. These campaigns would have to be brought to a successful conclusion before he could turn his attention to Antony, but in the meantime his associates in Rome kept him in the public eye. Buildings, roadworks, policing for personal safety and security of property, provision of food and clean water, and the proper control of the sewage system of Rome all became the concern of Octavian and his colleagues. Agrippa had been given high office and independent commands, but now assumed the lowly role of aedile in 33 in order to inspect and repair the sewers and put in water pipes and fountains. Antony's generals also built temples and improved public facilities, but somehow their achievements were marginalised, outshone by everything that Octavian's men did. Sosius held a triumph in 34 for his exploits in the Jerusalem campaign when Herod won back his kingdom, but although Antonian generals featured almost as often as Octavian's men in the self-congratulatory military displays, collectively they were farther away and their achievements were not so carefully orchestrated.

When he returned to Alexandria in the autumn of 34, Antony paraded through the streets in a chariot, with his Armenian captives walking behind him. Cleopatra watched while seated high above the procession, with Caesarion at her side. It has been described as less of a triumphal procession and more of a festival in honour of Dionysus, the supreme eastern deity. To the eastern kingdoms Antony's behaviour was perfectly acceptable, and the people could relate to a conqueror celebrating his victory by means of a parade with all honours to Dionysus, but the scenario as represented in Rome did Antony irreparable damage. It was too much like a parody of the Roman triumph for comfort, with sacrilegious undertones because the spoils of victory were traditionally dedicated to Jupiter Optimus Maximus, in his temple on the Capitol Hill in Rome. Antony therefore deprived the most important Roman god of this privilege by staging his pseudo-triumph in a foreign city in honour of a foreign god.[8]

After the parade through the streets of Alexandria, either on the same day or a short time later, Antony and Cleopatra staged another ceremony which is known to historians as the Donations of Alexandria.[9] Before a large gathering, seated next to Cleopatra on a high throne, with the children in front of them on smaller thrones, Antony redistributed territories, some of which were not yet conquered, to the immediate benefit of Cleopatra and her children. Alexander Helios was to rule Armenia, Media and Parthia. Since the latter states had not yet been conquered, this was more a declaration of future intent rather than a true statement of the status quo. Cleopatra Selene was to be ruler of Cyrenaica and Libya, and Ptolemy Philadelphus, aged about two, was given Syria and Cilicia. Over all of them was Cleopatra, 'Queen of kings and of her sons who are kings' or *Cleopatrae reginae regum filiorum regum* as the legend on Antony's coinage proclaims.[10] King of Kings was a well worn title in the east and not so megalomaniac as it sounds.

Antony did not proclaim himself king, being content with his position as Roman Triumvir and commander of the east. At some date, possibly just after the Donations of Alexandria, he issued coins in Syria with a Greek legend *Antonios Autokrator Trion Andron*,[11] which equates with his Roman titles Imperator and *Tresvir* or Triumvir, the basis of his authority in the east, but he was also playing the part of consort of the Queen of Egypt. Antony publicly recognised Caesarion's claim to the throne of Egypt, and declared that he was the legitimate heir of Caesar. This challenged Octavian as the one and only legitimate heir of Caesar, but at present the challenge was personal, not political. There were no grounds for Octavian to persuade the Romans to go to war. Egypt was not yet a Roman province, and Antony had not yet stepped too far outside the boundaries of Roman practice. Some of the territories in the list of Donations already belonged to Cleopatra, and the new additions to her domain were still governed by Romans and garrisoned by Roman troops.[12] Amongst the hyperbole of Augustan propaganda, it is easy to be swept along with the portrayal of Antony as a tyrannical megalomaniac aiming at world domination, acting in concert with the evil, scheming Queen of Egypt. No one can know whether Antony harboured overwhelming ambition to take over the whole Roman world, but at this stage he was acting within the terms agreed after Pharsalus and renewed when he and Octavian settled their differences. Antony had been charged with bringing order to the east, as Octavian had been charged with bringing order to the west. He had not usurped the authority of the Senate, and was acting within the terms agreed when he left Rome, having obtained ratification in advance for his arrangements for the eastern provinces and the client and free states. He had dealt with the territories in the usual Roman manner, making alliances with client states and installing rulers over them and adjusting boundaries, but he also acted in a way that was acceptable to the peoples of the east. He had adopted some of their customs, just as Pompey had done in allowing his image to appear on coins, and accepting a sort of semi-divine status that was perfectly understandable in the east. Antony's misfortune, or mistake, was to ally himself somewhat more intimately with one particular ruler, handing to Octavian the golden opportunity to create and concentrate on a foreign enemy and to attack Antony at the same time.

As soon as the campaigns in Illyricum were concluded in 33, Octavian embarked on a crusade of abuse against Antony, launched by a speech in the Senate early in the year.[13] He was consul in 33, but like Antony in the previous year, he held the office for only one day. He did not need the power that the consulship conferred on him, since he was now unassailable on account of his grant of tribunician sacrosanctity, one of the rewards for his victory over Sextus Pompey in 36. His first speech denouncing Antony would be a reliable test of the mood of the Senate and people of Rome, so he could estimate from its reception and the extent of the reaction how far he would have to go to achieve his aim. The timing of this inflammatory speech is not established beyond doubt and is consequently disputed. Some authors would place it at the beginning of 32, but it fits well with the situation in 33, when Antony was about to launch another attack on Parthia, and when the second term of the Triumvirate was coming to an end.

The terminal date of the Triumvirate is the subject of considerable ongoing debate, because it is not known what exactly was agreed when the Triumvirate was renewed, and the sources contradict each other.[14] Some modern scholars argue that the Triumvirate should

have expired on the last day of 32, on the supposition that the second
five year term was dated from January 36, but if this is correct the
Triumvirate suffered a break between November 37 and the beginning of the following year. Augustus declared in his *Res Gestae* that
he was Triumvir for ten consecutive years, implying that there was
no break in 37–36. The argument about the exact dating of the end
of the Triumvirate is now academic and insoluble. The most important aspect concerns Octavian's portrayal of himself as legitimate, law
abiding head of state. He emphasised the fact that he ceased to use
his power as Triumvir, possibly before the agreement came to an end,
whereas Antony continued as Triumvir. The broad general picture is
clear. Octavian was anxious to make an unequivocal statement that
he renounced his Triumviral power and did not intend to enter into
another agreement with Antony.

A decisive rupture between Octavian and Antony was fast
approaching. The timing was urgent. Two years after his disastrous
defeat in Parthia, Antony was ready to try again. He had prepared the
ground for the last few years by installing independent but trustworthy rulers in the territories of the east, and with Armenia converted
into a Roman province, his advance into Parthian territory would be
greatly facilitated. If he had to retreat again, then at least he would not
have to march through a potentially hostile country once he reached
Armenia, and he could spend the winter there. This time, Antony
might be successful in Parthia. If so, his prestige in Rome would
rise, and his power in the east would be immeasurably increased.
His legions were prepared and in position for the projected invasion
in the summer of 33. If Octavian was to stop him and prevent him
from gaining tremendous credit as well as military power that might
eclipse his own, then he had to do so very soon.

The grounds for a break with Antony were already present in his
treatment of his wife Octavia, but even though the situation could
be used to inflame the people, the repudiation of Octavia, like the
recognition of Caesarion as Caesar's heir, was still only a personal
problem and not a cause for war. Fortunately for Octavian, Antony's

long-term relationship with the Queen of Egypt could be exploited in the political arena. Octavian began to focus upon Cleopatra, arousing the fears of the people.[15] One of Cleopatra's frequent declarations was supposed to be 'When I dispense justice from the Capitol' by which she obviously meant to dominate Rome. The capital might be moved to Alexandria just as it was rumoured that Caesar intended. The prime political target was Antony, but it was much more acceptable to instigate a war against a foreign enemy, as Dio states more than once. In the speech that he invents for Octavian before the battle of Actium, Dio summarises the arguments for making war on Cleopatra, an enemy by reason of her conduct, and not on Antony, because it may have been possible to bring him back to reason.[16] In an earlier passage, Dio gives a more devious reason, in that when war was declared on Cleopatra, Antony was bound to follow her, and could therefore be charged with turning against his own country.[17] It was important for Octavian to present himself as the innocent, injured party. He had proclaimed an end to civil wars when he defeated Sextus Pompey, so he would lose face if he had to persuade the Roman people to embark on another civil war. It would be much easier to launch a civil war dressed up as a foreign one.

Something of the new feeling in Rome reached Antony while he was in Armenia in 33, making preparations for the Parthian campaign. He defended himself with a counterblast against Octavian that revealed that he had a firm grasp on political reality, much as he had shown himself fully aware of the situation when Cicero was stirring up hostility towards him before the battles of Mutina. Antony pointed out that Octavian had not returned the ships that he had borrowed before the battle of Naulochus, and he had not kept his word about the 20,000 soldiers that he was supposed to send as his part of the bargain. Belatedly taking up the cause of Lepidus, Antony castigated Octavian for his treatment of their third partner. Favourable publicity in Italy may have been one of the motives behind this accusation, since Lepidus had not been foremost on Antony's list of priorities until now. His veterans on the other hand were dearer to him, and he accused Octavian of partiality to his own veterans at the expense of Antony's troops. It may not have been true, but many people in Italy probably thought it was an accurate assessment, so Antony appealed to them when he protested about the situation in his letter. Reputedly he also blamed Octavian for not sharing Sicily with him. Here he was not standing on very firm ground. The story may be suspect, but it allowed Octavian to reply that he would partition Sicily just as soon as Antony gave him half of Armenia.[18]

Then the abuse became more personal. Octavian wrote to Antony reproaching him for his rejection of Octavia and his elevation of Caesarion, but most of all for his relationship with Cleopatra. Antony replied in kind, in a letter that is famously reproduced in Suetonius' life of Augustus. It is a crude soldier's letter, in which Antony says that sexual relationships do not really mean anything, since after all Octavian himself was known to have taken all sorts of women to bed, and as Antony goes on to say, 'Does it really matter where you get your erections?' But he also asks why there should be any surprise concerning Cleopatra, because '*uxor mea est*' which means literally 'she is my wife'. As mentioned above, convoluted theories have been proposed about this simple phrase and what Antony intended to convey by it.[19] One of the most serious problems concerns its authenticity. Suetonius wrote his biographies of the Emperors during the reign of Hadrian, over 150 years after the events he describes. Antony's letter may have survived for this length of time, and Suetonius may have seen it, but even that does not guarantee its authenticity. Forgery as a tool for condemning people has a long history.

If it is accepted that Antony did write these disputed words, on balance, it is best to take them at face value, since he could very easily have inserted '*non*' between '*mea*' and '*est*' to make himself crystal clear that he did not regard Cleopatra as his wife, nor had he undergone any ceremonial in Egypt that could be construed as a marriage. Acceptance of his statement for what it says means that he did regard Cleopatra as his wife, even if there had been no proper marriage. This is presumably how Octavian interpreted Antony's letter, and in broadcasting the facts in Rome he revealed to the Roman people how seriously Antony had damaged his reputation by this association, whether or not it was a marriage, because he was still married to the virtuous Octavia, who without complaint or reproach kept house for him in the city and looked after all his children. This was a situation that Octavian could use against Antony to great advantage.

A war of words followed, with accusations winging their way between Rome and Armenia, but by itself that would not have been a cause for concern. It had happened before. What finally brought Antony out of Armenia before he had begun any military activity in the east was the realisation that Octavian had won over too many people and had probably browbeaten the Senate into submission. Support in Rome was vital and Antony stood to lose too much if he allowed Octavian to go on alienating him. In the autumn of 33 he turned his face towards Rome and away from Parthia. He now had to win over the Senate, and though he did not need to do so, he began by asking once again for formal ratification of his acts in the east. It was a diplomatic move. More importantly he offered to lay down his Triumviral powers if Octavian would comply and lay down his powers as well.[20] It was Caesar and Pompey all over again, and people in Rome and Italy began to feel very tense.

By November 33, Antony had bowed to the inevitable and started to prepare for war. He ordered the faithful Canidius to bring the army out of Armenia, and he began to assemble troops around his winter base at Ephesus. Cleopatra joined him there. Her resources in money, ships and manpower would be very necessary, so when some of the Romans in Antony's army protested that she should be sent home to Egypt, Canidius for one countered that she had every right to stay, since she was paying the army. He was promptly accused of accepting bribes from the Queen to support her. A recent find supports the suggestion. A fragment of papyrus reused inside a mummy casing came to light in Berlin in 2001. It dates to 33, and concerns an agreement made with Canidius, allowing him to import wine and export wheat without paying the normal taxes. Cleopatra is not named in the document, but it is thought that the authorisation at the end of the document, written in Greek, may be in her own hand.[21]

If Canidius owed much to Cleopatra, at least he repaid his debts by never deserting her and Antony, but he was one of the few who remained faithful to the end. The seeds of dissension were firmly planted among Antony's officers, and perhaps could not be eradicated at this stage. Everything that Octavian said about Cleopatra would henceforth find its mark not only at Rome but also in Antony's army. The propaganda was causing considerable apprehension among Antony's friends in Italy, who despatched Gaius Geminius to persuade him to break with Cleopatra, but Antony would not listen.[22] If war were to be declared against either of them, Antony and Cleopatra would have to fight side by side, since neither of them could now hope for an independent reconciliation with Octavian.

At the beginning of 32, the Antonian generals Sosius and Domitius Ahenobarbus took up office as consuls. Theoretically, all should have gone well for Antony, but Octavian had been strengthening himself and was ready for any eventuality. The story goes that Antony had sent a despatch to his consuls to be read in the Senate but the two men decided that it was too infamous to be revealed.[23] Among other things, it purported to outline the Donations of Alexandria, which strictly speaking could not possibly have been unheard of in Rome by this time. There is considerable doubt about this tale; as it stands it condemns Antony for his character and behaviour, but in the absence of a fully documented description of the circumstances, it is open to speculation. Firstly it may not even be true, but might be a later shadowy interpolation to denounce Antony by vague but credible accusations against him. Secondly, if it is true that Antony's letter contained information too dangerous to reveal to the Roman public in January 31, it attests to the effectiveness of Octavian's steady campaign against Antony, suggesting that he had whipped up feeling to flashpoint.

This is implied in subsequent events. Octavian was not in Rome in February when Sosius made a speech denouncing him. If he did not dare to read out Antony's letter, Sosius apparently had enough courage to try to turn the tables on Octavian. It is not known what he said, but his speech may have reiterated something that Antony had pointed out in a letter to Octavian during their war of words in 33, namely that the major obstacle to the restoration of the Republic was Octavian himself and his single minded pursuit of power. Sosius probably asked the Senate to declare Octavian out of order, if not actually anything more serious. It is not suggested that he wished to declare Octavian an enemy of the state, and if there had been the merest suggestion of that, Octavian would have used it as the justification for the civil war. Whatever it was, the tribune Nonius Balbus vetoed the proposal.[24] No one knows whether Nonius was in the pay of Octavian to protect his interests, or in the pay of the Antonians to rescue them from an impossible situation if the speech in the Senate went badly wrong. The meeting broke up inconclusively.

Octavian lost no time now. His position is not clarified. If the Triumvirate had indeed ended in December 33, then he had no legal office, and should not have been able to command troops. But the legal niceties were perhaps never fully investigated or elucidated. The realities of power were clear enough and were after all the only things that counted now. Returning to Rome with a bodyguard, Octavian convened the Senate, entered the meeting in force, and sat between the two consuls. It was undoubtedly illegal, but the time for propriety was long past and it was very effective. He said that he would bring documentary proof to the next meeting that would condemn Antony out of hand.[25] No one knows what this evidence was, and Octavian was never put to the test of producing it; the mere threat was sufficient. The result was pandemonium. The two consuls and many senators fled to Antony.[26] It is said that 300 senators joined Antony, but the figure is only a guess, derived from the fact that Augustus later declared that 700 senators remained with him. The assumption is that the full Senate after Caesar had augmented it comprised 1,000 members, therefore subtraction of the number who remained loyal to Octavian gives the number that is thought to have gone to Antony at Ephesus.

On the face of it this immediate reaction was extreme, but there is no proper documentation of the background. Senators do not uproot themselves and sail to another part of the world because of a few speeches in the Senate House. They will have seen all the signs that are lost to a modern audience, and interpreted them correctly. Too many of them would remember the proscriptions of only a decade ago, when the world saw precisely how far both Octavian and Antony would go to gain their ends. To be caught in the cross-fire was not wise, and for some men neutrality would not be a viable option. That would be possible only if a long foundation of impartiality had already been laid. The choice was Octavian and war with Antony, or vice versa. There can be no record of what preceded these events because Octavian had a vested interest in obscuring the opening stages of the war. He had carefully engineered it for his own ends, so both for contemporaries and indeed retrospectively he had to make it seem that he was saving the state from a terrible menace. This menace was not specifically Antony but Cleopatra and the use to which she might put him. The vilification of the Egyptian Queen was actively pursued from now onwards. It was one way of unifying the opposition.

If the remaining senators needed any more urging to war, Octavian found the ideal tool. Sensing the way that the wind was blowing, Antony's generals Titius and Plancus deserted him and came to Octavian in Rome.[27] They perhaps could not tolerate the close relationship of Antony with Cleopatra, or at least could not tolerate the way in which her continued presence played into Octavian's hands. Antony finally divorced Octavia in 32. This seemed to alienate more of Antony's followers, perhaps because until the divorce they could believe that he was still committed to her and perhaps to Octavian, with the Egyptian Queen as a profitable ally. More likely they simply wanted to survive and therefore had to be on the winning side, which they now calculated would be Octavian's.

The final instalment on Octavian's list of grievances against Antony was about to be played out. Titius and Plancus told him that Antony had written his will and lodged it with the Vestals in Rome, as was the usual custom. Another variation on this tale is that the will was with a friend of Antony's, but wherever it was, its location was revealed to Octavian, who immediately searched for it and opened it. This was one more fortunate opportunity to reveal to the Romans just how depraved Antony had become. The enormity of Octavian's action was perhaps overshadowed by what he found in the will, or said that he had found.[28] He opened the will in private, but no contemporaries openly accused him of forgery, of the whole will, or parts of it. The main points in it were that Antony reaffirmed the legitimacy of the claims of Caesarion to be Caesar's son, and also heir to the Egyptian throne; he granted legacies to his children by Cleopatra, which meant that he acknowledged them, even though in Roman law they were illegitimate because marriage with a foreign woman was illegal. He clearly intended Antyllus to be his own heir, and had issued coins displaying his own head and that of his son. The most damaging part of Antony's will was his obvious determination to remain with Cleopatra, even after death, for he asked that he should be buried alongside her in Alexandria. He seemed now to have renounced Rome altogether, but it was also implied that his schemes for world domination involved supplanting Rome in favour of the Egyptian city. Just as rumours circulated that Caesar intended to relocate the capital city, it was said that Antony was going to remove the seat of government to Alexandria.[29] The threat was enough to make the Romans clamour for war, in unified antagonism towards Cleopatra and her bewitched consort Antony.

In emphasising the unanimous acclaim of the Roman people, Octavian was very thorough, revealing the caution with which he laid his plans. He arranged that all of Italy should swear an oath of allegiance to him, with the exception of those towns where Antony had many clients, the chief of which was Bononia (modern Bologna). There were precedents for using the Italian towns to pressurise the

Senate to act, as for instance when Pompey asked the municipalities to agitate for the recall of Cicero from exile. Octavian's use of the Italian municipalities was something different, in that what he extracted from them was an oath to an individual leader, not to Rome itself, and not to the Senate. It may have been the foundation of the oath sworn to each new Emperor, when the Empire had been firmly established. In 32 it was quite novel. It gave Octavian the moral authority to act as he did against Cleopatra, quite separately from any legal command he might be given. Augustus stated in his *Res Gestae* that the oath was sworn spontaneously by all of Italy, which simple declaration belies a great deal of preparation and paper work, not to mention some little coercion.[30]

The next problem was to declare war in a proper fashion. The excuse was that Cleopatra aimed at domination of the Roman world, and after the Donations of Alexandria and the redistribution of territory that seemed eminently plausible by now, so feelings ran high. It was therefore to be a just war, waged in self-defence, as all Roman wars were said to be, but there must be some ceremonial in declaring it. Octavian revived a very old ritual whereby a patch of earth was designated as enemy territory, and war was declared by throwing a spear into it. Characteristically, Octavian appealed to the distant Roman past to give his actions an unassailable authenticity. It was to be a constant theme of his supremacy that he modernised the Roman world only within the framework of ancient tradition, unsullied by foreign values or practices. That was where Antony had gone wrong, and his fate should be a lesson to all.

Antony spent the winter of 32–31 at Patrae, on the north coast of Achaea, watching over the Gulf of Corinth.[31] His troops were strung out along the coast of Greece from Corcyra to Methone, with the largest force camped near the Gulf of Ambracia. Two peninsulas, like encircling arms, guarded the narrow channel into the waters of the gulf. Antony's men watched the entrance from the southern peninsula, near Actium, which gave its name to the battle. Antony had built up a huge fleet of about 500 ships, perhaps the largest that had ever operated in one war. He had about eleven legions, though Plutarch says that he had sixteen; they were not all at full strength, but he had also recruited native levies, especially cavalry, so in terms of numbers he had no serious worries.[32] He had organised food depots and his naval communications were good, but he had to guard the long craggy coast of Greece with all its inlets and landing places. That was to prove an impossible task, and naturally reduced the number of ships and personnel at his disposal at the battle of Actium.

Antony had probably decided against repeating the pattern of the two previous civil wars, where battles were fought on land. He clung to the coast and did not withdraw into Macedonia, nor did he really pay much attention to the hinterland. Consequently he had little or no communication with the land to the rear of his army, but instead faced resolutely and exclusively westwards. He has been accused of putting the security of Egypt before everything else, or even worse, it has been suggested that he was primarily concerned for his own and Cleopatra's personal safety. The ancient sources for the campaign strategy and the battle of Actium are meagre, which leaves many questions unanswered. High sounding literature about it abounds, but it is retrospective and laudatory, epoch-making in intent and quite out of proportion with the actual events. It seems that there was no heroic battle but a series of skirmishes on land and a few exchanges at sea. Antony is portrayed almost as a man in a dream, completely unable to develop or carry out a plan.

From the evidence of the ancient writers, if what has come down to us can be called evidence, it is not feasible to reconstruct a coherent account of the campaign. It was a long and drawn out affair lasting for several months, but only some disconnected details are known. Antony did not use his fleet to engage Octavian at sea while he crossed from Italy in the spring of 31, but allowed him to sail unopposed from Brundisium across the Adriatic, and land most of his army not far from the point where Caesar disembarked in 48. Octavian's army and the fleet then progressed southwards down the coast, and Octavian himself was able to set up a base at Corfu, because the Antonian ships had withdrawn from the island. Quite rapidly, Octavian arrived at the northern peninsula of the Gulf of Ambracia. His first thought would have been to try to gain control over the mouth of the gulf, but it was too well defended by Antony's troops.[33] Octavian moved off further up the northern peninsula and dug in at Mikhalitzi. It may have been part of Antony's plan to lure him to the gulf, so that he could choose the battle ground himself, but if so he gained no advantage from it.

Antony and the bulk of his army joined the troops on the southern peninsula, made camp and almost immediately afterwards crossed the mouth of the gulf with the allied cavalry and some of the legionaries to try to cut off Octavian's camp from its water supply, but the attack failed, because Antony's native troops deserted to Octavian. A second attempt, led by Antony in person also failed because this time even Amyntas, who had been made king of Galatia thanks to Antony, went over to Octavian. Presumably very dispirited, Antony ferried his troops back over the entrance to the gulf and camped once again on the southern peninsula. The narrative sounds suspiciously simple, as though everything that Antony did was a supreme failure, but coin evidence shows that at some point he was hailed as Imperator by the troops. The coin issue dates to 31 but the dating of the proclamation by the troops is not secure; it could belong to a previous achievement, but equally it could indicate that Antony did enjoy at least one victory during the Actium campaign.[34] Perhaps the attempt to blockade and cut off Octavian's camp was not such a shambles as it has been described. There may have been some hard fighting which Octavian would rather have forgotten. One of the main problems is that there is no properly established chronology for the whole campaign, and only Octavian's successes are elaborated upon. Antony's little excursion across the gulf is made to seem transitory and wasteful.

Marcus Vipsanius Agrippa commanded Octavian's fleet, very practised and confident after the victory at Naulochus four and a half years earlier. He used his expertise and his fleet to good effect, first capturing Methone and gaining a base in the Peloponnese, and then going on to annihilate the Antonian ships at Leucas. Shortly afterwards he took Patrae and then Corinth, cutting off Antony's connections with Alexandria.[35] This left Agrippa's fleet free to block the mouth of the Gulf of Ambracia, where Antony's ships were bottled up. Sosius tried to break out with at least a part of the Antonian fleet, but he was defeated and driven back.[36] Thus from the landward side and then from the sea Agrippa and Octavian were able to tighten the circle around Antony, creating considerable difficulties for him in receiving supplies.[37] Octavian meanwhile built two walls from his camp to the sea, and thereby secured his own supplies.

Antony's most pressing need at the opening of the campaign was for a quick victory over Octavian, either on land or over the fleet. Once he had lost the initiative, he also seems to have lost the momentum. He needed to bring Octavian to battle, and perhaps stayed too long in trying to force the issue. By remaining at Actium instead of marching away and making Octavian follow or wait for him to come back, Antony had sealed his own doom. The position of his camp was not very salubrious, and his troops began to fall sick. Malaria and dysentery caused havoc as the hot weather arrived,[38] and morale plummeted to rock bottom. More of Antony's once trusted officers deserted him, including even Domitius Ahenobarbus, who was ill, and Dellius, who had a particular talent for discerning the precise moment to choose the winning side, having done it twice already. The demoralising effect on Antony must have been tremendous.[39]

The reasons for the continual desertions have not been elucidated in great detail. The allied levies of infantry and cavalry may have been subverted by Octavian long before he arrived at Actium. Inscriptions such as those from Aphrodisias show that Octavian was no stranger to the cities of the east, and that he could give what amounted to direct orders to them without reference to Antony. In that case he would have found it reasonably easy to infiltrate the consciousness of the ruling classes of several cities and states via his agents. How the various kings and high officials viewed him would depend very much on his successes at Rome and in his Illyrian campaigns, and very much more on his own self promotion and the amounts of money he could offer them. He would need to convince them that he was the most eminently dependable man, whiter than white, who could guarantee and support their future prosperity and security. One of the principal tools that he used in Rome was fear and loathing of Cleopatra, and he no doubt harped on the same theme in the east. It would be easy enough to keep agents on his payroll to whisper into the ears of Antony's allies, and the petty kings and noble rulers whom he had set up, that their future survival may be threatened if Antony succeeded in subduing Parthia and still kept up his association with Cleopatra. The Queen's track record so far would only support the suspicions. She had milked the prosperous areas of the east for whatever she felt that Egypt needed, and her influence over Antony was taken as read. The Donations of Alexandria would have been viewed by the eastern kings and princes with great suspicion, especially since there were already five offspring on whom it was likely that Antony would bestow further kingdoms, and it was quite possible that more children, all potential monarchs, might be born in the future. The fact that Antony had not succumbed to all Cleopatra's demands would carry no weight at all, once the initial misgivings were planted in men's minds.

It is notable that when Octavian turned his full attention to the east after the fall of Alexandria, he made few changes to the arrangements and dispositions that Antony had made. One reason is undoubtedly that Antony had been eminently sensible in his choice of rulers and officials, and had reorganised territorial boundaries with intelligence. Another reason might be that Octavian had already had some longstanding dialogue with these rulers before he annihilated Antony, offering them as their rewards continued unassailable sovereignty in their domains. All he had to do was to convince them that there was a real danger of territorial encroachment by Cleopatra, and then promise to protect them from it. Thus the oaths of loyalty that the allies swore to Antony in 31 were probably empty promises from the very beginning.

The Roman officers and senators who deserted to Octavian may have entertained the same fears once they saw Cleopatra in action. It is possible that they arrived on the scene with stories and rumours embedded in their minds that they were initially prepared to doubt, but then they would find that some of the tales were true. Even if they merely saw the innocuous traits, it would set them wondering if the more damaging stories may also be true. After the serious desertions of men like Dellius and Domitius Ahenobarbus, the remaining officers would feel very nervous. Antony further alienated both his allies and his senatorial colleagues by torturing Iamblichus, the king commanding his Arabian contingents, and by executing the senator Quintus Postumius.[40] It may have been necessary to assert himself and try to restore discipline, but the effect on those still with him would only have been to increase their doubts about whether they were on the right side in this war.

Canidius remained, and in a meeting of the high command he voted for a retreat eastwards into Macedonia, and then fighting a land battle, but that meant abandoning the huge fleet. Without it, there would be no means of getting back to Egypt except on foot, probably fighting all the way. According to Dio, Cleopatra considered that the best plan of action would be to garrison strategic locations, and use the ships to break out from Actium with the rest of the troops, not in secret, as if they were afraid, and not openly in case they should seem to be running away, but as if they were intended to fight a battle, and they could then force their way through the expected resistance and sail away.[41]

Since they were effectively blockaded in the Gulf of Ambracia, and the land behind them was a not much more that a malarial swamp, there was no other feasible solution. Antony committed himself to a break out, disguised as a naval battle. Since many of the sailors and soldiers had perished from disease, he could not man all his ships, so he selected the best ones and burnt the rest. It became an exercise in damage limitation, with a slight possibility that the break out might be converted into a real battle, one that Antony could even win. He ordered the crews to take their sails with them, and put on board his treasure chests. He said that the ships would need their sails to pursue the enemy in the open sea, but it is equally true that they would need sails to escape. Another possible explanation for the sails is that Antony intended to make use of the freshening winds that usually blew up in the afternoons, to enable him to get round Agrippa's fleet and turn it, rolling it up against the shore.

The weather was too unsettled to begin the proceedings until 2 September, when there was a calmer interlude in the morning. Antony came out in strength, putting himself and his flagship on his right, with which he tried to turn the enemy left commanded by Agrippa.[42] The two lines held their positions for a while, rowing now and then to keep their places. Agrippa made no move to close with Antony, so eventually the latter had to make a choice, to attack or to return to harbour. He moved forward with the right, leaving the slower centre behind. The race was now on, with Agrippa's left and Antony's right gradually stretching out, each trying to outdo the other. They engaged quite fiercely and there were losses on either side. Then in the rear, some of Antony's ships turned and went back into harbour, and Cleopatra, perhaps ordered to do so, took advantage of the thinning of the centre line,[43] and turned southwards to escape with a few ships. On her flagship the *Antonia*, she carried the treasure chests and probably important documents, and it may have been prearranged that if the battle did not go in Antony's favour, then she should sail for Alexandria.[44]

Her departure left Antony's right unsupported and hard pressed. His own ship was in the thick of the fighting, and when the time came to escape he could not safely disengage. He left the flagship and transferred to a smaller craft, and was rowed away to join Cleopatra's ship. In all, out of about 500 ships, he escaped to Egypt with perhaps less than 100. It is hardly surprising that Octavian made such political mileage out of the story via his literary circle, primarily his court poets, Vergil and Horace. Good poetry, shame about the facts.

Though the battle of Actium was over, as so often, the war was not yet won. Like Pompey after the battle of Pharsalus, Antony could base himself in Egypt, regain his strength, and regroup his army, which Canidius was to lead overland from Greece to Egypt. But reconstitution of a defeated fleet and army required energy, and from the moment when Antony transferred to Cleopatra's ship, his determination evaporated. Except for a brief attack by Octavian's pursuing ships, which he successfully evaded, Antony spent the entire voyage of three days in the bows of the ship, silent and probably beyond words. He had known defeat before, but had always revived his own and his soldiers' spirits, and emerged fighting fit, ready for anything, without losing credibility or the faith of the soldiers. This time he offered his friends money and the means of escape, which indicates that he thought his cause was lost, and he did not want to bring his friends down with him.[45] By now he was becoming accustomed to desertions, so perhaps he wanted to pre-empt any further disappointment by weeding out those who wished to leave before he reached Egypt. He could not know it yet, but Canidius's troops were purchased by Octavian's messengers, who caught up with them on their march. Mindful only of their own fate, the soldiers wrangled for profitable terms for seven days and eventually Octavian agreed to all that they asked. Negotiation was better than fighting unnecessarily, as both sides knew perfectly well, and Octavian gambled on making promises now and hoping to be able to fulfil them later. Canidius refused to join Octavian, and went on to join Antony in Egypt. His attachment to Antony ensured that when Octavian caught up with him again, he received no mercy. Hopefully, Antony appreciated the qualities of this loyal officer, and did not believe the rumour that Octavian spread that Antony's troops fought bravely but were betrayed when Canidius ran away.[46]

Approaching the coast of northern Africa, Antony and Cleopatra could not be certain of their reception in Egypt. They landed first at a small harbour far to the west of Alexandria, while they sounded out the state of affairs in the city, which was calm and ready to receive the Queen, and whether the legions of Cyrenaica were still favourable to Antony. They were not. Cleopatra sailed back to Alexandria, where she quickly asserted herself. There was no hint of the defeat at Actium as she entered the city; her ships were decorated for victory, and her demeanour was not subdued. She executed Artavasdes of Armenia, which would serve as an example to secure the loyalties of his rival Artavasdes of Media. For a while, Antony remained in the western desert. His state of mind can only be guessed.

It was certain that Octavian would eventually bring the war to Egypt, so there was much to be done before he arrived. Antony had little to hope for. His dreams of founding an eastern Empire, if he had ever entertained any, were shattered with the failure at Actium. He had probably never entertained any ambition for sole rule and mastery of Rome, but it was clear now that he had made his worst error in leaving the western half of the Roman world to Octavian. Unable to take any action, he built himself a little retreat on the shoreline, and called it the Timoneum, after Timon of Athens, whose claim to fame was his rejection of humanity and his life as a hermit.[47] For the moment he abandoned Cleopatra who had now to make preparation for the defence of her kingdom and her children, as well as her own life, by her own efforts. She did what she could to organise a united defence, presenting Caesarion to the people as Ptolemy XV, and at the same time Antyllus was recognised as an adult, by the Roman ceremony of assuming the *toga virilis*, exchanging his boy's clothing for the dress of a man. The purpose of declaring the two boys the adult heirs of the Queen of Egypt and her consort Antony was probably to foster the appearance of continuity, to give the impression that she thought there was a future to plan for. She tried to revive Antony by the usual methods – parties, drinking, and late night revels. He joined in, but the Society of Inimitable Livers was replaced now by the Society of the Inseparables at Death. His attitude was justifiable. He had pared down his associates to those who would perhaps remain with him, and he knew that this time it would be to the bitter end, which he anticipated would probably not be long in coming.

Octavian spent most of the winter on the island of Samos, interrupted by a hasty visit to Italy to settle disturbances there caused by the settlement of veterans. His friends Maecenas and Agrippa were unable to bring the situation under control. There was perhaps another problem. At some time which is not established beyond doubt, the younger Lepidus tried to raise revolt against Octavian on behalf of his father, who was still powerless and disgraced, living in enforced retirement on his estates. Some scholars prefer to date this event to the following year, and there is no way of proving whether it occurred before or after the fall of Alexandria. Whenever it happened, it is eloquent testimony to the fact that Octavian was not universally accepted in Italy or Rome, but it is also testimony to the fact that he was powerful enough to end attempts at opposition quite smoothly.

During the winter, embassies sped back and forth between Octavian and Antony,[48] and perhaps separately between Octavian and Cleopatra. Antony promised to do away with himself if Octavian would guarantee the safety of Cleopatra. If the story is true, it shows that he had lost all hope. He had lost most of his army to Octavian's bribery, and he could not trust the soldiers who were left, so he could not win the war. A return to Rome to win over the Senate and Italy was out of the question now that he understood how deeply ingrained prejudice against him had become. Instead he resorted to noble and heroic gestures, ultimately useless even if his proposal of suicide had been accepted. Perhaps he thought that once he was removed from the scene, Octavian could assume command of the entire Roman world, and there was just a slight chance that Egypt might remain independent. Octavian corroborated this judgement by writing to Cleopatra, offering lenient terms if she would lay down her arms and surrender Antony. She refused, either because she loved Antony very deeply, as he perhaps loved her in offering his life for hers, or because they both knew that what Octavian really wanted was Egypt itself, and he meant to have it no matter that he might have to scramble over their dead bodies to get it. Cleopatra judged from her own experience of treachery, intrigue and distrust, perfectly aware that Octavian would accept the surrender of Antony and then quickly find some excuse to renege on the terms he made with her. Now that all was lost, she would rather keep faith with Antony.

It is indicative of the success of Cleopatra's policies towards the people of Egypt that the whole country was united in its support for her. There were rumours of an intended uprising of the people on her behalf. She had always attended to the needs of the populace, to a far greater extent than the previous Ptolemies, and if she had given the word, there would have been an army of common people, marching to Alexandria, ready to do her bidding. She refused the offer, most likely because she did not want to involve her people in war and then subject them to the punishment that Octavian would hand out. She guessed correctly that Octavian would leave the people to get on with their lives if he could divert Egypt's wealth into his own coffers. One of the greatest worries that beset Octavian was that Cleopatra might destroy all her treasure before he could seize it.[49] He required astronomical sums of money to fulfil all the promises he had made to his own troops, to Antony's soldiers that he had bought, and to his allies. There was another factor in that control of the surplus food that Egypt could well afford would be of enormous advantage to him.

In the spring of 30 Octavian was ready to carry the war into Egypt. He returned to Greece and marched overland, reaching his objective by July. Cleopatra sent Caesarion, now aged sixteen, on a journey up the Nile into Upper Egypt, perhaps intending that he should cross the Red Sea, or travel into Ethiopia, and reach relative safety.[50] It must have been a heartbreaking moment, in a life which had witnessed so many similar moments and difficult decisions. The fact that she sent him away at this juncture reveals how little faith she had in her own and Antony's ability to win the war. She could not raise a fresh army, she would not rouse the populace to fight for her, and she did not trust Octavian to keep his word in any negotiations he might propose. She entertained few doubts about Caesarion's fate if and when he came face to face with Octavian.

Before the final engagement in battle between Antony and Octavian, one of Octavian's officers, Cornelius Gallus, attacked Egypt from the west. Antony took a squadron of ships and some infantry to meet him, but was defeated and lost the ships. In the east, Cleopatra's general Seleucus half-heartedly defended Pelusium, but gave up and let Octavian's troops pass by unopposed. Antony rallied, took some cavalry to clash with Octavian's advance guard, which he routed, and sent them fleeing back to the main army. He returned to Alexandria flushed with success, celebrating his victory in the old style.

But it was all desperate bravado. Antony knew when he was beaten. Allegedly he challenged Octavian to single combat, and received the supercilious reply that he could find better ways to die. The battle was to take place next day, on the first day of the month Sextilis, later renamed August, in honour of Octavian when he was awarded the title Augustus. Antony told his friends the night before the battle that he could not hope to win, and was merely looking for an honourable death. That same night, haunting music was heard in the streets of Alexandria, together with the noise of a procession of unseen people leaving the city by the eastern gate – the god Dionysus and his revellers deserting Antony, before he finally fell.

The next morning the army on the high ground at the Canopus gate watched the fleet sail out to engage Octavian's ships. They put up no fight. There was probably a prearranged signal, or perhaps some quick thinking captains copied each other in quick succession, as Antony's crews put up their oars and waited. Then the two fleets became one fleet as Antony's ships sailed towards Octavian's and joined them. The soldiers had perhaps expected something of the sort, and may even have known that it was going to happen. There was no reason why they should sacrifice themselves for a defeated man. If they went over to Octavian now, they would perhaps obtain good terms from him, rather than arousing his anger if they opposed him. The cavalry rode off with their swords sheathed. The legionaries fought desultorily for a while, then surrendered or ran away.

Antony rode back to Alexandria. It is said that he wondered if Cleopatra had betrayed him. She had retired to her mausoleum and barricaded the door, so when Antony was told that she was already dead, he had no real reason to doubt the story. He asked his slave Eros to kill him, but Eros killed himself instead, so Antony fell on his sword. Even a quick death deserted Antony, for he only succeeded in wounding himself painfully. When he had revived sufficiently for Cleopatra's slaves to communicate with him, he learned that she was not dead after all, but was waiting for him, so he had himself carried to her mausoleum on a stretcher. Somehow Cleopatra and her two servants Iras and Charmian hauled him up to the level of the window and dragged him inside. The romantic death in Cleopatra's arms is probably true.[51] Even if it could be proved beyond all doubt that it never happened that way, no one would be convinced. How and why the central characters arrived at this desperate point can be reinterpreted, amended, debated and disputed, but once they *had* arrived at that point, history shades off into legend, more enduring than mere prosaic fact.

Cleopatra survived for a few days after Antony's death. Octavian negotiated with her, and both Plutarch and Dio say that he went to see her in her mausoleum, but the story was probably invented in order to present historical points of view through the mouths of the main participants.[52] Cleopatra died most likely according to the traditional story, by the bite of the poisonous asp, which may have been arranged by or in consultation with Octavian. As soon as he heard of her death he sent for the *psylli* who were trained to suck out the poison from snake bites, a very prescient reaction if Cleopatra's death was supposed to have taken him by surprise. It is possible that Octavian allowed Cleopatra to choose her own way of death because it relieved him of the necessity of executing her.[53] From Cleopatra's point of view there was deep religious significance, since the bite of the asp bestowed divinity on the victim. In death, Cleopatra outdid anything that the Romans could have dreamed up for her. She was dressed in all her finery and wore her crown, which her devoted servants carefully arranged just before they too died with her. The whole scene is quite credible for a Queen who knew how important it was to cultivate and maintain an image.

A tradition survived that Octavian wanted to preserve Cleopatra alive for his triumph in Rome, but it is probably make-believe. It was much tidier to remove all possible contenders for the throne of Egypt, and take it over unopposed. The sympathies of the Egyptian people for their Queen might cause problems if she were allowed to survive, and those sympathies could also extend to her children. Caesarion was hunted down and killed. As heir to the Egyptian throne, and as Caesar's son, his fate was a foregone conclusion. Antony's son Antyllus, who was only fourteen years old, was dragged out of hiding and killed on the spot.[54]

Octavian spared the three younger children of Antony and Cleopatra. Alexander Helios, Cleopatra Selene, and Ptolemy Philadelphus were sent to Rome. Eventually Cleopatra Selene was married to king Juba of Mauretania and lived out the rest of her life in North Africa. The two boys may have gone with her, or they may have remained in Rome, keeping a low profile, but their ultimate fates are unknown. Iullus Antonius, Antony's second son by Fulvia, had a promising career, being married to Marcella, Octavia's daughter by her first husband. He was consul in 10, and went on to govern the province of Asia from 7 to 6. Unfortunately, he was implicated in a scandalous affair in 2 when Augustus' daughter Julia was accused of adultery with several eminent men. Julia was exiled. Iullus Antonius was executed, along with several of Julia's many other alleged lovers.

Besides his enduring administration, Antony left a personal legacy to the eastern kingdoms. His daughter by his first wife Antonia married Pythodorus, a wealthy Greek nobleman of Tralles, and in turn their daughter Pythodoris married Polemo of Pontus, and then Archelaus of Cappadocia. Her descendants became kings and queens of various states in the east. Antony had two more daughters by Octavia, Antonia major and Antonia minor. The elder Antonia married Lucius Domitius Ahenobarbus, the son of Ahenobarbus who deserted Antony before Actium. Gnaeus Domitius Ahenobarbus, the son of Antonia and Lucius, married his cousin Agrippina, and they produced the future Emperor Nero, who was thus Antony's great-grandson, but not exactly a credit to his illustrious ancestor. The younger Antonia married into Augustus's own household. Her husband was Drusus, the brother of Tiberius who succeeded Augustus as Emperor. Tiberius and Drusus were the sons of Livia and her husband Tiberius Claudius Nero, and became the stepsons of Augustus when he married Livia. Antonia minor and Drusus were the parents of the Emperor Claudius and his brother Germanicus, and the grandparents, through Germanicus, of Caligula, perhaps even less of a credit to Antony than Nero. Fortunately Claudius inherited his grandfather Antony's talents for sensible administration, his energy when engaged in any of his wide ranging projects, and his regard for humanity and humane treatment of those whom he considered deserving. Claudius could be cruel, like Antony, but also like Antony, he tried to be fair and just, and could be very generous. Antony would have approved of him.

Octavian honoured the last wishes of both Antony and Cleopatra and buried them side by side. Their tomb has never been found. Immediately afterwards, Octavian took over Egypt as his own preserve. He installed as governor the general Cornelius Gallus, who had attacked from the west in co-ordination with Octavian's advance from the east. Gallus was not a senator, but a member of the middle classes, the equites. Such an elevated command for an equestrian was an innovation, perhaps a hasty measure adopted because Gallus was on the spot and Octavian needed a suitable governor very quickly. If such it was, it became a regular equestrian post, one of the most sought after rewards of the equestrian career. Octavian-Augustus never readjusted the position of the governor of Egypt, nor the relationship of the province to himself. No senator was allowed to enter the country except by special dispensation from himself, and later Emperors saw no reason to relax this vigilance. Much of Rome's corn supply came from Egypt, and its wealth enabled Augustus to maintain his position in Rome, discharging his debts and paying all the promised donatives to his supporters and troops.

He could afford to be generous to the memory of Cleopatra, after having deliberately fomented war against her. The statue that Caesar had placed in the temple of Venus was allowed to remain there, and an Egyptian official, Cleopatra's friend Archibius, paid 1,000 talents to Octavian to save most of the other statues and portraits of her. Antony did not fare so well. The news of his death was read out in the Senate by Cicero's son Marcus. It cannot have been merely a fortuitous choice of reader. The Senate declared Antony's birthday *nefastus*, and decreed that all statues, busts and portraits of him should be destroyed. The few items which remain may perhaps have been overlooked, or they may even be wrongly identified by modern scholars. Only the coin portraits can legitimately claim to be unequivocal representations of Antony. His name was to be erased from all monuments all over the Roman world, and in their zeal to comply, some provincials chiselled out the name Antonius wherever it seemed to be connected to the name Marcus, perhaps because Octavian had decided that such thoroughness was only right and proper. Thus Antony's memory was damned for ever, and the world was instructed to forget about him. The world, however, did not comply. Many of the details are lost, but Mark Antony has never been forgotten, transformed from a historical political and military figure into a legendary lover, and eternally united with the Queen of Egypt, Cleopatra VII.

Notes

Chapter 1: Caesar's Lieutenant

1 Cicero (*Philippics*, 2.44) uses Antony's dissolute youth to discredit him. Plutarch (*Antony*, 2) blames Antony's friend Curio for leading him astray, setting the scene for a portrayal of Antony as weak and easily influenced by others (Pelling 1988, 118). Antony's dependence on strong women like Fulvia and Cleopatra probably stems from the strong character of his mother Julia (Huzar, 1978, 21).

2 Plutarch, *Antony*, 86.8.

3 A birth date in 83 is the more widely accepted alternative. This date would make Antony more or less the right age for the posts he occupied throughout his career, and coins issued in 43 and 42 support the date, since they bear the numerals 40 and 41, presumably Antony's age at those times (Pelling, 1988, 322). Chamoux (1986, 14) says that the coin evidence is not certain.

4 Appian (*Civil Wars*, 5.8) says that Antony was forty years old when he met Cleopatra at Tarsus, but both Pelling (1988, 322) and Chamoux (1986, 14) agree that this is a rounded figure.

5 Dio, 51.19.

6 Antony's grandfather, Antonius the orator, taught the young Cicero, who acknowledged him in his book on the making of an orator (Huzar, 1978, 14–15). Appian (*Civil Wars*, 1.72) tells the story of Antonius's death.

7 Plutarch, *Antony*, 1.

8 Pelling (1988, 117) says that the title Creticus was probably awarded to disguise the disaster. Huzar (1978, 15–16) labels Antony's father as an 'amicable incompetent' and interprets Creticus as a derisive title.

9 Cicero (*Brutus*, 235; 311) says Lentulus was an undistinguished orator and describes how he came back to Rome with Sulla. In a letter to Atticus describing the trial of Clodius, he says that Lentulus was twice acquitted, indicating that he was just as much of a bad lot as Clodius and Catilina (*Letters to Atticus*, 1.16).

10 Hybrida was prosecuted in 77 or 76 by Caesar, for extortion in Greece (Plutarch, *Caesar*, 4.1). He appealed to the tribunes and escaped condemnation but was ejected from the Senate a few years later (Huzar, 1978, 16).

11 Plutarch (*Pompey*, 26) says that Pompey was allowed 24 legates; Appian (*Mithridatica*, 94) sets the number at 25.

12 Dio (36.22) emphasises the seriousness of pirate activity before Pompey was appointed, and Rickman (1980, 5) explains how the corn supply of Rome was affected. See also, Plutarch *Pompey* 25-29; Appian, *Mithridatica*, 94–96; Dio, 36.37; Seager, 1979, 32–3; Greenhalgh, 1980, 77-80; de Souza, 1999, 97–148, 161–178.

13 Plutarch, *Pompey*, 30-42; Appian, *Mithridatica*, 97–119; Dio, 36.45–54; 47.1–23. Cicero argued for the appointment of Pompey in a published speech, *De Imperio Gn. Pompeii*.

14 Brunt, 1971, 127–131; Shotter, 1994, 56–60; Syme, 1939, 89.

15 The major ancient sources on the conspiracy of Catiline are Cicero's *In Catilinam*, which is naturally very biased, and Sallust's *The War with Catiline*; see also Appian, *Civil Wars*, 2.2–7. For reassessment and references see Gruen 1974; Wiseman 1992.

16 Gruen (1974, 138) says that fear of competitors does not fully explain the election of Cicero.

17 The so-called first conspiracy of Catilina: in summer 65, Cicero wrote to Atticus that he was thinking about defending Catilina (*Letters to Atticus*, 1.2), but by the time he made his electioneering speech in 64 he said that Catilina was implicated in a plot to assassinate the incoming consuls of 65, Lucius Aurelius Cotta and Lucius Manlius Torquatus. It is all very doubtful, especially as Torquatus defended Catiline in a later trial.

18 Appian, *Civil Wars*, 2.2.

19 Appian, *Civil Wars*, 2.4.

20 Appian, *Civil Wars*, 2.5.

21 Cicero (*Philippics*, 2.18) refers to Antony's accusation, and Pelling (1988, 118) points out that Cicero does not say that the other condemned conspirators were properly buried.

22 Cicero, *Philippics*, 2.48.

23 Cicero (*Philippics*, 2.44–47) devotes several paragraphs to Antony's alleged homosexual behaviour. Antony's accusation that Octavian sold his favours is related by Suetonius (*Augustus*, 68).

24 Appian (*Civil Wars*, 2.9) dates the association of the three men to 60, when Pompey and Crassus supported Caesar at the consular elections for 59; he describes how Varro wrote a pamphlet called *Tricaranus*, the Three Headed Monster, referring to the three powerful men.

25 Appian, *Civil Wars*, 2.15; Gruen, 1974; 244–46; 255–58; 294–99; Syme, 1939, 228; 244–6; 255–6.

26 Cicero reported to Atticus (*Letters to Atticus*, 1.12; 1.13) that a man in woman's clothing had been discovered at the Bona Dea ceremony, naming him in the first letter but not the second. Appian (*Civil Wars*, 2.14) says that Caesar refused to testify against Clodius, and made him tribune, implying that he already had plans to use him in this way in January 61 when the scandal occurred. In a letter written in January 60, Cicero (*Letters to Atticus*, 1.18) knew of the plans to transfer Clodius into the plebeian class .

27 Cyprus was part of the Ptolemaic Empire and was annexed by Rome on the pretext that the Mediterranean pirates were sheltered there.

28 Dio, 38.14.4; Appian, *Civil Wars*, 2.15–16; Plutarch, *Cicero*, 30.4. On his way to Brundisium Cicero received a copy of the bill on or before 13 April 58, and learned that an amendment had been made, extending banishment beyond 400 miles from Rome (*Letters to Atticus*, 3.4).

29 Plutarch, *Antony*, 2.7. The date is merely inferred from the context Pelling, 1988, 119. Cicero (*Philippics*, 2.48) describes Antony's split with Clodius but gives no reason for it, and does not mention Antony's journey to Greece.

30 Plutarch, *Antony*, 2.8.

31 Suetonius, *Augustus*, 86.2–3.

32 Dio, 50.17.

33 Plutarch, *Antony*, 3.2 inflates Antony's role; see Pelling, 1988, 121.

34 Suetonius, *Julius Caesar*, 54.3.

35 The story that Gabinius received ten thousand talents is polemical (Pelling, 1988, 121), and more than Caesar himself is said to have received from Ptolemy Auletes. Grant (1972, 16) suggests that Ptolemy expected Gabinius would make up the full amount by plunder and bribes; Huzar (1978, 32) says that Rabirius would be able to pay Gabinius from the taxes he collected.

36 Plutarch, *Antony*, 4.1–3.

37 Appian, *Civil Wars*, 5.8.

38 Reporting on the so-called conference at Lucca a few years later Cicero (*Letters to his Friends*, 1.9) says that Caesar had already talked with Crassus at Ravenna a short while before Pompey went to Lucca to meet him. Appian implies (*Civil Wars*, 2.17) that Caesar, Pompey and Crassus all conferred together at Lucca.

39 Caesar, *Gallic War*, 7.81.

40 Gruen (1974, 494–5) points out that Caesar's statement after Pharsalus that he

would have been prosecuted and had to defend himself is merely self-justification for the war, but it has embedded itself irretrievably in the views of modern historians. Gruen thinks it unlikely that Caesar would have been brought to trial, since there is no mention in Cicero's correspondence of any impending case being prepared against Caesar.

41 Cicero, *Philippics*, 2.49.

42 Cicero, *Philippics*, 2.21; 2.49; Dio, 45.40.

43 Appian (*Civil Wars*, 2.19;23) says that it was thought that Pompey was waiting for the situation to worsen, so that he would be made dictator, but he was satisfied with the sole consulship.

44 Cicero (*Letters to Atticus*, 8.3) refers to the law of ten tribunes in a letter written three years after the event, enumerating how Pompey had striven to keep faith with Caesar and expedite his wishes. On this law and the *lex de iure magstratuum* see Gruen, 1974, 455–58.

45 Gruen, 1974, 458.

46 Caesar, *Gallic War*, 8.2.

47 Caesar, *Gallic War*, 8.24.

48 Caesar, *Gallic War*, 8.38.

49 Caesar, *Gallic War*, 8.23.

50 Caesar, *Gallic War*, 8.48.

51 Cicero, *Philippics*, 2.4.

52 Caesar, *Gallic War*, 8.50.

53 Dio, 41.1., Caesar, *Gallic War*, 8.52, written by Aulus Hirtius who makes Curio refer to Pompey's *dominatio et arma*.

54 Caesar, *Gallic War*, 8.50; Plutarch, *Antony*, 5.1; Cicero, *Philippics*, 2.4; 2.51; Cicero, *Letters to his Friends*, 8.14.1. Huzar (1978, 4)3 says that the Pompeians must have realised that Antony as tribune and augur now possessed enormous legal power.

55 Cicero, *Letters to Atticus*, 7.8

56 Dio, 41.3; Caesar, *Civil Wars*, 1.2–5; Plutarch, *Antony*, 5.8.

57 Dio, 41.4, says that when Caesar was informed of events in Rome, he came to Ariminum, crossing the boundary of his province for the first time, thus explaining the very thing that Caesar manages to avoid saying in his published account of the beginning of the civil wars. Rawson (1992, 424) points out that no one knows where the Rubicon ran.

58 Protection of tribunician rights became Caesar's justification for the war, and he makes much of this in the first chapters of the *Civil Wars*. While he was at Ravenna, still in his province, he heard of the tumult in Rome and that the tribunes had fled the city and were coming to join him, and he used this to insert a passage explaining the enormity of silencing and threatening the tribunes (*Civil Wars*, 1.5). He made a speech to the soldiers, once again emphasising the violation

of tribunician rights (*Civil Wars*, 1.7), then he crossed the Rubicon and marched to Ariminum, where Curio, Antony and Cassius joined him (*Civil Wars*, 1.8).

59 Caesar, *Civil Wars*, 1.11.

60 Caesar, *Civil Wars*, 1.18; Cicero, *Letters to Atticus*, 8.4.

61 Caesar, *Gallic War*, 8.52; Dio, 41.4.

62 Dio, 41.18; Appian, *Civil Wars*, 2.41.

63 Cicero (*Letters to Atticus*, 10.8 and 8a) refers to Antony's 'odious letter'.

64 Cicero, *Letters to Atticus*, 10.10.

65 Cicero, *Philippics*, 2.58; *Letters to Atticus*, 10.16.

66 Cicero, *Letters to Atticus*, 10.13.

67 Caesar, *Civil Wars*, 3.10; Appian, *Civil Wars*, 2.45.

68 Caesar, *Civil Wars*, 3.10; Appian, *Civil Wars*, 2.47.

69 Dio, 41.46; Appian, *Civil Wars*, 2.57.

70 Dio (41.46) says that Caesar harboured suspicions that the troops at Brundisium did not put to sea because they were waiting to see who would emerge victorious; Appian (*Civil Wars*, 2.56–7) carries no such tale of suspicion, but says that Caesar tried to go to Italy because he considered that he was the best person to bring the troop ships across the sea.

71 Antony at Brundisium: Caesar, *Civil Wars*, 3. 24–30; Plutarch, *Antony*, 7; Appian, *Civil Wars*, 2.58–59; Dio, 41.48.

72 Caesar, *Civil Wars*, 3.26.

73 Caesar, *Civil Wars*, 3.29.

74 Caesar, *Civil Wars*, 3.30; Dio, 41.49.

75 Caesar, *Civil Wars*, 3.62–65; Dio, 41.50.

76 Caesar, *Civil Wars*, 3.65.

77 Caesar, *Civil Wars*, 3.85–97; Dio, 41.53–61. Appian, *Civil Wars* 70–82. Caesar (*Civil Wars*, 3.89) says that Antony commanded the right wing at Pharsalus, but there is no further mention of him in the account of the battle.

78 Dio, 42.21.

Chapter 2: Caesar's Lover

1 Strabo, 17.796.

2 Grant (1972, 3) suggests that Cleopatra V Tryphaena was the wife of Ptolemy Auletes, and their eldest daughter was Cleopatra VI Tryphaena, contradicting Strabo's statement that there were only three daughters.

3 Plutarch (*Antony*, 27.3–5) describes Cleopatra and her immense charm. Pelling (1988, 190) quotes Becher (1966, 72), who says that this is the most critical

and objective description of Cleopatra in ancient literature. Plutarch was not a contemporary of Antony and Cleopatra but he was only two generations away from people who would be able to remember them. By the third century, the legend of Cleopatra had subsumed reality, and Dio (42.34–35) described her as supremely beautiful, whilst also acknowledging her charms and ability to make herself agreeable to everyone.

4 Caesar (*Civil Wars*, 3.107) reminded his audience that during his consulship an alliance had been formed with Ptolemy Auletes, by law and by a decree of the Senate (*et lege et senatusconsulto societas erat facta*).

5 From January to February 56, Cicero's letters to Publius Lentulus Spinther, who was governor of Cilicia from 56 to 53 (*Letters to his Friends*, 1.1–6) document the changing circumstances with regard to Auletes. In August 56, Cicero opted for immediate action, on the grounds that the Senate originally chose Lentulus to restore Ptolemy, and no senatorial decree had been passed to remove the task from him. Cicero urged to Lentulus to go to Alexandria with troops, pacify the city, then invite Ptolemy to return, so technically he could be said to have been restored without an army (*Letters to his Friends*, 1.7).

6 Strabo, 17.1.11; Cicero, *Pro Caelio*, 10.23.

7 Grant (1972, 16) accepts that Gabinius was offered ten thousand talents, but suggests that not all the money was paid because Auletes expected Gabinius to make good the shortfall by looting; Huzar (1978, 32) suggests that only travelling expenses were paid and the rest would be collected by Rabirius as part of the taxes he gathered. Pelling (1988, 121) doubts the sum and describes it as polemic.

8 Caesar (*Civil Wars*, 3. 103; 110) refers to the troops of Gabinius left behind in Egypt, and describes how they had married local women and raised children, forgetting Roman ways. They fought in the army of Achillas against Caesar in the Alexandrian War.

9 According to Caesar (*Civil Wars*, 3.108) in his will Auletes named his elder daughter and elder son as his heirs, and asked the Roman people to ensure that his wishes were carried out. A copy of the will was sent to Rome to be placed in the Treasury but in the troubled times it could not be stored there and was given to Pompey instead. Another copy was kept in Alexandria under seal. When he installed Cleopatra and Ptolemy XIV as rulers, Caesar referred once again to the will of Auletes, naming his elder son and daughter, but since Ptolemy XIII was dead by this time, he chose the younger boy and arranged a brother–sister marriage between him and Cleopatra (*Alexandrian War* 33). According to Dio (42.35) Caesar read the will to the audience, directing Cleopatra and Ptolemy to live together according to the Egyptian custom.

10 Grant 1972, 29; 254, n.78 quoting H. de Meulanaare, *Chronique d'Egypte* XLII, 1967, 297.

11 There were precedents for keeping the death of the ruler secret: Grant 1972, 30; 254 nn.1–2. Marcus Caelius Rufus wrote to Cicero informing him that the death of Auletes was known at Rome at the beginning of August 51 (Cicero, *Letters to his Friends*, 8.4.5) but Egyptian records of 28 August 51 were issued in Cleopatra's name only, with no mention of Ptolemy XIII (Grant 1972, 47; 256, nn. 49 and 50).

12 Strabo visited Alexandria not long after the deaths of Cleopatra and Antony, and described the city in detail (17.1.8ff). See also Empereur (1998) and La Riche (1996).

13 Caesar acknowledged that no one could enter the great harbour without the consent of those who occupied Pharos island (*Civil Wars*, 3.111).

14 Plutarch *Antony* 27.4–5. Pelling (1988, 191) accepts that Cleopatra spoke Egyptian, but thinks the range of languages is 'suspiciously conventional'.

15. Bradford (1971, 13) says that Cleopatra spoke Latin, but Grant (1972, 258 n.9) points out that there is no proof.

16 Grant 1972, 46–7.

17 Two papyri from different places in Egypt attest that the third year of Cleopatra's reign was the first year of the reign of Ptolemy XIII: *P. Berl.* Inv. 16277 and *P. Lond.* 827.

18 Valerius Maximus (4.1) says that Bibulus sent the culprits who had executed his two sons to the Senate for judgement. Caesar subtly manages to shift the blame for the deaths of Bibulus's sons from the Gabinian troops to the runaway slaves and dissidents in the Alexandrian army (*Civil Wars*, 3.110).

19 Grant, 1972, 49.

20 The only ancient reference to Cleopatra's whereabouts after she was expelled from Alexandria and then the kingdom comes from an account of world history from the Creation to the sixth century, written by the Byzantine John Malalas (*Chronica* 10). No one knows the sources that he used for the tale.

21 Caesar, *Civil Wars*, 3.103.

22 Appian, *Civil Wars*, 2.84.

23 The rolled up carpet story is related by Plutarch (*Caesar* 8); Dio (42.35) merely says that Cleopatra entered the city by night without the knowledge of Ptolemy.

24 Dio (42.34) says that Cleopatra had contacted Caesar through agents, but when she knew his disposition towards women she resolved to meet him.

25 Caesar (*Civil Wars*, 3.107) says that the quarrel of the Egyptian rulers affected the Roman people and himself as consul.

26 According to Dio (42.34–35) Cleopatra set out to seduce Caesar from the very beginning and Caesar was utterly captivated. Appian (*Civil Wars*, 2.90) dismisses the whole Alexandrian episode in one chapter without even hinting that Caesar and Cleopatra were lovers. Caesar himself (*Civil Wars*, 3.108) sedately affirms that before he arrived in Alexandria he sent word that it would please him if Ptolemy

and Cleopatra would settle their differences before him instead of by armed conflict.

27 Dio, 42.35.

28 Dio, (42.35) claims that Caesar granted Cyprus to Arsinoe and the younger Ptolemy because he was full of fear at his predicament in Alexandria, so he not only refused to take over Egypt but gave away parts of the Roman territories as well. Suetonius (*Julius Caesar*, 35) says that Caesar did not annexe Egypt because he foresaw that some ambitious governor could use the wealth of the land and make it a headquarters for rebellion.

29 Grant (1972, 64) portrays Pothinus as a nationalist dedicated to keeping the Romans out of Egypt. Dio (42.36) depicts him as over-ambitious, and already guilty as the prime agitator of the Egyptians.

30 When Achillas brought up the Royal army to Alexandria, Caesar (*Civil Wars*, 3.109–110) says that he took control of Ptolemy to make it seem that the war was being waged by a small group of private individuals. Significantly he does not say that he brought the Queen under his control, nor does he even acknowledge her presence at this stage.

31 Caesar, *Civil Wars*, 3.111.

32 Caesar, *Alexandrian War*, 1.

33 Caesar, *Civil Wars*, 3.110–112.

34 Caesar, *Civil Wars*, 3.112; Dio, 42.40.

35 Appian (*Civil Wars*, 2.90) makes it seem as though Pothinus and Achillas were killed at the same time as soon as Caesar reached Alexandria. Dio (42.36) describes how Pothinus urged Achillas to attack and how Caesar put him to death to prevent him from kidnapping Ptolemy and using him as a figurehead (42.39). In Caesar's account, Pothinus was executed for communicating secretly with Achillas (*Civil Wars*, 3.112).

36 Caesar, *Alexandrian War*, 4; Dio, 42.40.

37 Caesar implies that he took the Pharos island (*Civil Wars* 110–112) but in reality he held only a part of it around the lighthouse (*Alexandrian War*, 17). In the battle for the causeway Caesar had to swim for his life when the Alexandrians repulsed the Romans (*Alexandrian War*, 21). The account is devoid of the heroics added to it by later authors: Plutarch (*Caesar*, 38) relates that Caesar left his cloak behind and the Alexandrians hung it up as a trophy, and also that he swam with one arm, holding aloft some important documents to keep them out of the water. Appian (*Civil Wars*, 90) repeats the story of the cloak used as a trophy and Dio (42.40) includes both tales.

38 Caesar, *Alexandrian War*, 23; Dio 42.42.

39 Caesar, *Alexandrian War*, 27–32; Dio 42.43.

40 Caesar, (*Alexandrian War*, 23) acknowledged the loyalty of Cleopatra who had remained with him in his headquarters (*quae manserat in fide praesidiisque eius*).

41 Dio (42.44) says that Caesar really intended Cleopatra to rule alone, but added Ptolemy to the equation to appease the people who did not want to be ruled by a woman. Then he arranged a marriage between brother and sister as a pretence, to disguise the fact that he was living with Cleopatra himself.

42 According to Appian (*Civil Wars*, 2.90) Caesar and Cleopatra were accompanied on their Nile cruise by 400 ships, and Suetonius (*Julius Caesar*, 52) says that they took an army with them. All this would be appropriate for protection. See Grant (1972, 81) on the political benefits of the cruise.

43 Caesar spent nine months in Egypt from the time he landed at Alexandria to his departure for Syria and war against Pharnaces (Appian, *Civil Wars*, 2.90). Literally interpreted, this ought to mean that he left in July 47. Cicero wrote to Atticus from Brundisium on 19 June 47 (*Letters to Atticus*, 9.18) saying that Caesar had not left Alexandria, but this may simply mean that the news was on its way and had not yet reached Italy. There is evidence that Caesar was already in Syria by June (Grant, 1972, 82).

44 The first reference in the surviving ancient literature to Caesarion is in Cicero's correspondence (*Letters to Atticus*, 14.20) written on 11 May 44, cryptically mentioning that he hoped it was true about Cleopatra and Caesar's son, without elaborating on what had happened. The problem is with the Latin text, which could be read either as *de Caesare filio* or alternatively *de Caesare illo*. If the first interpretation is correct, it does show that Cicero accepted Caesarion as the son of Caesar, since he was not referring to Octavian and the adoption in this context. On the other hand if *illo* is to be preferred, the meaning is altogether different and Grant (1972, 95–6) proposes that Cicero is not referring to Caesarion at all, but 'that Caesar', a child of Caesar's conceived by Cleopatra, but miscarried. The passage follows immediately after a reference to a miscarriage of Tertia, wife of Cassius and half sister of Brutus.

45 Caesarion was born after Caesar left for Syria (Plutarch *Caesar* 49.10). In a passage devoted to Caesar's love affairs, Suetonius (*Julius Caesar* 52.2) says that Caesar allowed Cleopatra to give his name to the son she bore, and that according to some Greek writers Caesarion resembled Caesar in looks and deportment. He goes on to say that Mark Antony declared to the Senate that Caesar had acknowledged Caesarion and several of his friends knew this, including Gaius Matius, and his secretaries Balbus and Oppius. Grant (1972, 84–5) points out, in favour of Caesar as the true father of Caesarion rather than any number of casual lovers, that Ptolemaic women kept their affairs within the Royal family, adding that unlike Roman Imperial women who were murderous and adulterous, Ptolemaic women were murderous and chaste.

46 On the Caesareum see Boethius and Ward-Perkins 1970, 459.

47 See note 43 above on the date of Caesar's departure.

Chapter 3: A Time in Rome

1 Dio, 42.22–25.

2 Antony's administration of Italy 'mingled competence and recklessness' (Huzar 1978, 64) He adopted military dress and wore his sword and armour in public: Dio, 42.27–8. Chamoux (1986, 78) theorises that Antony wanted to accustom people to the appearance of monarchy, prefiguring his attempts to make Caesar accept the crown at the Lupercalia. See also Plutarch *Antony*, 9.3–6; Cicero, *Philippics* 2.61–3; 2.67–8; Dio, 45.28

3 Huzar (1978, 68) says that Antony never thought that he would have to pay for Pompey's house. Cicero (*Philippics*, 2.64, 66–9) accuses Antony of squandering the contents of the house in a matter of days, and in a later passage (*Philippics*, 2.74), of sulking when Caesar forced him to pay for Pompey's house and possessions. He links it with the discovery of an assassin in Caesar's house. Everyone assumed that Antony intended to kill Caesar, and Caesar denounced him in the Senate. No other source backs up this tale. Plutarch (*Antony*, 9.5–8; 10) relates Antony's bad behaviour, but places it in the previous year (Pelling 1988, 137–8).

4 Dio, 42.29–32; Plutarch, *Antony*, 9.3–4.

5 Cicero (*Philippics*, 2.99) attributes Antony's hatred for Dolabella (Cicero's son-in-law) to the fact that he seduced his wife Antonia, for which he denounced Dolabella at a meeting of the Senate on the Kalends of January, but he does not give the year. Pelling (1988, 137) says that Plutarch (*Antony*, 9) invented the context for this without any proof of dating, so that he could use the personal quarrel to underline Antony's objection to Dolabella as colleague.

6 Plutarch *Antony* 10.

7 Dio, 43.19–23; Plutarch, *Caesar*, 55; Suetonius, *Julius Caesar*, 37.

8 Dio, 43.19 describes Arsinoe in Caesar's triumph, saying she was spared for the sake of her brothers, and in another passage he says that it was her brothers, again in the plural who were dragged from the sanctuary at Ephesus and killed on the orders of Antony and Cleopatra. Appian (*Civil Wars*, 5.9) says that Arsinoe was killed at Miletus in the sanctuary of Artemis. Plutarch omits the story altogether (Pelling, 1988, 192).

9 Grant (1972, 83–4) suggests an inscription from Memphis naming King Ptolemy Caesar and a birth date of 23 June refers to Caesarion. He admits that the inscription has no other date and could belong to any period, so that the title could be that of any of the later Roman Emperors, and also if it does concern Caesarion it was presumably set up after 44, when he did become king. Extrapolating further, Grant assumes that the date of 23 June is reckoned on the new solar calendar, after Caesar changed from the lunar calendar in 46. This means that on the old Roman reckoning, Caesarion would have been born in

September 47, which means that he was less than a month old when Caesar held his four triumphs, and therefore Cleopatra was not in Rome at the time.

10 Dio, 43.27

11 Antony married Fulvia at an unknown date between 47 and 45. Cicero (*Philippics*, 2.70 and 77) implies that Antony carried on his affair with the actress Cytheris even after he married Fulvia. On Fulvia see also Plutarch, *Antony* 10; Appian, *Civil Wars*, 4.29; Dio, 47.8.

12 Dio, 41.1; Gelzer, 1968, 287ff for Caesar's legislation and reforms at this time.

13 Cicero, *Letters to Atticus*, 12. 18a; *Philippics*, 2.76–7.

14 Plutarch, *Antony*, 10.

15 Cicero, *Philippics*, 2.77.

16 Cicero, *Philippics*, 2.34, implies that Antony consented to the plot to kill Caesar when Trebonius approached him.

17 Plutarch, *Antony*, 11; Cicero, *Philippics*, 2.78.

18 Huzar, 1978, 74.

19 Plutarch, *Antony*, 11.3; Cicero, *Philippics*, 2.79–84.

20 It was rumoured that Caesar was going to move the capital to Alexandria or Ilium (Suetonius, *Julius Caesar*, 79) and that he was going to marry Cleopatra (Nicolaus of Damascus, *Life of Augustus*, 28).

21 The tribune Helvius Cinna said that Caesar had asked him to present a bill to the people allowing Caesar to marry any woman in order to beget children (Suetonius, *Julius Caesar*, 52).

22 Suetonius, *Julius Caesar*, 76; Appian, *Civil Wars*, 2.106; Dio, 43.44.

23 Antony as *flamen dialis* and priest of the Lupercal: Huzar 1978, 76. Caesar created several patricians to fill the ranks depleted by the civil wars (Suetonius, *Julius Caesar*, 41). See also Weinstock, 1971.

24 The Lupercalia incident: Suetonius, *Julius Caesar*, 79; Appian, *Civil Wars*, 2.109; Plutarch, *Antony*, 12; Cicero, *Philippics*, 2.85–7. Plutarch (*Caesar* 61) says that Caesar wanted the kingship, and the Lupercalia was staged to test the waters, ending in failure because the people clearly did not want him to become king. According to Dio (44.11) Antony told Caesar that the people offered him the crown through him, and in a later passage he uses a speech by Calenus (46.17) to suggest that Antony wanted to make Caesar realise that he had gone too far towards the monarchy for safety. For an analysis of all the permutations and intentions see Pelling (1988, 144).

25 Appian, *Civil Wars*, 2.117; Dio, 44.19.

26 Appian, *Civil Wars*, 2.118.

27 Lepidus was willing to help Antony: Appian, *Civil Wars*, 2.118; Dio, 44.22, but elsewhere Dio accuses Lepidus of being eager for revolution (44.34). Suetonius (*Julius Caesar*, 82) says that fear of Lepidus and Antony prevented the assassins from dragging Caesar's corpse to the Tiber.

28 Cicero, *Letters to Atticus*, 14.21; see also, 14.14.

29 Appian, *Civil Wars*, 2.125; 3.5; Dio, 44.53. Plutarch, *Antony*, 15 sets the event a little later, perhaps to avoid the impression of unseemly haste, but it would be imperative to act quickly and Antony probably collected the documents on the night of 15 March or at latest next day (Pelling, 1988, 155).

30 Cicero refers more than once to Antony's robbery of the treasury of the temple of Ops (*Philippics*, 2.35–6; 5.11–12). He accuses Antony of taking 700 million sesterces, and paying all his debts with the proceeds. On the Ides of March he owed forty million, and yet by the beginning of April he had settled the score (*Philippics*, 2.93).

31 Appian (*Civil Wars*, 2.127–28) provides a long account of the debate in the Senate on 17 March. Antony pointed out that virtually everyone in the Senate owed his position to Caesar and the men currently in office and those soon to take up office would have to step down if all Caesar's acts were annulled. Then he mentioned that the same chaos would result in the provinces and allied states if Caesar's dispositions were cancelled (Appian *Civil Wars*, 2.133). Dio (44.34) says that the conspirators promised the soldiers that they would not change any of Caesar's laws concerning them. Antony suggested that all Caesar's acts and intentions should be ratified and the Senate agreed, because it would be beneficial for the Republic (Appian, *Civil Wars*, 2.134–35). On 12 April 44 Cicero wrote to Atticus (*Letters to Atticus* 14.6) 'Are we to have consuls and tribunes for the next two years selected by him (Caesar)?'

32 Dio, 44.34.

33 Caesar's will was read by Piso, Caesar's father-in-law and executor, in Antony's house (Suetonius, *Julius Caesar*, 83). The senators urged Piso not to make it public and not to give Caesar a state funeral but then capitulated (Appian, *Civil Wars*, 2.135–36), and the will was read at the funeral (Appian, *Civil Wars*, 2.143; Dio, 44.35).

34 Dio, 44.36–49.

35 Appian, *Civil Wars*, 2.144–47. Pelling (1988, 153–54) points out that Appian is correct from the point of view of Roman ritual. Cicero (*Letters to Atticus*, 14.10) reminded Atticus at a later date how he had foretold that if Caesar was given a public funeral it would be fatal to the Liberators.

36 Suetonius, *Julius Caesar*, 84.

37 Syme (1939, 107) says that thoughtful men would know that the Dictatorship could be revived under another name, and Dio (45.24) reports a speech of Cicero's in which he said that it was not the name of Dictator that did the harm, and in any case Antony was behaving like one without the title.

38 Cicero, *Letters to Atticus*, 14.9, and again in 14.14.

39 Syme, 1939, 97–111; Yavetz, 1969, 69–73; Pelling, 1988, 156.

40 Huzar, 1978, 66; Chamoux, 1986, 120–21.

41 Appian (*Civil Wars* 3.5) and Dio (44.53) take it as read that Antony manipulated

Caesar's notes and documents to gain the favour of many people including foreign princes and cities.

42 Cicero, *Letters to Atticus*, 14.10; 14.14.

43 Cicero, *Letters to Atticus*, 14.13; *Philippics*, 2.95; 5.11–12.

44 Cicero, *Letters to Atticus*, 14.8.

45 Cicero, *Letters to Atticus*, 15.1 on 17 May 44; 15.4 on 24 May 44.

46 Cicero, *Letters to Atticus*, 15.15 on 13 June 44; 15.17 on 14 June 44.

47 Suetonius, *Julius Caesar*, 72.

48 Cicero wrote that people had started to call Octavian by the name of Caesar, 'but Philippus doesn't so I did not' (*Letters to Atticus*, 14.12 on 22 April 44). On 2 November 44 he wrote (*Letters to Atticus*, 16.8) that he had received a letter from Octavian (*ab Octaviano*).

49 Syme declared that testamentary adoption did not exist and was therefore not legal (*Epigraphia e Ordine Senatorio* I, 1982, 397ff, reprinted in R. Syme *Roman Papers* IV, 1988, 159ff). The legal problems of Octavian's adoption were examined by Schmitthenner, W., *Oktavian und das Testament Caesars: eine Untersuchung zu den Politischen Anfangen des Augustus*, (Munich: C.H. Beck'sche Verlag, 1952).

50 Cicero, *Letters to Atticus*, 14.10.

Chapter 4: Separate Ways

1 Papyrus evidence (P.Oxy., 14.1629) indicates that Ptolemy XIV was still alive and his name was being added to official documents on 25 July 44 (Grant, 1972, 97; 261 n.10). By September he was dead (Porphyry *FGH* 260). Josephus (*Against Apion*, 2.58; *Jewish Antiquities*, 15.39) was certain that Cleopatra had murdered her brother. Grant (1972, 98) points out that Ptolemy's death was so fortuitous that it could not have been an accident. Cleopatra was able to elevate Caesarion as Ptolemy XV, and at a later date she obtained recognition from Rome that he was king of Egypt (Dio, 47.31).

2 Cicero wrote to Atticus (*Letters to Atticus*, 15.13), highly pleased that Cassius was approaching Egypt. Defending herself against Antony's charges that she had helped the Liberators, Cleopatra said she was threatened twice by Cassius (Appian, *Civil Wars*, 5.8), and her governor of Cyprus went over to him of his own accord (Appian, *Civil Wars*, 5.9). See also Syme, 1939, 124; Grant, 1972, 101–03.

3 Attending to the needs of the veteran soldiers was very important for both Antony and Octavian, for the political and military support that these large numbers of men represented, but they had to be kept in order in case they caused trouble;

in May 44 Antony canvassed the veterans to take an oath to support all Caesar's acts, and to remain in their camps (Cicero, *Letters to Atticus*, 14.21). Syme (1939, 119) says that the pressures on Antony made him choose between the Senate and the veterans. Caesar's project for draining the Pontine Marshes was continued by Antony (Dio, 45.9) and created more land for settlement. Land bills and legislation to ease veteran settlement and give allotments to the urban poor surfaced repeatedly in Roman history; Huzar (1978, 107) points out that although Antony's acts as consul in 44 were repealed, the land bills were too important to discard and were passed again.

4 Appian, *Civil Wars*, 3.5; 3.12; Dio, 44.53. Cicero told Atticus that Antony had accepted huge bribes from the Sicilians to grant them full Roman citizenship instead of the Latin rights that Caesar had planned, and in the same letter he hinted that Fulvia had arranged matters for Deiotarus; he thought the king worthy of any kingdom but not one bought through Fulvia (*Letters to Atticus*, 14.12).

5 Plutarch (*Antony* 16.2–3) describes the meeting between Octavian and Antony without inventing speeches for them as does Appian (*Civil Wars*, 3.15–3.20).

6 Appian *Civil Wars* 2.124; 3.7–8.

7 Brutus and Cassius were put in charge of the corn supply to keep them out of Rome (Appian, *Civil Wars*, 3.6). Cicero waxed indignant on their behalf when they were given this task (*Letters to Atticus*, 15.10), but as Pelling (1988, 157–58) points out the presence of the two Liberators in Italy complicated everything for Antony, especially his dealings with Octavian. The sources give conflicting evidence about which provinces Brutus and Cassius were to govern, Appian (*Civil Wars*, 3.8; 3.12) says Cyrenaica, Crete and Bithynia; Dio (47.21) mentions only the last two.

8 Cicero (*Letters to Atticus*, 14.14) informed Atticus that Antony was to bring a bill before the Senate on 1 June 44 to reallocate the provinces, giving himself Gaul and Dolabella Syria, with extended terms. Many of the senators did not attend the meeting so Antony got his way by a tribunician law (Appian, *Civil Wars*, 3.27). Plutarch's account (*Antony* 14) is confused (Pelling, 1988, 152). Octavian canvassed for Antony after the soldiers urged them to co-operate (Appian, *Civil Wars*, 3.30).

9 Antony took over the Macedonian legions and sent Gaius Antonius to arrange their transfer, and to govern the province because Decimus Brutus refused to go there (Appian, *Civil Wars*, 3.24–25; Dio, 45.9; 45.22; Cicero, *Philippics*, 3.10).

10 Octavian was intent on pursuing the assassins of Caesar, and said that no one had prosecuted them but if anyone did they would receive the support of the people (Appian, *Civil Wars*, 3.13).

11 Appian, *Civil Wars*, 3.28.

12 Appian, *Civil Wars*, 3.31.

13 Dio, 45.7.

14 Dio (44.53) sneers that Antony despised Octavian for his youth and inexperience.

15 Appian, *Civil Wars*, 3.23

16 Appian, *Civil Wars*, 3.39; Suetonius, *Augustus*, 10.

17 Antony called a meeting of the Senate on 1 September to confer more honours on Caesar, to which Cicero objected (*Philippics*, 1.6) and therefore did not attend. The next day he delivered the first of the *Philippics*. Antony's reply has not been preserved. Dio (45.18–47) reports Cicero's attack on Antony and the answering defence of Antony made by Fufius Calenus (46.1–28).

18 Appian (*Civil Wars*, 3.40) says that the troops at Brundisium were angry with Antony for not pursuing the murderers of Caesar, a point to which he returns when Antony made a speech to the soldiers and offered them money, but the soldiers said it was not enough. Antony ended by punishing the ringleaders; he asked the military tribunes to search their records and bring him a list of all the troublesome characters (*Civil Wars*, 3.43), and chose by lot the names of those to be executed.

19 Appian, *Civil Wars*, 3.45.

20 Syme (1939, 127) says that Antony withdrew to Gaul confident in his abilities and his troops. See also Dio, 45.13; Appian, *Civil Wars*, 3.46.

21 Decimus had been ordered by the Senate to remain in his province when Antony proposed that they should swap provinces, so that Antony would obtain Cisalpine Gaul and Decimus should govern Macedonia. Decimus stuck to the letter of the law (Appian, *Civil Wars*, 3.27; 3.49). Syme (1939, 162) points out that not even Cicero could dispute the fact that Antony was entirely within his legal rights in asking Decimus to surrender the province to him.

22 Appian, *Civil Wars*, 3.49; Dio, 46.35–6.

23 In order to elevate Octavian to senatorial status, the Senate conferred on him the rank of ex-quaestor, though he had not held the office (Dio, 46.29; Appian, *Civil Wars*, 3.64).

24 The war against Antony was entrusted to the new consuls for 43, Hirtius and Pansa. Octavian was given the rank of propraetor which allowed him to command troops, but when the consuls were with him his power was nullified (Appian, *Civil Wars*, 3.51; 3.64–5).

25 Piso and Calenus proposed sending an embassy to Antony (Appian, *Civil Wars*, 3.54; 3.62). Antony's reply was shredded point by point by Cicero (*Philippics*, 8.8–9), but in Syme's estimation (1939, 169–70) Antony's offer was 'neither unreasonable nor contumacious'. Dio (46.30–1) says that Antony made offers that he knew could not be accepted, and that another embassy was proposed, this time with Cicero as one of the party but it never took place.

26 Appian, *Civil Wars*, 67–70. On the battles around Mutina see Roberts 1988, 123–38.

27 Death of Hirtius: Appian, *Civil Wars*, 3.71; Dio 46.37–8. Antony's withdrawal to Transalpine Gaul: Appian, *Civil Wars*, 3.72; Plutarch, *Antony*, 17.

28 Appian (*Civil Wars*, 3.74) says that fifty days' thanksgiving were voted at Rome at Cicero's suggestion; Dio (46.39) says sixty days.

29 Pelling (1988, 161) points out that Antony did not cross the Alps, but the greatest difficulties were encountered in crossing the Apennines to reach the coastal route into Transalpine Gaul.

30 Fulvia was sheltered by Atticus: Nepos, *Atticus*, 9.

31 Appian (*Civil Wars*, 3.66) has an otherwise unattested tale that Ventidius intended to march to Rome and seize Cicero, but there is no mention of such a plot in the *Philippics*. Ventidius's meeting with Antony's troops is described retrospectively (Appian, *Civil Wars*, 3.80; 83).

32 Appian, *Civil Wars*, 3.83.

33 Appian, *Civil Wars*, 3.83–4; Dio 46.50–51. Plutarch (*Antony*, 18) emphasises Antony's talent for inspiring troops (Pelling 1988, 163).

34 Appian (*Civil Wars*, 3.85) says that the Senate appointed Octavian as general with Decimus to pursue Antony, even though they were afraid that he might join forces with Antony.

35 Brutus wrote to Cicero explaining that Octavian had heard about the clever remark (*Letters to his Friends*, 11.20); see also Velleius Paterculus (2.62) and Suetonius (*Augustus*, 12). Cicero allied himself with Octavian to prevent him from joining forces with Antony (Huzar, 1978, 95), and thought that he could use him to overthrow Antony and then discard him (Syme 1939, 143).

36 Appian (*Civil Wars*, 3.94) explains how it was possible in Rome to have adoption ratified by a law of the people, and says that Octavian was eager to put it into effect because he then obtained control of Caesar's freedmen, and many of them were rich. See also Dio 46.47.

37 Octavian sent some of his soldiers to Rome to ask the Senate for the consulship (Appian, *Civil Wars*, 3.88; Dio 42–3). Dio also says (46.41 and 43) that Octavian also contacted Antony and Lepidus and made a secret pact with Antony.

38 Syme (1939, 165) calls Plancus 'a time server' but he did eventually join Antony (Appian, *Civil Wars*, 3.97).

39 Dio (46.53) says that Decimus was killed by a personal enemy, but according to Appian (*Civil Wars*, 3.98) the Gallic chieftain Camilus captured him and contacted Antony, who told him to kill Decimus.

40 Appian, *Civil Wars*, 4.2. Dio (46.41) says that Octavian had already made a secret alliance with Antony when he first asked for the consulship, and then he made a pretence of war against Lepidus and Antony (46.50).

41 As consul Octavian pursued the murderers of Caesar, not making his intentions known until all the legacies had been paid, then in order to remain within legal limits he proposed a law to bring them to trial, and established courts to try them, even though many of them were not present (Dio, 46.48).

42 Brutus and Cassius collected troops in the east (Appian, *Civil Wars*, 3.78), and
the Senate confirmed them as legitimate governors of Macedonia and Syria
respectively (Dio, 46.40). Both Appian (*Civil Wars*, 4.57–82) and Dio (47.20–21)
give an account of the activities of Brutus and Cassius from the Ides of March to
the beginning of the civil war.

43 The meeting of Antony, Octavian and Lepidus is described by Dio (46.54–6) and
Appian (*Civil Wars*, 4.2) who says that a new magistracy was to be created for
the calming of the civil dissension. Plutarch (*Antony*, 19–20) also describes the
meeting at Bononia, but as Pelling (1988, 165) points out, he had no interest in
the formal details of the Triumvirate.

44 Appian, *Civil Wars*, 4.7.

45 Appian, *Civil Wars*, 4.2.

46 Appian, *Civil Wars*, 4.3; Dio, 46.55.

47 Dio, 46.56; Plutarch, *Antony*, 20.

48 Appian, *Civil Wars*, 4.3; Dio, 46.56.

49 Appian (*Civil Wars*, 4.3) names some of the eighteen cities chosen for veteran
settlement. A special commission was set up to divide the land, which made
the soldiers more loyal to the Triumvirs (Dio, 47.14). There were at least 80,000
veterans to settle and sixteen more towns were added later (Huzar, 1978, 117). For
a detailed account of veteran settlement at this period see Keppie (1983).

50 Appian (*Civil Wars*, 4.5.31) and Dio (47.1–19) wax lyrical about the tales of horror,
betrayal, and bravery during the proscriptions. Syme (1939, 191) says that the numbers
of people killed was probably exaggerated both by contemporaries and later historians.

51 Appian, *Civil Wars*, 4.19–20; Dio 47.8; 47.11. Plutarch (*Cicero*, 46) says that Octavian
argued to save Cicero for two days and then gave in.

52 Antony takes most of the blame for the worst excesses of the proscriptions
(Pelling 1988, 168). Dio (47.7–8) says that although Octavian had no ambition to
kill so many men, he was carried along because he was allied to Antony, but he
saved as many lives as he could.

53 Appian, *Civil Wars*, 4.7; Dio, 47.2.

54 Dio, 47.14–17.

55 Appian, *Civil Wars*, 4.32–4.

56 Dio, 47.18–19; Weinstock, 1971.

57 Southern, 1998, 62–3. The divine honours voted to Caesar while he still lived and
his deification after his death may or may not be linked. Octavian made political
mileage from his divine ancestry.

58 On the first day of the year the Triumvirs swore an oath to Caesar, and made
everyone else swear that they would consider all his acts binding, which Dio
(47.18) says is the origin of the oath sworn each year to the Emperors.

59 Appian, *Civil Wars*, 3.79; 4.75; Dio, 47.21; 47.23–4.

60 Appian, (*Civil Wars*, 3.78) says that Dolabella sent Allienus to bring the legions from Egypt; Dio (47.31) says that Cleopatra sent them and in return she gained the right to call her son, who she pretended was the son of Caesar, king of Egypt. Huzar (1978, 124) doubts that Cleopatra actually sent any help at all, suggesting that she prevaricated while she waited to see who would win.

61 Appian, *Civil Wars*, 3.78; 4.59–63; Dio, 47.30.

62 Appian, *Civil Wars*, 4.85; Dio, 48.18; see Syme, 1939, 202 n.5 for sling bullets with Q. Sal[vidienus] on them.

63 Dio, 48.24.

64 Appian, *Civil Wars*, 4.82; 5.8.

65 Appian, *Civil Wars*, 4.86.

66 Appian, *Civil Wars*, 4.105–106.

67 Dio, 47.37.

68 Appian, *Civil Wars*, 4.109–110.

69 Plutarch, *Antony*, 22; Appian, *Civil Wars*, 4.110–113; Dio, 47.42–6.

70 Appian, *Civil Wars*, 4.121–31; Dio, 47.48–9; see Roberts, 1988, 170–73 for Antony's planning.

71 According to Plutarch (*Antony*, 22) and Appian (*Civil Wars*, 4.135) Antony treated Brutus's body with respect, but Suetonius (*Augustus*, 13) says that Octavian had the head cut off to have it thrown down at the foot of Caesar's statue in Rome.

72 Appian, *Civil Wars*, 5.3.

73 Plutarch, *Antony*, 23.

74 Appian, *Civil Wars*, 5.4–5. For Antony in the east see Buchheim 1960 and Bengtson 1977.

75 Appian (*Civil Wars*, 5.4–6) invents a speech for Antony while he was at Ephesus, which summarises the state of affairs in the east after the civil wars.

76 Appian, *Civil Wars*, 5.6.

77 Appian, *Civil Wars*, 5.7

78 Plutarch, *Antony*, 25; Appian, *Civil Wars*, 5.8; Dio, 44.39.

Chapter 5: Reunion

1 Antony appears as Hercules on coins (*BMCR* II 395 no.4; 396 no.48; Grant, 1972, 262 n.16). Dio (50.5) describes Antony as the new Dionysus. Egyptian queens equated themselves with Isis; Plutarch (*Antony*, 54) describes Cleopatra as Isis, and gives this far less weight than the Donations of Alexandria, when Antony made her Queen of large areas of the east (Pelling 1988, 251–52). Grant (1972, 118–19)

stresses the importance of this supreme goddess throughout the ancient world.

2 Plutarch, *Antony*, 26; Socrates of Rhodes, in Athenaus IV 147.

3 Appian, *Civil Wars*, 5.8.

4 On the political arrangements at Tarsus see Grant 1972, 120-21 and Huzar, 1978, 153.

5 Appian (*Civil Wars*, 5.9–10) accuses Antony of irresponsibility in his raid on Palmyra, and then leaving without pacifying the east properly. Grant (1978, 122) agrees that Antony did not make arrangements with the client kings, but perhaps this was deliberate since everything would be upset again when the Parthian campaign began.

6 Appian (*Civil Wars*, 5.11) devotes a few lines to Antony in Alexandria; Plutarch (*Antony*, 28–9) provides a series of stories about him and Cleopatra, which as Chamoux (1986, 248–49) points out are probably reliable, because Plutarch heard them from his grandfather whose great friend Philotas was a medical student in Alexandria while Antony was there.

7 Appian, *Civil Wars*, 5.13; Keppie, 1983, 60; Syme, 1939, 207–08.

8 Dio, 48.3.

9 Dio, 48.1–15; Appian *Civil Wars* 5.14; 5.18–49. According to Appian (*Civil Wars*, 5.30; 5.43) Lucius undertook the war to restore the Republic.

10 Appian, *Civil Wars*, 5.54.

11 Dio (48.5) says that Octavian made no charge against Antony because Lucius and Fulvia acted contrary to Antony's wishes. Huzar (1978, 132) suggests that Fulvia could see that Octavian was more dangerous than Antony thought, and that she was the driving force behind the events leading to the Persusine war. Chamoux (1986, 255–57) agrees that Fulvia took the lead.

12 Pelling (1988, 198) says that Antony was kept informed by Octavian about the activities of Fulvia and Lucius, but thought it best not to send clear instructions. Huzar (1978, 134) thinks that Antony did not stir up the trouble but he was aware of it and feigned ignorance. According to Dio (48.27) Antony knew but chose not to act; Appian (*Civil Wars*, 5.52) says that he did not find out about the troubles until after he had left Alexandria; Chamoux (1986, 259) accepts this view.

13 Appian, *Civil Wars*, 5.19.

14 The Parthians overran Syria, encouraged by Labienus (Dio 48.24–6). Antony may have heard the news late in 41; he planned to leave Alexandria in the spring of 40 but had to depart earlier (Grant 1972, 123; Buchheim 1960, 118).

15 Dio, 48.25.

16 Grant, 1972, 127–29; Huzar, 1978, 162–67.

17 Appian, *Civil Wars*, 5.50; Dio, 48.15.

18 Plutarch, *Antony*, 30; Appian, *Civil Wars*, 5.54. Dio (48.28) says that after Fulvia's death Octavian and Antony made peace; Appian (*Civil Wars*, 5.59) depicts Antony

as full of grief.

19 Appian, *Civil Wars*, 5.51; Dio, 48.15. Huzar (1978, 135–37) says that although Antony looked favourably on an alliance with Sextus Pompey, he changed his mind because it could never be as profitable as an alliance with Octavian.

20 Appian, *Civil Wars*, 5.55; Dio, 48.7; 48.16.

21 Appian, *Civil Wars*, 5.56; Dio, 48.28. Huzar (1978, 137) points out that Domitius had attacked Brundisium in the previous year, so the inhabitants would be suspicious of him.

22 Appian, *Civil Wars*, 5.59; 5.64; Dio, 48.28.

23 Octavian took over the troops of Fufius Calenus because he did not want to leave them without a commander during the conspiracy of Lucius (Appian, *Civil Wars*, 5.61; Dio, 48.20).

24 Plutarch, *Antony*, 30.6–31.5; Appian, *Civil Wars*, 5.65; Dio, 48.29; Pelling, 1988, 201.

25 Huzar, 1978, 139; *BMCR* II 497–99, nos 114–30.

26 Plutarch, *Antony*, 31; Appian, *Civil Wars*, 5.65; Dio, 48.31.

27 Appian, *Civil Wars*, 5.65.

28 Suetonius, *Augustus*, 66.

29 Appian, *Civil Wars*, 5.67–8.

30 Plutarch (*Antony* 32) and Appian (*Civil Wars*, 5.69; 5.72–3) describe the agreement with Sextus, and how Menodorus urged Sextus to sail away with his guests; Dio (48.38) has the same story but calls him Menas.

31 Appian, *Civil Wars*, 5.73; Plutarch, *Antony*, 32. Antony was supposed to yield the Peloponnese to Sextus Pompey, but never did so (Appian, *Civil Wars*, 5.76; Plutarch, *Antony*, 33).

32 Appian, *Civil Wars*, 5.75.

33 Appian, *Civil Wars*, 5.76; Dio, 58.39.

34 Appian, (*Civil Wars*, 5.65) says that Ventidius was sent to the east after the Treaty of Brundisium; Dio (48.39) says after Misenum.

35 Pelling, 1988, 201; Reynolds, 1982, nos. 10; 12;13.

36 Appian, *Civil Wars*, 5.79–80; Plutarch, *Antony*, 34.

37 Dio, 49.19–20. Grant (1972, 131) praises Ventidius as one of the most remarkable generals of the age.

38 Plutarch, *Antony*, 34; Dio, 49.19–22. Huzar (1978, 174)and Pelling (1988, 211) point out that Ventidius would not accept bribes and make terms when Antony was so close to Samosata and would decide what to do.

39 Plutarch, *Antony*, 35; Dio, 48.54. Appian (*Civil Wars*, 5.93–5) describes the terms agreed at Tarentum, but omits the events at Brundisium, as though Antony aimed directly for Tarentum. Huzar (1978, 143) describes the Tarentum meeting as the final attempt to make peace. Pelling (1988, 214) redates the event to July–August rather than the traditional September–October.

40 Huzar (1978, 143) suggests that the extension of the Triumvirate was perhaps legalized just as the first one had been, and points out that the Triumvirs made no plans to extend it further. Instead they arranged the consulships in advance, Sosius and Ahenobarbus for 32, and Antony and Octavian for 31. Syme (1939, 225) says that it was assumed that the state would have been set in order by 33.

41 Dio, 48.44.

42 Grant (1972, 442–43) stresses the religious and political significance of the choice of names for the twins.

43 Huzar (1978, 168) and Chamoux (1986, 285) think that Antony and Cleopatra may have married according to Egyptian rites, and Pelling (1988, 219-20) suggests that living together as man and wife would be interpreted in the east as a marriage. Grant (1972, 153; 186–87) quotes Antony's letter to Octavian, reported by Suetonius (*Augustus*, 69), in which Antony writes *uxor mea est*, literally 'she is my wife', but some scholars dispute this and translate it with a question mark attached, to mean '*is* she my wife?'

44 Plutarch, *Antony*, 23. Pelling (1988, 217) points out that Cleopatra's territorial gains formed part of Antony's settlement of the east, which Huzar (1978, 148–49) describes as sensible and long lasting.

45 Huzar, 1978, 159–60.

46 Plutarch, *Antony*, 34; Dio, 49.24.

47 Plutarch devotes much of his biography to the Parthian campaigns (*Antony*, 37–52). Dio (49.23) describes the rise of Phraates.

48 Pelling, 1988, 222–23.

49 Grant (1972, 146) accepts that Antony followed Caesar's plan. Huzar (1978, 176) says it is not known how much Caesar influenced Antony's planning.

50 Dio (49.25–6) describes the loss of the siege train. Velleius Paterculus (2.82) says that two legions were lost. Plutarch (*Antony* 39) describes the flight of Artavasdes, saying that he was one of the prime instigators of the war.

51 Dio, 49.27. Chamoux (1986, 290–91) suggests that Antony planned to aim for Ctesiphon after capturing Phraaspa.

52 Dio (49.27) says that Phraates was threatened by internal dissension.

53 Huzar (1978, 179) praises Antony, at his best when crisis loomed.

54 Plutarch (*Antony*, 40–51) and Dio (49.28–9) detail the retreat.

55 Plutarch (*Antony*, 51) gives the losses at this point as 3000 dead and 5000 wounded.

56 Dio (49.31) accuses Antony of fawning upon Artavasdes, but as Pelling (1988, 240) points out Antony faced a long march, and needed the goodwill of the king to cross his territory.

57 Grant, 1972, 150.

58 Dio (49.31–2) says that Cleopatra brought money but it was not enough, and Antony used his own funds, and cash that he raised from his allies to pay the

troops, but pretended it came from her.

59 According to Dio (49.33) Artavasdes of Media pretended he wanted to fight against the Parthians but was more interested in war against Armenia.

60 Appian, *Civil Wars*, 5.123–28.

61 Appian, *Civil Wars*, 5.133–34.

62 Grant (1972, 151–52) says that when Octavia brought so few soldiers and ships compared to what he was owed, Antony justifiably interpreted it as an insult. Huzar (1978, 181) agrees that Octavian deliberately provoked Antony.

63 Plutarch (*Antony*, 54) says that Octavia, by raising all Antony's children and repeatedly trying to intercede on his behalf, ultimately did Antony considerable harm because he was blamed for deserting such a virtuous woman.

Chapter 6: Caesar's Heir

1 Dio, 49.39.

2 Plutarch, *Antony*, 54; Dio, 49.44; Huzar, 1978, 182.

3 Dio, 49.39.

4 Josephus *Jewish Antiquities* 15.97–103; Grant, 1972, 158–59.

5 Grant, 1972, 169–70; *BMCR* II p525, no.179.

6 Huzar (1978, 182) says that the Armenian conquest was ignored in Rome, and Grant (1972, 157) argues for its great success.

7 Huzar (1978, 183) points out that no one made any effort to reconquer Armenia.

8 Huzar (1978, 182–23) labels the procession a Dionysiac revel; Grant (1972, 161) says that Antony never acted the part of a Roman general while he was in Alexandria, and did not intend to hold a Roman triumph, but celebrated his victory in honour of and as the personification of Dionysus.

9 Plutarch, *Antony* 54; Dio 49.40–41. Both Grant (1972, 162–74) and Chamoux (1986, 316–25) argue for the mature planning behind the Donations of Alexandria and the fact that Antony's arrangements were not made on a whim to satisfy Cleopatra's demands.

10 This coin has the legend *Armenia Devicta* on one side and Cleopatra as Queen of Kings on the other (*BMCR* II p525, no.179). Grant (1972, 160–70) points out that it is remarkable for the Queen's head on it, and although Antony had portrayed Fulvia and Octavia on coins, these were Roman women, whereas Cleopatra was a foreign Queen.

11 Grant 1972, 168–170.

12 Pelling (1988, 249) and Huzar (1978, 199) insist that the Roman controlled territories underwent no change of government after the Donations of Alexandria, but according to Grant (1972, 165–66) coin evidence indicates that

although the government and the military occupation of the provinces did not change, the Roman officials acknowledged the supremacy of the Ptolemaic rulers.

13 Plutarch, *Antony*, 55. The propaganda of 33 was just a continuation of the sporadic campaign that had started ten years earlier (Pelling, 1988, 252–53) See Suetonius, *Augustus*, 28; Dio, 49–41; 50.7.

14 For political reasons Octavian stopped using the title before Antony did (Huzar, 1978, 205; Bleicken, 1990, 68). Exasperated with what he calls excessive debate about the expiry of the Triumvirate, Syme (1939, 277–78, n.6) points out that the exercise of power by consuls and a tribune at the beginning of 32 indicate that the Triumvirate had ended, but Antony chose to continue to use his Triumviral powers until 32, just as he and Octavian had extended their appointment at the end of 37.

15 Huzar (1978, 186–90) blames Cleopatra for dragging Antony down and alienating his allies.

16 Dio (50.24–26) makes up a speech for Octavian at the end of the civil wars, where he says that Cleopatra aimed at domination of Rome, but he still believed that Antony could be brought round, so he did not declare war on him. Here Dio repeats the motives he ascribes to Octavian in earlier passages, where he says (50.4–5) that Cleopatra swore to dispense justice from the Capitol, and conceived a hope of ruling the Romans, so Octavian declared war against her.

17 Dio, 50.6.

18 Dio, 50.1.

19 Suetonius, *Augustus*, 69.

20 Dio, 49.41.

21 Chamoux (1986, 336) accepts the story that Canidius was bribed, whereas Pelling (1988, 256) discounts it. For the discovery of the fragment of papyrus detailing concessions to Canidius see *Sunday Times*, 22 October 2001.

22 Plutarch, *Antony*, 59.

23 Dio (49.41) suggests that Antony's consuls tried to hush up the Donations of Alexandria, which Pelling (1988, 249) says is incredible, given that the news must have been current in Rome by then.

24 Dio (50.2) does not elaborate on what was proposed.

25 Dio, 50.2.

26 Huzar (1978, 201–02) says that most of the Patrician clans were represented in Antony's following.

27 Dio, 50.3.

28 Plutarch, *Antony*, 58. Syme (1939, 282 n.1) does not dismiss the idea that Octavian forged the will; Grant (1972, 193) says that Antony would not be so stupid as to trust even the Vestals with inflammatory statements such as Octavian revealed, and also suspects forgery; Huzar (1978, 208) questions whether this really was Antony's will.

29 Dio, 50.4

30 *Res Gestae*, 25.2. Suetonius (*Augustus*, 17) doubted the spontaneity of the oath that Octavian insisted upon. Pelling (1996, 53) accepts the military character of the oath, while Brunt and Moore (1967, 67) reject the idea that it formed the basis of the annual oath of loyalty to the Emperors.

31 Dio, 50.9.

32 Plutarch, *Antony*, 61–62. Dio (50.7) says that Antony had the larger forces.

33 According to Dio (50.12) Antony built towers on each side of the gulf and stationed his own ships at intervals so he could sail in and out.

34 *BMCR* II p.531 no.227; p583 no.1–3; Grant (1972, 201) suggests that the salutation as Imperator may belong to the Antonian defeat of an attack by Octavian.

35 Dio, 50.11–12; Grant (1972, 204) says that the attack on Methone took Antony by surprise; Roberts (1988, 306) thinks that Antony never conceived of such an attack launched from Italy.

36 Dio, 50.13.

37 Plutarch, *Antony*, 68.

38 Dio (50.12) says that more men died during the summer than the winter.

39 Ahenobarbus had a grievance against Cleopatra according to Dio (50.13); on Dellius see Grant (1972, 209).

40 Dio, 50.13.

41 Dio, 50.15.

42 Dio, 50.32–35; Plutarch *Antony* 65–68. Roberts (1988, 316–28) gives a very detailed account of the battle.

43 Grant (1972, 208) thinks that Antony's only hope was to escape to fight somewhere else, and gives references to the main debates about whether Actium was intended to be a naval battle or a break out (1972, 274 n.23).

44 Dio (50.33) says that Cleopatra rode at anchor behind the ships but could not bear to wait, and fled.

45 Plutarch, *Antony*, 67.

46 Plutarch, *Antony*, 68; Grant, 1972, 212.

47 Plutarch, *Antony*, 69.

48 Plutarch, *Antony*, 72; Dio, 51.6; 51.8.

49 Plutarch, *Antony*, 74.

50 Plutarch, *Antony*, 81.

51 Plutarch, *Antony*, 77.

52 Plutarch, *Antony*, 83; Dio 51.12–13.

53 Plutarch, *Antony*, 85–86; Huzar (1978, 227) says that Octavian needed Cleopatra's suicide; Grant (1972, 225) says that it was better if Cleopatra died but Octavian did not want to be responsible for her death; Pelling (1988, 318–20) discusses the possibility that Octavian wanted Cleopatra to feature in his triumph.

54 Plutarch, *Antony*, 81; Dio, 51.16.

Bibliography

A Note on Sources

Mark Antony

There is no contemporary account of Antony's life, but certain episodes were described by various writers. When he joined Caesar in Gaul, some of Antony's exploits were deemed worthy of inclusion in the *Commentaries*, better known to us as Caesar's *Gallic War*. Thereafter, the only surviving contemporary information concerning Antony is embodied in the letters and speeches of Cicero, none of which were favourable to Antony, but the letters provide an unparalleled account of the political and social developments in Rome, while the speeches allow an insight into the turbulent war-mongering against Antony. Some correspondence from Antony has been preserved, for instance, the letter which he sent from northern Italy is quoted and shredded paragraph by paragraph in the *Philippics*, and his communications with Cicero are repeated, ostensibly verbatim, in Cicero's letters to Atticus.

The history of the Triumvirate will never be entirely recovered, not least because the last of the Triumvirs, Octavian, was not particularly interested in preserving the information for posterity. From 44 onwards, the historical record for a reconstruction of a life of Antony is fraught with difficulties, because the facts were distorted, or in some cases suppressed, to suit the tastes of Augustus, who rewrote his own part in the civil wars. Antony was written off as a failure, influenced and led by Cleopatra, the sinister and dangerous enemy of Rome.

Later authors used works that are now lost to us, or known only in fragments. These include Plutarch, who wrote during the second half of the first century, and the second century historian Appian, whose work has survived only in part; only eleven of his original twenty-four books are extant. His history of the civil wars beyond 35BC, when Sextus Pompey was executed, has been lost. Neither of these two authors are entirely hostile to Antony. Plutarch was influenced by the experiences of his grandfather, who was forced to take part in a convoy, carrying supplies by hand to Antony's camp at Actium, when the encirclement by Octavian and Agrippa cut the Antonians off from easier sources of supply.

The history of Rome written by Titus Livius, known as Livy, fails us for the period of Antony's life. Some fragments survive from the later copyists, and perhaps much of his work is preserved in Dio's Roman history, who wrote in the early third century. By then, the depiction of Antony as debauched, irresponsible, incompetent and most of all as a failure was indelible, so any departure from this theme depended upon personal opinion.

Modern scholars are assisted by the archaeological and numismatic evidence. Although the Senate decreed that Antony's memory was to be eternally damned, and his portraits were to be destroyed, nothing could be done to eradicate the coinage, which has much to tell us about the political history and the self-promotion of the great men of the day. The coin portraits are not totally accurate, but can still reveal something of the character of the main participants in the civil wars and political upheavals in the second half of the first century BC.

Cleopatra

There is no single ancient source for the life of Cleopatra, which is somewhat surprising in view of the fact that she is so well known in modern times. She is mentioned in the works of several ancient authors, but even then her life is not documented from beginning to end in any coherent fashion, and most of the stories about her are of the fabulous or anecdotal kind.

Contemporaries who knew her and wrote about her include Julius Caesar, the tutor of her children Nicolaus of Damascus, and Herod, king of Judaea. The historian Asinius Pollio lived through the civil wars between Pompey and Caesar and Octavian and Antony, and wrote an account of his times that extended probably to the mid thirties BC. Of these, Caesar's narrative of the Alexandrian war gives scarcely any detail of Cleopatra as a person, and mentions her only in passing, and the work of Nicolaus and the memoirs of Herod are known only in quotation in the works of other authors. Asinius Pollio's work is also lost, save for a few fragments contained in other writings. Marcus Tullius Cicero knew Cleopatra from her time in Rome as Caesar's guest, and though he wrote of her in his letters to Atticus, there is little in the way of solid information about her, only gossip, unexplained allusions and prejudice.

Later authors who mentioned Cleopatra were already imbued with the Augustan tradition that she was the greatest enemy that Rome ever faced. They were also hostile to Antony. Livy and Velleius Paterculus both pleaded the cause of Octavian-Augustus, and in turn downgraded the achievements of Antony and Cleopatra. Livy's history covered the period but this part of his work has not survived. Velleius' work is an abbreviated account denying any credit at all to Antony and Cleopatra. The Jewish historian Flavius Josephus, who wrote in the first century AD, is hostile to Cleopatra on behalf of king Herod, whose territories she wanted to take over, and so Josephus has no good word to say of her.

Much of the information about the life of Cleopatra derives from Plutarch's *Life of Antony* where he waxes lyrical about the more fabulous of Cleopatra's attributes and activities. Plutarch was born about seventy to eighty years after the deaths of Cleopatra and Antony, and had access to some first hand information passed down from relatives and friends who had witnessed events or even known or seen the Queen herself. The narrative is an entertaining read, and it inspired Shakespeare, the main source of western tradition about Cleopatra.

Much of the Augustan literature on the period presents Cleopatra in an ambivalent light, condemning her alleged hostility to Rome and her acquisitive territorial ambitions, but admiring her determination and bravery. Quintus Horatius Flaccus (Horace) and Vergilius Maro (Vergil) refer to the Queen via indirect allusions, but spread a general picture of danger from the most artful woman of her age. Current opinion denies that these poets were closely directed by Augustus himself, scarcely able to write a word unless he vetted it first, but nonetheless, in general they take the line that Augustus saved the world from a dire threat.

Besides the works of the ancient authors, there are the official administrative sources, not abundant for the reign of Cleopatra, comprising papyri, inscriptions, sculptures and coins. As archaeological excavations progress in Alexandria and elsewhere, it is likely that more of this sort of material will come to light, to be added to the corpus of knowledge already gleaned from these useful tools. Portraits of Cleopatra are not numerous, and not always securely identified, but from her unflattering coin portraits comparison can be made with her distinctive Alexandrian hairstyle and her prominent nose.

Cleopatra as she emerges from the available information is comparable to the internationally famous film stars of the great age of cinema, so extremely well known, yet so elusive, fascinating to ancient and modern authors alike. There are a great number of books and articles about Cleopatra, but not all of them restrict themselves to a description of her life and times. She has been depicted through the ages by the important artists of the western world, and a great number of books are concerned only with the Shakespearian Cleopatra, and not with the Queen of Egypt who existed alongside Caesar, Antony and Octavian.

Ancient sources

Appian	*Mithridatica*
	Roman History, Loeb
Athenaus	
Caesar	*Alexandrian War*, Loeb
Caesar	*Civil Wars*, Loeb
Caesar	*Gallic War*, Loeb
Cicero	*In Catilinam*
	Letters to Atticus, Loeb (3 vols)
	Letters to His Friends, Loeb (3 vols)
	Philippics, Loeb
	Pro Caelio
Dio	*Roman History*, Loeb
Horace	*Carmen Saeculare*
	Odes and Epodes, Loeb
Josephus	*Against Apion*, Loeb
	Jewish Antiquities, Loeb (3 vols)
	Jewish War, Loeb (3 vols)
Nepos	*Atticus*
Nicolaus of Damascus	*Life of Augustus*, translated with commentary by Hall, C.M., Smith College Classical Studies No.IV, Northampton, Massachusetts
Plutarch	*Life of Antony* ed. Pelling, C.B.R. (Cambridge University Press, 1988)
Sallust	*The War with Catiline*, Loeb
Strabo	*Geography*, Loeb
Suetonius	*The Lives of the Caesars*, Loeb
Velleius Paterculus	*Compendium of Roman History*, Loeb
Vergil	*Aeneid*, Loeb
	Georgics, Loeb

Modern Works

Becher, I., *Das Bild der Kleopatra in der Griechischen und Lateinischen Literatur* (Berlin, 1966).

Bell, H. Idris, *Egypt From Alexander the Great to the Arab Conquest* (Oxford University Press, 1938).

Bengtson, H., *Marcus Antonius: Triumvir und Herrscher des Orients* (Munich: Beck, 1977).

Bleicken, J., *Zwischen Republik und Principat: zum Charakter des Zweiten Principats* (Göttingen, 1990).

Boethius, A. and Ward Perkins, J.B., *Etruscan and Roman Architecture* (Harmondsworth: Penguin, 1970).

Bradford, E., *Cleopatra* (Hodder and Stoughton, 1971).

Braund, D.C., *Rome and the Friendly King* (London, 1984).

Brunt, P.A., *Social Conflicts in the Roman Republic* (New York and London: W.W. Norton and Co., 1971).

Brunt, P.A. and Moore, J.M., *Res Gestae Divi Augusti: the Achievements of the Divine Augustus* (Oxford, 1967).

Buchheim, H., *Die Orientpolitik des Triumvirs Marcus Antonius* (Heidelberg: C. Winter, 1960).

Cambridge Ancient History, Vol.IX: *The Last Age of the Roman Republic 146–43 BC*, edited by Crook, J. A. (*et al.*) (Cambridge University Press 2nd ed., 1992).

Cambridge Ancient History, Vol.X: *The Augustan Empire, 43 BC–AD 69* edited by Bowman, A. K. (*et al.*) (Cambridge University Press 2nd ed., 1996).

Carter, J. M., *The Battle of Actium*, (London: Hamish Hamilton, 1970).

Chamoux, F., *Marc Antoine* (Paris: Arthaud, 1986).

Earl, D., *The Age of Augustus* (Elek; reprinted by Ferndale editions 1980).

Empereur, J.Y., *Alexandria Rediscovered* (British Museum Press, 1998).

Fielding, S., *The Lives of Cleopatra and Octavia* (London, 1928).

Flamarion, E., *Cleopatra: from history to legend* (London: Thames and Hudson, 1997).

Foss, M., *The Search for Cleopatra* (Michael O'Mara Books, 1997).

Fraser, P.M., *Ptolemaic Alexandria* (Oxford, 1972).

Gelzer, M., *Caesar* (Oxford, 1969).

Grant, M., *Cleopatra* (Weidenfeld and Nicolson, 1972).

Grant, M., *Roman History from Coins* (Cambridge University Press, 1968).

Greenhalgh, P., *Pompey: the Roman Alexander* (London: Weidenfeld and Nicolson, 1980).

Gruen, E. S., *The Last Generation of the Roman Republic* (University of California Press, 1974; reprinted in paperback 1995).

Gurval, R. A., *Actium and Augustus: the politics and emotions of civil war* (University of Michigan Press, 1995).

Hamer, M., *Signs of Cleopatra* (Routledge, 1992).

Hughes-Hallett, L., *Cleopatra: histories, dreams and distortions* (Pimlico, 1990).

Huzar, E.G., *Mark Antony: a biography* (University of Minnesota,1978; reprinted by Croom Helm 1986).

Keppie, L., *Colonization and Veteran Settlement in Italy 47–14BC* (British School at Rome, 1983).

La Riche, W., *Alexandria: the sunken city* (Weidenfeld and Nicolson, 1996).

Lindsay, J., *Cleopatra* (Constable, 1971).

Lindsay, J., *Mark Antony and his Contemporaries* (London, 1936).

Lintott, A.W., *Violence in Republican Rome* (Oxford, 1968).

Marshall, B.A., *Crassus: a Political Biography* (Amsterdam, 1976).

Meier, C., *Caesar* (Harper Collins, 1995).

Mundy, T., *Queen Cleopatra* (London, 1929).

Payen, L., *Cleopatra* (New York, 1915)

Pelling, C. (ed.), *Plutarch: Life of Antony* (Cambridge University Press, 1988).

Pelling, C., 'The Triumviral period' in CAH^2 Vol.X, 1996, pp.1–69.

Reynolds, J., *Aphrodisias and Rome* (London: Society for the Promotion of Roman Studies, 1982).

Richardson, G.W., 'Actium', *Journal of Roman Studies* 27 (1937), pp.153–64.

Roberts, A., *Mark Antony: his life and times* (Malvern Publishing Co., 1988).

Scullard, H. H., *From the Gracchi to Nero* (Methuen 3rd ed., 1970).

Seager, R., *Pompey: a Political Biography* (Oxford: Blackwell, 1979).

Shotter, D., *The Fall of the Roman Republic* (London: Routledge, 1994).

Sherwin-White, A.N., *Roman Foreign Policy in the East 168 BC to AD 1* (London, 1984).

Southern, P., *Augustus* (Routledge, 1998).

Southern, P., *Mark Antony* (Tempus, 1998).

Souza, P. de, *Piracy in the Graeco-Roman World* (Cambridge University Press, 1999).

Stockton, D., *Cicero: a political biography* (Oxford University Press, 1970).

Syme, R., *The Roman Revolution* (Oxford University Press, 1939).

Tarn, W.W., 'The Battle of Actium', *Journal of Roman Studies* 21, (1931), pp.173–99.

Tarn, W. W., 'Antony's legions', *Classical Quarterly* (1932), pp.75–89.

Ward, A.M., *Marcus Crassus and the Late Roman Republic* (Columbia and London, 1977).

Weigall, A., *The Life and Times of Cleopatra* (London, 1914).

Weigall, A., *Mark Antony: his life and times* (London, 1931).

Weinstock, S., *Divus Julius* (Oxford, 1971).

Wiseman, T. P., 'The Senate and the *populares*, 69–60 BC', in *CAH* IX^2 (1992), pp.327–367.

Yavetz, Z., *Plebs and Princeps* (Oxford, 1969).

Abbreviations

BMCR	*Catalogue of Coins of the Roman Republic in the British Museum.*
FGH	*Fragmente der Griechische Historiker*, Jacoby, F. (ed.), Berlin.
JRS	*Journal of Roman Studies.*
OGIS	*Orientis Graeci Inscriptiones Selectae.*
P.Berl	Moller, S. (ed.), *Griechische Papyri aus dem Berliner Museum* (Gothenburg, 1929).
P.Grenf.	Grenfell, B. P. and Hunt, A. S. (eds), *New Classical Fragments and Other Greek and Latin Papyri* (Oxford, 1897).
P.Lond.	Kenyon, F. G. and Bell, H. I. (eds), *Greek Papyri in the British Museum* (London, 1893–1917).
P.Oxy.	Grenfell, B. P., *et al.*, *The Oxyrhynchus Papyri* (London, 1898–).

List of Illustrations

1 Head of Julius Caesar from Egypt, carved in green slate. Courtesy Berlin Museen.

2 The siege works surrounding the Gallic citadel of Alesia, the context of the first mention of Mark Antony by name in Caesar's *Gallic War*. Antony and Gaius Trebonius rushed troops to threatened points during a night attack, and repulsed the Gauls. Drawn by Jan Shearsmith.

3 Head of Mark Antony from Rome. This damaged sculpture is probably securely identified as Antony since it bears more than a passing resemblance to his coin portraits, with his square jaw, thickset neck, and his fleshy face wearing a determined stare. Courtesy Capitoline Museum, Rome.

4 Coin in the Macedonian Ptolemaic style representing Cleopatra's father, Ptolemy XII Auletes. Drawn by Jacqui Taylor.

5 Silver coin from Alexandria with an unflattering portrait of Cleopatra. Her prominent hooked nose was inherited from her father. Drawn by Jacqui Taylor.

6 Plan of Alexandria. Drawn by Graeme Stobbs.

7 On this relief from the temple at Dendera in Upper Egypt, Cleopatra is portrayed as the goddess Isis, the supreme deity of the east, with whom the Ptolemaic Queen is strongly identified. The cartouche at the top left displays Cleopatra's name in Egyptian hieroglyphics. Photograph courtesy of David Brearley.

8 Silver denarius of Caesar Imperator. Although portraits of individuals regularly appeared on coins in the east, the Romans usually restricted their coin portraits to gods. In the final months before his assassination Caesar started to issue coins bearing his own image, setting the precedent for the Imperial coinage. Drawn by Jacqui Taylor.

9 Caesar as dictator for the fourth time on this silver denarius issued in 44BC. Drawn by Jacqui Taylor.

10 Silver denarius of 44, showing the earliest coin portrait of Mark Antony. He is
bearded and veiled, as augur. A *lituus*, one of the symbols of the augurs, is shown
under his chin. On the reverse, the two galloping horses and the rider wearing
a cap are associated with the Games of Apollo, but the full meaning of this
representation is not understood. The design is very similar to one of Caesar's
coins, issued shortly before this one, showing him also veiled and looking to the
right. Drawn by Jacqui Taylor.

11 This silver denarius of 43 shows the head of Antony's younger brother Gaius
Antonius, in Macedonian dress with a cap and a Greek style chlamys, or cloak.
Gaius Antonius was sent to Macedonia as governor in 44. The legend proclaims
him *C. ANTONIUS.M.F. PRO. COS.* (Gaius Antonius, son of Marcus, Proconsul).
The reverse shows religious symbols and the word *pontifex*, an office which Gaius
held from 45 until his execution by Marcus Junius Brutus before the battle of
Philippi. Drawn by Jacqui Taylor.

12 Map of northern Italy. After the battles of Mutina in April 43, Antony retreated
into Gaul over the Apennines, joining up with Ventidius Bassus about thirty miles
west of Genoa, and arriving in Gaul at Forum Julii (Frejus) in May. Drawn by
Graeme Stobbs.

13 Obverse of a gold aureus of 42. Antony is styled as *IIIVIR. R.P.C.* or *Tresvir Rei
Publicae Constituendae*. On the reverse the god Mars is depicted, with the name of
Lucius Mussidius Longus, who was one of the officials who issued gold coinage
with portraits of the Triumvirs from 42 to 40. Drawn by Jacqui Taylor.

14 Map of Macedonia and Greece where Antony fought several battles. He was with
Caesar at Dyrrachium and Pharsalus; he fought and defeated Brutus and Cassius at
Philippi, and he met disaster at Actium. Drawn by Graeme Stobbs.

15 The head of Marcus Junius Brutus on the obverse of a gold aureus of 42. Casca
Longus, named on the reverse, was one of Brutus's legates, and the military
trophies celebrate the raising of troops in the east. Drawn by Jacqui Taylor.

16 Plans of the two battles of Philippi showing the various stages of the main
episodes.

a Philippi First Battle October 42. Antony builds a causeway across the marsh to cut
the communications of Brutus and Cassius, and get behind Cassius' camp.

b Antony defeats Cassius and drives him from his camp. Cassius withdraws to the
north-east, and later commits suicide. At the same time Brutus defeats Octavian
and captures his camp, but Octavian survives by hiding in the marsh.

c Philippi Second Battle November 42. Brutus moves into Cassius's camp, and Antony
continues his outflanking movement. Brutus builds small posts to keep pace with
him, but offers battle in mid-November. Antony and Octavian eventually encircle
him and drive him off. Drawn by Graeme Stobbs.

17 A gold aureus dated to 41, issued by Gnaeus Domitius Ahenobarbus, with a

portrait perhaps of himself. The temple of Neptune on the reverse epitomises Ahenobarbus' career, first as a naval officer of Brutus, and then an independent admiral after Philippi. He made an alliance with Antony in 40, adding his naval power to Antony's forces. Drawn by Jacqui Taylor.

18 Full face and profile of a head of Cleopatra in classical Greek style, and reminiscent of portraits of Alexander. Cleopatra combined her Egyptian heritage with her Macedonian Greek ancestry, and portrayed herself in both styles. From the Berlin Antikensammlung, courtesy of Berlin Museen.

19 Head of Mark Antony, older and more rugged and experienced, with double chin and worry lines between his eyebrows. Courtesy Musée Archéologique, Narbonne. Photograph Jean Lepage. Courtesy of Musées de Narbonne

20 Portrait of Antony on an intaglio, showing marked resemblance to the images on his coins. Drawn by Jacqui Taylor.

21 Quintus Labienus, the son of Caesar's general Titus Labienus, was sent to Parthia by Brutus, to try to organise an alliance with the Parthian king Orodes. After Philippi Labienus remained with the Parthians and was instrumental in instigating the invasion of Syria. His title Parthicus proclaims his alliance with King Orodes. When Antony's general Ventidius Bassus drove the Parthians out, Labienus disappeared and his ultimate fate is unknown. Drawn by Jacqui Taylor.

22 Antony's eastern campaigns. The Parthians invaded Syria in 40–39, but were driven out by Ventidius, who besieged the last remaining fugitives in Samosata. During the offensive against Parthia in 36, Antony assembled his troops at Zeugma as though he wished to invade Mesopotamia from the west, but then he marched rapidly north eastwards then south into Media, finally arriving at Phraaspa, to which he laid siege. If he had been successful, he would probably have marched on Ecbatana, the Parthian capital, but with the loss of his siege engines he had little chance of bringing the war to such a rapid close. When he prepared for the abortive campaign of 33, he had overrun Armenia and converted it into a Roman province, and forged an alliance with Media, so he perhaps planned to invade eastwards from Syria and southwards from Media. Drawn by Graeme Stobbs

23 Gold aureus issued *c*.40, when Antony and Octavian settled their differences and Antony married Octavian's sister. On the obverse, the legend proclaims Antony as Imperator and Triumvir (*M. ANTONIUS IMP.IIIVIR. R. P. C.*), and the reverse bears the unlabelled portrait of his wife Octavia. Drawn by Jacqui Taylor.

24 Antony and Octavia are shown together on this silver coin, with the legend, partly worn away in this example, *M. ANTONIUS. IMP. COS DESIG. ITER. ET. TERT.* referring to his military command as Imperator, and the fact that he was consul designate for 38. The reverse shows Bacchus flanked by two intertwined serpents. Drawn by Jacqui Taylor.

25 On this gold aureus issued *c*.37 Octavian proclaims himself *CAESAR DIVI.F.*

IIIVIR. ITER. R.P.C., son of the divine Caesar, and Triumvir for the second time, after the extension of the Triumvirate for another term of five years. Drawn by Jacqui Taylor.

26 Cleopatra and her son Caesarion from the temple at Dendera. They are depicted as Isis and Horus, in the ancient regalia and pose of the Pharaohs, and firmly embedded in Egyptian tradition. Photograph David Brearley.

27 Antony and Cleopatra on opposite sides of a silver denarius of 32. Antony celebrates the conquest of Armenia by the legend *ANTONI ARMENIA DEVICTA*. He garrisoned the country and opened Armenia to Roman traders, but Octavian dismissed the conquest as worthless. The portrait of Cleopatra and the accompanying legend forms one of the most important icons of her history. She is proclaimed Queen of Kings and of her sons who are kings (*CLEOPATRAE REGINAE REGUM FILIORUM REGUM*), referring to the territorial arrangements made by Antony in the ceremony of the Donations of Alexandria. Drawn by Jacqui Taylor.

28 One example among many of a series of coins issued in the east *c.*37–33. The dates of issue and the particular mints are hard to identify. The Greek legend proclaiming Cleopatra Queen, and the younger Thea (transliterated from the Greek: *BASILISSA CLEOPATRA THEA NOTERA*. These coins predate and postdate the Donations of Alexandria, but the legend makes Cleopatra's territorial ambitions quite clear. Her title 'the younger Thea' makes reference to the earlier Cleopatra Thea, daughter of Ptolemy VI. She married three successive Seleucid rulers of Syria, and was widely known in the east. The message on these coins indicates that Cleopatra VII portrayed herself as ruler of Egypt and Syria. Drawn by Jacqui Taylor.

29 Map of Egypt and the surrounding kingdoms and provinces. Cleopatra's interest in acquiring control of certain territories was most probably driven by economic considerations rather than pure and simple Imperialistic urges. When she succeeded to an impoverished throne her aim was to reconstitute the Ptolemaic Empire and its trading potential. With Antony's help, in his capacity as Triumvir with legally approved control of the eastern half of the growing Roman Empire, she achieved much, but not all, of what she desired in order to revive and sustain the economy of Egypt. Drawn by Graeme Stobbs.

30 Another of the series of coins proclaiming Cleopatra Queen and the younger Thea, though in this example the second part of the legend has worn away. On the reverse of these coins, Antony is shown with the Greek version of his titles Imperator and Triumvir (transliterated from the Greek it reads *ANTONIOS AUTOKRATOR TRION ANDRON*). Drawn by Jacqui Taylor.

31 Portrait from Alexandria identified as Cleopatra. The features such as the nose and the shape of the face support the identification as the Queen. Photograph David Brearley.

32 On the obverse of this silver denarius of 31 Antony depicts one of his war galleys, and proclaims himself Triumvir, in contrast to Octavian who ceased to use this title. The standards of the Seventh Legion (*Legio VII*) are depicted on the reverse, just one example of Antony's numerous coin issues naming his legions. Drawn by Jacqui Taylor.

33 Silver denarius issued by Antony and his general Scarpus in 31. The legend round the head of Jupiter Ammon, an amalgamation of the chief Roman and eastern deities, runs *M. ANTONIO. COS III. IMP.IIII*, naming Antony as consul for the third time in 31, but Octavian had deprived him of the office. The abbreviated *IMP.IIII* indicates that Antony had been hailed as Imperator for the fourth time. It is not established which particular event gave rise to the proclamation by the troops, but the context must be one of his battles fought in 31. An optimistic portrait of the goddess Victory is shown on the reverse. Drawn by Jacqui Taylor.

34 The battle of Actium, 2 September 31. Before the naval battle was fought, there was a prolonged series of skirmishes on land, which cannot be documented in detail. Antony crossed the entrance to the Gulf of Ambracia to try to cut off Octavian's water supply, but he had to withdraw as his allies deserted him. Octavian built protective walls from his camp to the sea to ensure his supplies, and meanwhile Agrippa captured several ports and harbours, including the island of Leucas to the south of Actium. As the stranglehold on Antony grew more serious, he was forced to try to break out. Instead of retreating into Macedonia as Canidius advised, he chose to fight at sea. He burnt the ships that he could not man, and shortly after the battle started, many of his ships turned back into harbour, while he and Cleopatra sailed away to Egypt. Drawn by Graeme Stobbs

35 Silver denarius of uncertain date, *c.*31BC or perhaps slightly earlier, issued by Octavian, with a fine portrait of himself. The reverse (not shown) bears the legend *CAESAR DIVI F.* and a depiction of Venus Victrix, the divine ancestress of the Julii. Octavian probably began to use the title *Divi Filius* as soon as he claimed his inheritance, but the earliest coin examples date from the period after Philippi when he was settling the veterans in Italy. Drawn by Jacqui Taylor.

36 Plain and unadorned head of Cleopatra, showing her severe hairstyle as depicted on coins. Courtesy Vatican Museums, Vatican City.

37 Bronze equestrian statue of Octavian from Greece. Courtesy National Archaeological Museum, Athens.

38 On this gold aureus of 27 issued three years after the fall of Alexandria, Octavian reminded the Roman world that he had captured Egypt (*AEGVPT CAPTA*). He styled himself *CAESAR. DIVI.F. COS. VII*, (Caesar, son of the divine Caesar, consul for the seventh time). Drawn by Jacqui Taylor.

Index

Note: Antony, Cleopatra and Octavian are denoted by the abbreviations A., C. and O.

Achillas 81, 83, 85–87, 89, 123, 242, 244
Actium 203, 208, 215–6, 217, 218, 220–1,
    223, 235, 260, 262, figs 14, 34.
Aemilius Lepidus, Marcus 28, 31
    urban praetor 51
    proposes Caesar be made Dictator 53
    consul with Caesar 98
    magister equitum 98, 104
    blockades assassins of Caesar on
    Capitol Hill 110
    Brutus as guest 113
    governor of Gaul 134, 136
    joins A. 137, 140
    Triumvirate 141–2, 144–5
    consul 146
    remains in Rome during Philippi
    campaign 150
    receives Africa as province156, 176
    tries to hold Sicily 196
    disgraced and exiled from Rome 196
Africa 14, 16, 18, 25, 38, 53, 75, 96, 98–9,
    139, 141, 143, 156, 176, 196, 222, 228

Agrippa, see Vipsanius Agrippa, Marcus
Ahenobarbus, see Domitius
    Ahenobarbus, Gnaeus
Alesia 40, fig. 2
Alexander Helios 188, 201, 205, 228
Alexander the Great 62, 68, 163
Alexandria 37, 62, 65–7, 69, 70, 72, 73–
    76, 78, 79, 82, 83, 93, 94, 101, 105, 151,
    162, 166, 168–70, 194–5, 198, 201, 208,
    214, 218, 219, 221, 222–3, 225–6, 227,
    242, 243, 244, 245, 247, 255, 258–9, fig.
    6, siege of 85–91,
    Donations of 204–5, 211, 219, 255,
    258, 259
Amyntas, king of Galatia 189, 197, 217
Annius Milo, Titus 42–43, 95
Antioch 35–6, 188, 189, 191
Antiochus, king of Commagene 183
Antonia, daughter of Gaius Antonius
    Hybrida, marries A. 28
    A. divorces her 96, 246
Antonia, A.'s daughter by Antonia, 28,

228

Antonia *major* A.'s elder daughter by
  Octavia 188, 229
Antonia *minor* A.'s younger daughter by
  Octavia 188, 229
Antonius, Gaius, A.'s brother 22, 51, 126,
  255
  praetor 103
  killed by Brutus 149, 155, fig. 11
Antonius Hybrida, Gaius, A.'s uncle 23,
  25, 26, 28, 33, 238
Antonius, Iullus, A.'s younger son by
  Fulvia 188, 228
Antonius, Lucius, A.'s brother 22
  tribune 103, 124
  retreat into Gaul 136
  designated consul 148
  Perusine war 170–1, 175, 255, 256
Antonius, Marcus, A.'s grandfather 21
Antonius, Marcus, A.'s father 20–22
Antony, Mark,
  birth and family 20–1, 237–8
  mother remarries 22, 238
  death of stepfather Lentulus Sura 27
  friendship with Curio 28–9
  goes to Greece to study 33–4
  Gabinius offers cavalry command 35
  in Judaea 35–6, 239
  takes Pelusium 37
  goes to Gaul to join Caesar 39
  quaestor 42, 45, 49
  receives surrender of Commius 46
  elected augur 46–7
  tribune 48–9, 240
  flees to Caesar 49
  watches Italian ports 52
  ferries troops to Greece 54
  241, joins Caesar 55
  command at Pharsalus 57–8
  returns to Rome as *magister equitum*

59
  riots in Rome 59, 95–7
  in disgrace for behaviour in Rome
  98, 246
  C. in Rome 99–100
  marries Fulvia 100, 247
  back in favour with Caesar 103
  Lupercalia 107–8, 246, 247
  Caesar assassinated 108–9
  restores order after the murder of
  Caesar 110–11
  takes charge of Caesar's papers 111,
  248
  summons Senate 112, 248
  Caesar's funeral 115
  abolishes Dictatorship 116, 248
  quarrels with O. 125
  withdraws to Cisalpine Gaul 130–1,
  251
  siege of Mutina 131, 252
  Forum Gallorum 134
  retreats to Transalpine Gaul 134–5,
  252
  joins Lepidus 136
  alliance with O. 139, 252
  formation of Triumvirate 140–5, 253
  proscriptions 144, 253
  taxation schemes 146–7
  Senate confirms Caesar's acts 148
  prepares for war with Brutus and
  Cassius 149–50
  Philippi campaign 151–7
  governor of Gaul via legates 156
  summons Cleopatra to Tarsus 161,
  164
  organisation of the East 158–61, 254
  goes to Egypt 169–71, 255
  Lucius and Fulvia in Perusine War
  170–1, 175, 255
  leaves Fulvia in Greece 173

allies with Domitius Ahenobarbus 174, 194
treaty of Brundisium 175–6, 177, 256
loses command of Gaul 175, 256
priest of the cult of divine Caesar 176
marries Octavia 176
Treaty of Misenum 178
winters at Athens 180
Ventidius and Parthians 180, 182–3, 256
renewal of Triumvirate 185, 256–7
alleged marriage ceremony with C. 188, 257
winters at Antioch with C. 188
Parthian campaign 190–3, 257
summons C. after retreat 194, 257
repudiates Octavia 198, 258
breaks with O. 199
Armenian campaign 201–3
victory procession in Alexandria 204, 258
Donations of Alexandria 204–5, 211 215, 219, 255, 258, 259
problems over expiry date of Triumvirate 206–7, 259
O. reads A.'s will 214, 259
O. declares war 215
Actium campaign 217–221, 260
flees to Alexandria 222
retreats to Timoneum 223
embassies from O. 224
offers to commit suicide to save Cleopatra 224
troops go over to O. 226
death 227, figs 3, 10, 13, 19, 20, 23, 24, 28, 30
Antyllus, A.'s elder son by Fulvia 198, 202
Aphrodisias 181, 218

Apollodorus 82
Apollonia 54, 57, 122, 130
Archelaus, husband of Berenice 68–9
Archelaus, king of Cappadocia 161, 190, 228
Ariarathes, king of Cappadocia 161–2, 190
Aristobalus 35
Armenia 92, 162, 190, 192–5, 201–5, 207, 208–9, 210, 223, 258
Arsinoe 64, 69, 82–3, 85, 86, 87, 90, 99, 124, 168, 244, 246
Artavasdes, king of Armenia 190, 192, 194, 195, 201–2, 223, 257
Artavasdes, king of Media 190, 195, 201, 223, 258
Ascalon 80
Asinius Pollio, Gaius 104, 134, 137, 139, 148, 156, 174, 263
Athens 20, 33, 34–5, 157–9, 172, 179, 180–1, 184, 198, 223
Atticus, see Pomponius Atticus, Titus
Augustus, see Octavian
Aulus Gabinius, see Gabinius, Aulus

Balbus, see Cornelius Balbus, Lucius
Berenice 64, 65, 68–70, 72
Bibracte (Autun) 45
Bibulus, see Calpurnius Bibulus, Marcus
Bononia (Bologna) 133, 214, formation of Triumvirate 140, 145, 157, 253
Brundisium 51, 54, 96, 130, 151–2, 177, 182, 184, 216, 239, 241, 245, 251
closes gates to A. 174, 256
treaty between O. and A. 175–6, 177, 256
Brutus, see Junius Brutus, Marcus, Junius Brutus, Decimus
Buchis 77, 163

Caelius Rufus, Marcus 72, 95, 97, 242
Caesareum 94, 245
Caesarion, son of Caesar and Cleopatra
  93–4, 99, 118, 122–4, 162–3, 165–6,
  204, 205, 207, 209, 214, 223, 225–6,
  228, 245, 246, 249
Calendar, Caesar's reforms 101, 246
Calenus, see Fufius Calenus, Gaius
Caligula, Emperor 229
Calpurnia, wife of Caesar 105, 108, 111
Calpurnius Bibulus, Marcus 43
  consul with Caesar 31
  sons killed in Alexandria 78, 243
  commands Pompeian fleet 53
Calpurnius Piso, Lucius 133, 248, 251
Calvinus, see Domitius Calvinus,
  Gnaeus
Canidius Crassus, Publius 190, 194,
  210–11, 220, 222, 259
Cappadocia 92, 161–2, 190, 228
Cassius Longinus, Gaius,
  assassin of Caesar 110, 113, 116, 151
  seizes eastern provinces 124, 140, 142,
  146
  takes over Syria 149–50
  Philippi 152–3
  death 154
Cassius, Quintus 49–50
Catilina, see Sergius Catilina, Lucius
Cato, see Porcius Cato, Marcus
Cicero, see Tullius Cicero, Marcus
Cilicia 21, 38, 44, 67, 72, 89, 154, 164,
  180, 189, 205, 242
Cisalpine Gaul 17, 31, 38, 103, 106,
  125–6, 132–3, 141, 145, 156, 251,
  see also Gaul, Transalpine Gaul
Claudius, Emperor 229
Claudius Marcellus, Marcus 48
Cleopatra VI Tryphaena 64–5, 68, 241
Cleopatra VII,

early years 61, 63–4
expedition of Gabinius 69–70
joint rule with Auletes 71–2, 242–3
attends ceremony of Buchis at
  Hermonthis 77–8
puts off joint rule with Ptolemy XIII
  78–9
attention to population of Egypt 76
languages 77
driven out of Alexandria 79, 243
refuge in Ascalon 80
goes to Caesar in Alexandria 82, 243
Caesar's lover 84
made Queen of Egypt 90
siege of Alexandria 85–91, 244
Nile journey with Caesar 92, 245
birth of Caesarion 93, 245, 247
in Rome 99–10
statue in temple of Venus Genetrix
  104
assassination of Caesar 108–9
Caesar's will 114–5
death of Ptolemy XIV 123
administration of Egypt 162–3
sends legions to aid Dolabella
  149–50, 254
sends fleet to aid Triumvirs 151
summoned by A. to Tarsus 161, 164
entertains A. on Royal Barge 167–8
visits Alexandria 169–71
twins Alexander Helios and
  Cleopatra Selene 169, 188
A. invites her to Antioch 188
alleged marriage ceremony 188, 209,
  257
A. summons her after failure of the
  Parthian campaign 194
visit to Herod 202
victory procession in Alexandria 204
Donations of Alexandria 204–5

O. begins political campaign against
A. and C. 205–8, 259
C. accompanies A. to Greece 215
campaign of Actium 217–21, 260
returns to Egypt with A. 222
prepares for war with O. 223–4
refuses to give up A 224–5
death 227, figs 5, 7, 18, 27, 28, 30, 31,
36
Cleopatra Selene, daughter of A. and C.
99, 188, 205, 228
Clodius Pulcher, Publius 29, 31–2, 34,
42, 100, 142, 238, 239
Cocceius Nerva, Lucius 175
Commius, leader of the Atrebates 46
Cornelius Balbus, Lucius 94, 111, 245
Cornelius Dolabella, Publius 32, 97–8,
104, 114, 126, 149–50, 246, 250, 254
Cornelius Gallus 226, O. installs as
governor of Egypt 229
Cornelius Lentulus Sura, Publius, A.'s
stepfather 22–3, 238
conspiracy of Catilina 26
condemned to death by Cicero 27
Cornelius Sulla, Lucius 10, 14–16, 24, 25,
30, 66, 106, 116, 131, 144, 238
Crassus, see Licinius Crassus, Marcus
Curio, see Scribonius Curio, Gaius
Cyprus 33, 62, 85, 90, 124, 239, 244, 249

Decidius Saxa, Lucius 151–2, 169, 172
Decimus Brutus, see Junius Brutus,
Decimus
Deiotarus, king of Galatia 124, 161, 162,
250
Dellius, Quintus 164, 218, 220, 260
Dendera, Upper Egypt 93, 231, fig. 26
Dictatorship 10, 104, 106, 110, 127, 141
Pompey accused of wanting office
43, 240,

Lepidus proposes Caesar made
Dictator 53
Caesar accepts one year term 59
for ten years 101, 104
for life 107
A. abolishes the office 116, 248
Dionysus 148, 158, 163, 166, 187, 204
226, 254, 258
Dolabella, see Cornelius Dolabella,
Publius
Domitius Ahenobarbus, Gnaeus 47
commands Pompeian fleet 151–2, 155
allies with A. 174, 194, 211, 257
deserts A. 218, 220, 260, fig.17
Domitius Ahenobarbus, Gnaeus, A.'s
grandson 229
Domitius Calvinus, Gnaeus 92, 148
Donations of Alexandria 204–5, 211,
219, 255, 258, 259
Dyrrachium 54–5, 58, 152–3

Egypt 62–3, 66–7, 72–3, 75–7, 79, 80,
83–4, 90–1, 93, 99, 105, 117, 121–3,
162, 165–6, 172, 188–9, 216, 219, 222,
230, 242, 243, 244, 249, fig. 29
Gabinius's expedition 36–8, 69–71,
78, 239, 242
Pompey flees to 10, 58–9, 81
A. visits Cleopatra 169–71
corn supplies 163, 196, 230
O. carries war into 223–5
installs Cornelius Gallus as governor
229

Faberius, Caesar's secretary 111, 117
Flavius Josephus 202, 249, 258, 263
Forum Gallorum, battles 134
Fufius Calenus, Quintus 107, 133, 156,
175, 247, 251, 256
Fulvia 131, 142, 147, 177, 188, 237, 250

wife of Clodius 29, 32, marries
Curio 43
death of Curio 53
A. marries her 100, 247
A. pretends to be his own messenger
102
takes refuge with Atticus 135, 145,
252
death of Cicero 144
Perusine war 170–3, 176, 255
death 173

Gabinius, Aulus 34–9, 69–71, 78, 239,
242
Galatia 124, 161–2, 189, 197, 217
Gallus, see Cornelius Gallus
Ganymedes 87–8
Gaul 17, 26, 32, 33, 38, 39, 40, 41, 43,
45, 46, 48, 81, 98, 103, 104, 130, 132,
134–6, 175, 177, 184, 193, 197, 250–2,
261
see also Cisalpine Gaul, Transalpine
Gaul
Germanicus 229
Glaphyra, mother of Archelaus 161

Helvius Cinna, tribune 127, 247
Herod 159, 172, 183, 189, 202, 204, 263
Hermonthis 77–8, 93, 163
Hirtius, Aulus 47, 71, 89, 103, 133–4, 240,
251, 252
Horatius Flaccus, Quintus 155, 264
Hortensia, protests about tax 147
Hortensius, Quintus 47
Hyrcanus of Judaea 35, 38, 159

Illyricum 31, 197–8, 203, 206
Isis 92–3, 162, 166, 188–91, 254
Iullus Antonius, see Antonius, Iullus

Jerusalem 35, 172, 204
Juba, king of Mauretania 53, 98
Juba, son of above, in Caesar's triumph
99, marries Cleopatra Selene 99, 228
Judaea 35, 38, 80, 159, 172, 189, 202, 263
Julia, A.'s mother 21, 22, 237, 238
protests about tax 147
flees to Sextus Pompey after
Perusine war 173
Julia, Caesar's aunt 16
Julia, Caesar's daughter,
marries Pompey 17, 31
death 40
Julia, Caesar's sister 115
Julia, O.'s daughter 182, 228
Julius Caesar, Gaius,
early career 14–16
advocates leniency for Catilinarian
conspirators 27–8
forms alliance with Pompey and
Crassus 31, 239
consul in 59BC 31–2
backs Clodius as tribune 32–3
A. joins him in Gaul 39–40
conference at Lucca 38, 239
Pompey's laws on provincial
command 43–5, 240
terminal date for command in Gaul
48
crosses Rubicon 49
in Italy 50
to Spain 51, 101
Dictator 53
Dyrrachium and Pharsalus 53–9
Dictator for one year 59
A. in disgrace 59, 95
Egypt 79, 81–93
siege of Alexandria 85–91
war with Pharnaces 97

war in Africa 98

Dictator for ten years 101, 104

adopts his great–nephew Octavius 101, 115, 122

Dictator for life 107

refuses crown at Lupercalia 107–8

increases numbers of senators 110

assassination 109

Senate confirms all his acts 113

funeral 115, figs. 1, 8, 9

Julius Caesar, Lucius, A.'s maternal grandfather 21

Julius Caesar, Lucius, A.'s uncle 144

Junius Brutus, Decimus 103, 108, 109, 125–6, 132–3, 134, 136–9, 152

Junius Brutus, Marcus, assassin of Caesar 109, 110, 113, 116, 124–6, 140, 142, 143, 146, 149, 151–5, 159, 161, 165, 172, 233, 245, 250, 252, 253, 254, fig. 15

Labienus, Titus 40, 46, 50, 101, 151, 172, 180, 233, 255

Labienus, Quintus, son of above 151, 172, 180, 233, 255, fig. 21

Lentulus Sura, see Cornelius Lentulus Sura

Lepidus, see Aemilius Lepidus, Marcus

Leuke Come 194

Libo, see Scribonius Libo, Lucius

Licinius Crassus, Marcus 22–4, 31, 149, 179, 191, 192

forms alliance with Caesar and Pompey 38, 239

Parthian campaign 39, 78

death 40

Lighthouse see Pharos

Livia Drusilla, O.'s wife 186, 229

Lupercalia 107–8, 246, 247

Macedonia 41, 126, 130, 149, 151, 169, 177, 216, 220, 251, 253

Maecenas 174, 184, 224

Magister equitum 174, 184, 224

Manius, executed by A. 172, 176–7

Marcellus, see Claudius Marcellus, Marcus

Marius, Gaius 10, 14–16, 21, 24, 116, 144

Marseilles 96

Menodorus (Menas), Sextus Pompey's admiral 178, 182, 256

Misenum, Treaty of 178, 234

Mithradates of Pergamum 89

Mithradates, king of Pontus 15, 24, 34, 203

Munatius Plancus, Lucius 103, 134, 137, 139, 146, 148, 165, 173, 197, 213, 214, 252

Munda, battle of 101

Mutina (Modena) 132–3, 134, 135, 138, 193, 208, 252

Nabataea 189

Naucratis 73

Naulochus, naval battle 196–7, 208, 217

Nero, Emperor 186, 229

Nicolaus of Damascus 247, 263

Nile 37, 62, 69, 73–4, 77, 89, 92, 162, 225, 245

Nonius Balbus, tribune 212

Norbanus Flaccus, Gaius 151–2

Octavia, O.'s sister, A.'s wife 176, 179, 184, 187–8, 198, 207, 209, 210, 213, 229, 258, figs. 23, 24

Octavian, adoption by Caesar 18, 101, 115, 122

legal problems of the adoption 119, 249, 252

divi filius 127, 147

quarrels with A. 125–9, 250

granted *imperium* by Senate 123, 251, 252

support of Cicero 130–3

battles of Mutina 131

hailed as Imperator 134

refuses to help Decimus Brutus 138

consul 139, 252

Triumvirate 140–5, 233

proscriptions 143–4, 185, 213, 253

Philippi campaign 153–6

agreement with A. at Brundisium 175–6, 177, 256

marries Scribonia 175

takes over A.'s legions in Gaul 175, 256

renewal of Triumvirate 185, 257

marries Livia 186

battle of Naulochus 196–7, 208, 213

reads A.'s will 214, 259

oath of loyalty 214, 260

declares war on Cleopatra 215, 259

Actium campaign 217–221, 260

takes over Canidius's troops 222

winters on Samos 224

embassies to Egypt 224

takes over Egypt 229, figs. 35, 37, 38

Oppius, Gaius 94, 111, 245

Oppius Statianus 192

Orodes, king of Parthia 151, 190

Pacorus, son of Orodes of Parthia 172, 180, 182, 190

Pansa, see Vibius Pansa, Gaius

Paraetonium 73

Parthia 39, 40, 46, 104, 151, 161, 162, 168, 172, 205,

A.'s campaigns and plans 126, 157, 179, 180, 184, 189, 190–2, 195, 197, 202, 206, 207, 210, 219

Patrae 215, 218

Pedius, Quintus 114, 128, 139, 140, 143, 146

Pelusium 37, 69, 80, 89, 226

Perusia (Perugia) 148, 171, 173, 175

Pharnaces 92, 93, 97–9

Pharos island 74, 88, 243, 244

Pharos lighthouse 74, 86, 87

Pharsalus 10, 18, 53–9, 71, 79, 81, 82, 151, 152, 174, 175, 205, 222

Philippi campaign 151, 152–5, 157, 165, 169, 170, 172, 197, fig. 16

Philippics, Cicero's orations against A. 27, 29, 42, 96, 129, 144

Phraates, king of Parthia 190–1, 193, 195, 202–3, 257

Plancus, see Munatius Plancus, Lucius

Polemo, king of Pontus 189, 192, 195, 228

Pollio, see Asinius Pollio, Gaius

Pompeia, Caesar's wife 32

Pompey (Gnaeus Pompeius Magnus),

early career 14–16

consul in 70BC 22–3

defeats pirates 23–4, 238

gains eastern command 24–5, 238

returns to Rome 30

allies with Crassus and Caesar 31, 239

marries Julia, daughter of Caesar 31

death of Julia 40, and Cicero 33, 38,

and Ptolemy Auletes 36, 67–8, 69,

and Gabinius 36, 39, 69

conference at Lucca 38, 239

sole consul 43, 48

laws on provincial commands 43–5, 240

sets terminal date for Caesar's command in Gaul 48

A. makes speech against 49

abandons Italy 51, 81

Pharsalus campaign 53–9

flees to Egypt 81

death 81

A. buys his house 96, 98, 125, 246

Pompey, Gnaeus, elder son of Pompey the Great 55

Pompey, Sextus, younger son of Pompey the Great 101, 137, 141, 143, 148, 155, 156, 175–9, 182–3, 196–7, 206, 256

shelters A.'s mother 173

A. chooses not to ally with him 150, 173–4, 184, 256

disrupts food supply of Rome 156, 174, 177, 182, 185

death 197

Pomponius Atticus, Titus 49, 50, 115–9

gives refuge to Fulvia 135, 145, 252

Porcius Cato, Marcus 17, 33, 47, 68, 85, 114

Pothinus 81, 83, 85–7, 123, 244

Proscriptions 10

Marius and Cinna 21

Triumvirs 143–4, 185, 213, 253

Ptolemais 73

Ptolemy I Soter 62–3, 73–4, fig. 5

Ptolemy XII Auletes, C.'s father 36–8, 58, 61, 63–4, 66–7, 69, 71–8, 81, 89, 163, 239, 241, 242

Ptolemy XIII 10, 78–9, 81–3, 85, 88–90, 168, 242, 243

Ptolemy XIV 89, 90, 99, 123, 242, 249

Ptolemy Philadelphus 189, 194, 205, 228

Rabirius Postumus, Gaius 36, 71, 239, 242

Rufio 91

Rullus, see Servilius Rullus, Publius

Salvidienus Rufus, Quintus 150, 170

executed 177

Samosata 183, 192, 256

Sardinia 13, 141, 156, 176, 178, 182

Scribonia, sister of Lucius Scribonius Libo, marries O. 175, 178

birth of Julia and divorce from O. 182, 186

Scribonius Curio, Gaius 28–9, 32, 43, 47–9, 51, 100, 237, 240

death in Africa 53

Scribonius Libo, Lucius, blockades A. in Brundisium 54–5

sister marries O. 175, 178

Senate 10–11, 13, 15, 23, 25, 27, 29, 30, 36, 39, 41, 48–9, 59, 67–9, 85–6, 91, 101, 107–8, 132, 136, 160, 165, 172–3, 176, 185, 206, 215, 242–3, 251

Caesar increases numbers of senators 106, 110, 213

A. and Senate 20, 29, 59, 96–7, 104, 111–3, 118, 122, 129, 131, 133, 144, 206, 211–2, 224, 230, 245, 246, 248, 250, 251

ratifies Caesar's will 114

grants *imperium* to O. 132

tries to block O. from consulship 138–9

confirms Caesar's acts 117, 126, 134

ratifies A.'s acts past and future 179, 210

legalise position of Brutus and Cassius 140, 253

senators flee to A. 212–3

Sergius Catilina, Lucius 25–7, 42, 238

Sertorius, Quintus 16

Servilius Isauricus, Publius 53, 148, 170

Servilius Rullus, Publius 174

Sicily 13–4, 16, 38, 51, 53, 126, 141, 150, 152, 156, 176, 178, 196, 209

Sosigenes 101

Sosius, Gaius 204, 211–2, 218, 257
Spain 13–18, 30, 38, 48, 51, 53, 56, 81, 95,
    99, 101–2, 104, 122, 134, 137, 139, 143,
    156, 170–1, 197
Staius Murcus 151–2
Sulla, see Cornelius Sulla, Lucius
Syria, 66, 69, 78, 80, 89, 93, 97, 158, 189,
    245, 253
    Gabinius as governor 34–5, 38,
    Crassus takes over 38–9
    Dolabella as governor 126, 149, 250
    Brutus and Cassius legitimised in
    command 253
    campaigns of Ventidius Bassus 180–2
    A. and Syria 168–9, 172, 18–3, 191,
    194–6, 197, 205, 255
    given to Ptolemy Philadelphus in
    Donations of Alexandria 205

Tarentum, Treaty of 184, 186, 256
Tarsus, C. meets A. 20, 164–8, 237, 255
Terentius Varro, Marcus, handbook on
    senatorial procedure for Pompey 22,
    pamphlet *Tricaranus* 239
Thapsus, battle of 98
Tiberius, Emperor 186, 229
Timoneum 223, fig. 6
Titius, Marcus 141, 196–7, 213–4
Transalpine Gaul 17, 31, 103, 133–4, 137,
    141, 252,
    see also Cisalpine Gaul, Gaul
Trebonius, Gaius 40, 102, 103, 109, 149,
    231, 247
Tribune, military 29, 251
Tribune of the plebs 12, 15, 43–5, 63,
    68–9, 238, 240, 248, 259, sacrosanctity
    of 50, 240
    Clodius 32, 34, 42, 239, A. elected 47,
    240
    Curio 47–8

A. and Quintus Cassius flee to
    Caesar 49
Lucius Antonius 103, 124
O. suspected of wanting to be
    tribune 127, 247
Publius Titius 141
O. receives tribunician sacrosanctity
    206
Nonius Balbus 212
Triumvirate, so–called first Triumvirate,
    A. and O. and Lepidus form alliance
    140–5, 253
    renewal 185, 256–7
    expiry date 206–7, 259
Tullius Cicero, Marcus 14, 24, 29, 32, 47,
    49, 72, 115, 117, 126, 128, 137, 139,
    149
    Catilina 25–8, 238
    Clodius 32, 238
    banished 33, 239
    recalled 38
    supports A. for quaestorship 42
    defends Milo 43
    governs Cilicia 44
    joins Pompey 52
    hostility to A. 96, 102, 129, 130,
    133–5, 155, 208, 237, 238, 246, 251,
    and C. 99, 104, 107, 117–8, 245
    proposes amnesty after assassination
    of Caesar 112
    supports O. 119, 130–3, 138, 252
    proscribed and death 144–5

Varro, see Terentius Varro, Marcus
Ventidius Bassus, Publius,
    raises legions and joins A. 136, 252,
    governor of Gaul 156
    campaign against the Parthians 173,
    180, 182–3, 256
Venus Genetrix, temple 104–5, 230

Vibius Pansa, Gaius 103, 133–4, 138–9,
  251
Vipsanius Agrippa, Marcus 170, 174, 177,
  184, 186, 196, 197, 204, 217–8, 221,
  224
Volusenus, Gaius 46

TEMPUS – REVEALING HISTORY

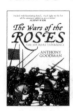   

The Wars of the Roses
The Soldiers' Experience
ANTHONY GOODMAN
'Sheds light on the lot of the common soldier as
never before' *Alison Weir*
'A meticulous work'
The Times Literary Supplement
£12.99   0 7524 3731 3

D-Day
The First 72 Hours
WILLIAM F. BUCKINGHAM
'A compelling narrative' *The Observer*
A *BBC History Magazine* Book of the Year 2004
£9.99   0 7524 2842 2

English Battlefields
500 Battlefields that Shaped English History
MICHAEL RAYNER
'A painstaking survey of English battlefields... a
first-rate book' *Richard Holmes*
'A fascinating and, for all its factual tone, an
atmospheric volume' *The Sunday Telegraph*
£18.99   978 07524 4307 2

Trafalgar Captain Durham of the Defiance: The
Man who refused to Miss Trafalgar
HILARY RUBINSTEIN
'A sparkling biography of Nelson's luckiest
captain' *Andrew Lambert*
£17.99   0 7524 3435 7

  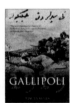 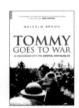

Battle of the Atlantic
MARC MILNER
'The most comprehensive short survey of the
U-boat battles' *Sir John Keegan*
'Some events are fortunate in their historian, none
more so than the Battle of the Atlantic. Marc
Milner is *the* historian of the Atlantic Campaign...
a compelling narrative'
Andrew Lambert
£12.99   0 7524 3332 6

Okinawa 1945 The Stalingrad of the Pacific
GEORGE FEIFER
'A great book... Feifer's account of the three
sides and their experiences far surpasses most
books about war' *Stephen Ambrose*
£17.99   0 7524 3324 5

Gallipoli 1915
TIM TRAVERS
'The most important new history of Gallipoli for
forty years... groundbreaking' *Hew Strachan*
'A book of the highest importance to all who would
seek to understand the tragedy of the Gallipoli campaign' *The Journal of Military History*
£13.99   0 7524 2972 8

Tommy Goes To War
MALCOLM BROWN
'A remarkably vivid and frank account of the
British soldier in the trenches' *Max Arthur*
'The fury, fear, mud, blood, boredom and bravery
that made up life on the Western Front are vividly
presented and illustrated' *The Sunday Telegraph*
£12.99   0 7524 2980 9

If you are interested in purchasing other books published by Tempus, or in case you have difficulty finding any
Tempus books in your local bookshop, you can also place orders directly through our website
www.tempus-publishing.com

TEMPUS – REVEALING HISTORY

Private 12768 Memoir of a Tommy
JOHN JACKSON

'Unique... a beautifully written, strikingly
honest account of a young man's experience of
combat' *Saul David*
'At last we have John Jackson's intensely personal
and heartfelt little book to remind us there was
a view of the Great War other than Wilfred
Owen's' *The Daily Mail*

£9.99   0 7524 3531 0

The German Offensives of 1918
MARTIN KITCHEN

'A lucid, powerfully driven narrative' *Malcolm Brown*
'Comprehensive and authoritative... first class'
Holger H. Herwig

£13.99   0 7524 3527 2

Verdun 1916
MALCOLM BROWN

'A haunting book which gets closer than any
other to that wasteland marked by death'
Richard Holmes

£9.99   0 7524 2599 4

The Forgotten Front
The East African Campaign 1914–1918
ROSS ANDERSON

'Excellent... fills a yawning gap in the
historical record'
The Times Literary Supplement
'Compelling and authoritative'
Hew Strachan

£12.99   978 07524 4126 9

Agincourt
A New History
ANNE CURRY

'A highly distinguished and convincing account'
Christopher Hibbert
'A *tour de force*' *Alison Weir*
'*The* book on the battle' *Richard Holmes*
A *BBC History Magazine* Book of the Year 2005

£12.99   0 7524 3813 1

The Welsh Wars of Independence
DAVID MOORE

'Beautifully written, subtle and remarkably
perceptive' *John Davies*

£12.99   978 07524 4128 3

Bosworth 1485 Psychology of a Battle
MICHAEL K. JONES

'Most exciting... a remarkable tale' *The Guardian*
'Insightful and rich study of the Battle of
Bosworth… no longer need Richard play the
villain' *The Times Literary Supplement*

£12.99   0 7524 2594 3

The Battle of Hastings 1066
M.K. LAWSON

'Blows away many fundamental assumptions
about the battle of Hastings… an exciting and
indispensable read' *David Bates*
A *BBC History Magazine* Book of the Year 2003

£12.99   978 07524 4177 1

If you are interested in purchasing other books published by Tempus, or in case you have difficulty finding any
Tempus books in your local bookshop, you can also place orders directly through our website

www.tempus-publishing.com

TEMPUS – REVEALING HISTORY

Freaks
JAN BONDESON

'Reveals how these tragic individuals triumphed over their terrible adversity' *The Daily Mail*
'Well written and superbly illustrated' *The Financial Times*

£9.99   0 7524 3662 7

Bollywood
MIHIR BOSE

'Pure entertainment' *The Observer*
'Insightful and often hilarious' *The Sunday Times*
'Gripping' *The Daily Telegraph*

£9.99   978 07524 4382 9

King Arthur
CHRISTOPHER HIBBERT

'A pearl of biographers' *New Statesman*
£12.99   978 07524 3933 4

Arnhem
William Buckingham

'Reveals the reason why the daring attack failed' *The Daily Express*

£10.99   0 7524 3187 0

Cleopatra
PATRICIA SOUTHERN

'In the absence of Cleopatra's memoirs Patricia Southern's commendably balanced biography will do very well' *The Sunday Telegraph*

£9.99   978 07524 4336 2

The Prince In The Tower
MICHAEL HICKS

'The first time in ages that a publisher has sent me a book I actually want to read' *David Starkey*

£9.99   978 07524 4386 7

The Battle of Hastings 1066
M. K. LAWSON

'A *BBC History Magazine* book of the year 2003
'The definitive book on this famous battle' *The Journal of Military History*

£12.99   978 07524 4177 1

Loos 1915
NICK LLOYD

'A revealing new account based on meticulous documentary research' *Corelli Barnett*
'Should finally consign Alan Clark's Farrago, *The Donkeys*, to the waste paperbasket' *Hew Strachan*
'Plugs a yawning gap in the existing literature... this book will set the agenda for debate of the battle for years to come' *Gary Sheffield*

£25   0 7524 3937 5

If you are interested in purchasing other books published by Tempus, or in case you have difficulty finding any Tempus books in your local bookshop, you can also place orders directly through our website

www.tempus-publishing.com

TEMPUS – REVEALING HISTORY

  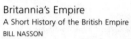  

Britannia's Empire
A Short History of the British Empire
BILL NASSON

'Crisp, economical and witty' *TLS*
'An excellent introduction the subject' *THES*

£12.99   0 7524 3808 5

Madmen
A Social History of Madhouses,
Mad-Doctors & Lunatics
ROY PORTER

'Fascinating'
The Observer

£12.99   0 7524 3730 5

Born to be Gay
A History of Homosexuality
WILLIAM NAPHY

'Fascinating' *The Financial Times*
'Excellent' *Gay Times*

£9.99   0 7524 3694 5

William II
Rufus, the Red King
EMMA MASON

'A thoroughly new reappraisal of a much
maligned king. The dramatic story of his life is
told with great pace and insight'
John Gillingham

£25   0 7524 3528 0

To Kill Rasputin
The Life and Death of Grigori Rasputin
ANDREW COOK

'Andrew Cook is a brilliant investigative historian'
Andrew Roberts
'Astonishing' *The Daily Mail*

£9.99   0 7524 3906 5

The Unwritten Order
Hitler's Role in the Final Solution
PETER LONGERICH

'Compelling' *Richard Evans*
'The finest account to date of the many twists
and turns in Adolf Hitler's anti-semitic obsession'
Richard Overy

£12.99   0 7524 3328 8

Private 12768
Memoir of a Tommy
JOHN JACKSON
FOREWORD BY HEW STRACHAN

'A refreshing new perspective' *The Sunday Times*
'At last we have John Jackson's intensely
personal and heartfelt little book to remind us
there was a view of the Great War other than
Wilfred Owen's' *The Daily Mail*

£9.99   0 7524 3531 0

The Vikings
MAGNUS MAGNUSSON

'Serious, engaging history'
BBC History Magazine

£9.99   0 7524 2699 0

If you are interested in purchasing other books published by Tempus, or in case you have difficulty finding any
Tempus books in your local bookshop, you can also place orders directly through our website
www.tempus-publishing.com

TEMPUS – REVEALING HISTORY

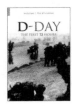 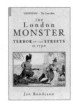  

D-Day The First 72 Hours
WILLIAM F. BUCKINGHAM

'A compelling narrative' *The Observer*
A *BBC History Magazine* Book of the Year 2004

£9.99   0 7524 2842 x

The London Monster
Terror on the Streets in 1790
JAN BONDESON

'Gripping' *The Guardian*
'Excellent... monster-mania brought a reign of terror to the ill-lit streets of the capital'
The Independent

£9.99   0 7524 3327 x

London
A Historical Companion
KENNETH PANTON

'A readable and reliable work of reference that deserves a place on every Londoner's bookshelf'
Stephen Inwood

£20   0 7524 3434 9

M: MI5's First Spymaster
ANDREW COOK

'Serious spook history' *Andrew Roberts*
'Groundbreaking' *The Sunday Telegraph*
'Brilliantly researched' *Dame Stella Rimington*

£9.99   978 07524 3949 9

Agincourt
A New History
ANNE CURRY

'A highly distinguished and convincing account'
Christopher Hibbert
'A *tour de force*' *Alison Weir*
'*The* book on the battle' *Richard Holmes*
A *BBC History Magazine* Book of the Year 2005

£12.99   0 7524 3813 1

Battle of the Atlantic
MARC MILNER

'The most comprehensive short survey of the U-boat battles' *Sir John Keegan*
'Some events are fortunate in their historian, none more so than the Battle of the Atlantic. Marc Milner is *the* historian of the Atlantic campaign... a compelling narrative' *Andrew Lambert*

£12.99   0 7524 3332 6

The English Resistance
The Underground War Against the Normans
PETER REX

'An invaluable rehabilitation of an ignored resistance movement' *The Sunday Times*
'Peter Rex's scholarship is remarkable'
The Sunday Express

£12.99   0 7524 3733 X

Elizabeth Wydeville: England's Slandered Queen
ARLENE OKERLUND

'A penetrating, thorough and wholly convincing vindication of this unlucky queen'
Sarah Gristwood
'A gripping tale of lust, loss and tragedy'
Alison Weir
A *BBC History Magazine* Book of the Year 2005

£9.99   978 07524 3807 8

If you are interested in purchasing other books published by Tempus, or in case you have difficulty finding any Tempus books in your local bookshop, you can also place orders directly through our website

www.tempus-publishing.com

TEMPUS – REVEALING HISTORY

Quacks Fakers and Charlatans in Medicine
ROY PORTER

'A delightful book' *The Daily Telegraph*
'Hugely entertaining' *BBC History Magazine*

£12.99   0 7524 2590 0

The Tudors
RICHARD REX

'Up-to-date, readable and reliable. The best
introduction to England's most important
dynasty' *David Starkey*
'Vivid, entertaining... quite simply the best short
introduction' *Eamon Duffy*
'Told with enviable narrative skill... a delight for
any reader' *THES*

£9.99   0 7524 3333 4

The Kings & Queens of England
MARK ORMROD

'Of the numerous books on the kings and
queens of England, this is the best'
Alison Weir

£9.99   0 7524 2598 6

The Covent Garden Ladies
Pimp General Jack & the Extraordinary Story of Harris's List
HALLIE RUBENHOLD

'Sex toys, porn... forget Ann Summers, Miss
Love was at it 250 years ago' *The Times*
'Compelling' *The Independent on Sunday*
'Marvellous' *Leonie Frieda*
'Filthy' *The Guardian*

£9.99   0 7524 3739 9

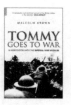
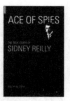

Okinawa 1945
GEORGE FEIFER

'A great book... Feifer's account of the three
sides and their experiences far surpasses most
books about war'
Stephen Ambrose

£17.99   0 7524 3324 5

Tommy Goes To War
MALCOLM BROWN

'A remarkably vivid and frank account of the
British soldier in the trenches'
Max Arthur
'The fury, fear, mud, blood, boredom and
bravery that made up life on the Western Front
are vividly presented and illustrated'
The Sunday Telegraph

£12.99   0 7524 2980 4

Ace of Spies The True Story of Sidney Reilly
ANDREW COOK

'The most definitive biography of the spying
ace yet written... both a compelling narrative
and a myth-shattering *tour de force*'
Simon Sebag Montefiore
'The absolute last word on the subject' *Nigel West*
'Makes poor 007 look like a bit of a wuss'
The Mail on Sunday

£12.99   0 7524 2959 0

Sex Crimes
From Renaissance to Enlightenment
W.M. NAPHY

'Wonderfully scandalous' *Diarmaid MacCulloch*
'A model of pin-sharp scholarship' *The Guardian*

£10.99   0 7524 2977 9

If you are interested in purchasing other books published by Tempus, or in case you have difficulty finding any
Tempus books in your local bookshop, you can also place orders directly through our website
www.tempus-publishing.com